Dear Lucy,

This is just a token to say thank you for you're hard work & dedication throughout your time as campaigns officer in Manchester. I know that the last 6 months were particularly difficult but you should know that your moral compass & principled attitude proceed you & I only hope that we see you in some campaigning capacity in the future.

Remember to stick to your gut!

Carly
UJS campaigns director
2009

A STATE
BEYOND
THE PALE

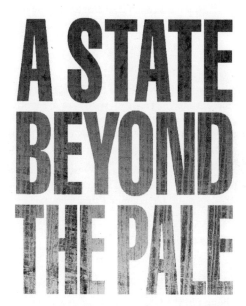

A STATE BEYOND THE PALE

EUROPE'S PROBLEM WITH ISRAEL

ROBIN SHEPHERD

Weidenfeld & Nicolson

LONDON

First published in Great Britain in 2009
by Weidenfeld & Nicolson

1 3 5 7 9 10 8 6 4 2

A CIP catalogue record for this book
is available from the British Library.

ISBN-13   978 0 297 85664 1

Typeset by Input Data Services Ltd, Bridgwater, Somerset

Printed and bound in the UK by CPI Mackays, Chatham ME5 8TD

Weidenfeld & Nicolson

The Orion Publishing Group Ltd
Orion House
5 Upper Saint Martin's Lane
London, WC2H 9EA

An Hachette Livre UK Company

The Orion Publishing Group's policy is to use papers
that are natural, renewable and recyclable products and
made from wood grown in sustainable forests. The
logging and manufacturing processes are expected to
conform to the environmental regulations of the
country of origin.

www.orionbooks.co.uk

I dedicate this book to Zuzana and our beautiful
newborn baby daughter Sofia

CONTENTS

ACKNOWLEDGMENTS

There are a number of people I would like to thank for helping bring this project to fruition. First among them are David and Richard Bolchover who encouraged me to write the book in the first place. Their help and support throughout the whole process has been invaluable. Rarely did a day go by when I did not speak to David in particular about something or other related to it – a quotidian reality which became a source of some amusement in our respective families. Several people, including the above, read the manuscript in full or in part. I would therefore like to thank the Bolchover brothers as well as Paul Lewis, Manfred Gerstenfeld, David Horovitz, Emanuele Otto-lenghi, Ben Cohen, Ed Joseph, Will Rosen, David Benson and Anthony Julius for all their thoughts and comments. (Anthony Julius and Alexandra Fawcett at Mishcon de Reya deserve my additional and sincerest thanks for helping me through some difficult times, when I found myself under severe pressure due to the nature of my views on the subject of my research.) I should also like to thank Laura Wilton and Jaroslaw Wisniewski who interned for me and provided some important help in the early stages of my research.

Grateful as I am to all of the above, it goes without saying that any errors, shortcomings and oversights in this book are my responsibility alone.

In a broader sense, a number of institutions and associated individuals were helpful in giving me food for thought. Tom Gross, of tomgrossmedia.com, deserves a special mention for the extraordinary hard work he puts in with his regular email alerts and essays outlining the way in which the Western media reports on the conflict. In similar vein, Just Journalism provided many insights on the British media in particular. I would also like to thank Michael Dickson (StandWithUs) and Astar Sobol (ELNET) for setting up a whole series of meetings in Israel in the summers of 2007 and 2008. They are particularly to be applauded for introducing me to such a wide variety of people with diverging views.

In researching a book of this kind the vast bulk of the material I have been looking at has, of course, been drawn from an anti-Israeli perspective. Given my conclusions, however, it would be invidious of me to acknowledge them by name even though, perversely, their influence has been enormous!

Finally, I owe a huge debt of thanks to George Weidenfeld, who saw the value of the project as soon as I described it to him. His colleagues at Weidenfeld & Nicolson – Alan Samson and Lucinda McNeile especially – have been a pleasure to work with.

PREFACE

It does not take long in this debate before it starts to get personal. That is partly because of the passions it arouses, and this debate is nothing if not passionate. But it is also because there is a common assumption – a fair one sometimes – that many of those engaging in the discussion about Israel, the Palestinians and the wider Muslim world are personally and emotionally tied in to the positions they hold. Our starting points should be irrelevant. Arguments stand or fall on their own merits, not because of the background of the people putting them. Nonetheless, experience teaches that such questions are asked in any case. For those that are interested, then, here is a thumbnail sketch of my personal route map into this subject.

To begin with, a few negatives. I am not Jewish, nor do I have the slightest intention of converting. I am not a Christian Zionist, nor do I have any other religious affiliation beyond my upbringing in the Anglican tradition. Coming from a small town in northern England, as a child and a young teenager I was largely unaware of Jews and Judaism. Until I went to university I do not remember meeting a single person who identified themselves as Jewish. I knew of the Holocaust, of course. I also seem to remember some conversations with my paternal grandfather about anti-Semitism before the war, about Jews not being accepted in certain golf clubs and about how, in his own early years, he remembered seeing children make fun of the Hassidim for the way they dressed. There was Shylock in *The Merchant of Venice*. There was Fagin in *Oliver Twist*. There were great scientists such as Einstein and there were great financiers such as the Rothschilds. As far as my knowledge of Jews went, that was about it. I had no strong views one way or the other either on Jews themselves or on the State of Israel.

If anything, I knew even less about the Palestinians, or Arabs generally. It probably came down to the *Tales from the Arabian Nights* and the exploits of T. E. Lawrence in the film *Lawrence of Arabia*. I also knew that Arab countries had a great deal of oil because my uncle worked for BP and kept travelling to the Gulf. I know that I had heard of the Palestinians because I have vague recollections of the hijacking which led to the Israeli rescue mission at Entebbe in 1976 (at which time I was eight) and because the PLO would periodically crop up in the news. But as with the Jews and Israel, the Arabs and Palestine were entirely peripheral matters.

It would remain this way for quite some time. My early political interests were dominated by the political and social revolution associated with Margaret Thatcher in the Britain of the 1980s and with the Cold War stand-off between the West and the Soviet Empire. I am pretty sure that I can trace the first, tentative beginnings of my interest in Israel to my under-graduate days. As a student of the Russian language and Soviet politics and history, the question of the Soviet Jews (the Refusniks) who were being prevented from emigrating from the Soviet Union loomed large.

On a half-year study trip to Moscow in 1988 and 1989, I also remember reading my first book on Israel – *The Siege* by Conor Cruise O'Brien. It was lent to me by a fellow student and roommate, himself a Jew and a Zionist with whom I would while away the Russian winter in long and fascinating con-versations about Israel and the Jews.

If these were my early pro-Israeli influences they were at least counterbalanced by the anti-Israeli atmosphere that pervaded a British university system heavily dominated by the radical Left. Though I was not involved in student politics in an active sense,

I remember the attempts to ban Jewish student societies for their adherence to Zionism. I remember the leafleting, the pro-Palestinian gatherings, the student resolutions. With particular clarity, I remember the justification put forward for all this that 'Zionism was racism'. It was a charge that would put anyone with even mildly pro-Israeli leanings right on the back foot. It was a verbal jab to the chin. It was a way of telling you to conform to the anti-Israeli orthodoxy or be vilified.

But I also remember with great clarity that the people and groups making that accusation screamed 'fascist' or 'racist' at more or less anyone who got in their way, more or less regardless of the subject at hand. They were the same people who, while talking loudly about human rights, wore T-shirts and badges glorifying Lenin and Trotsky, the architects of the world's first totalitarian state. In the 1980s they joined and ran 'peace movements' whose primary aim was to make Western countries disarm unilaterally in the face of Soviet imperialism. My senses told me that people whose judgement (let alone moral compass) was so unreliable on the great issues of the day that I did have a feel for could not necessarily be trusted to get it right on those issues about which I knew little, such as the Israel–Palestine conflict. Nonetheless, I decided to sift the arguments from both sides and see what I would come up with.

In the summer of 1989 – during the first Intifada – I made my first trip to Israel, spending a month on a Moshav working in a small chair-making factory and another month travelling around the country. I spent much of my time in east Jerusalem, making several trips to the West Bank proper.

One such trip took me to a refugee camp in Jericho where I remember being taken by a UN worker into the home of a Palestinian family whose six-year-old son, they told me, had been shot dead accidentally in a gunfight between Israeli soldiers and militants. I remember their kind hospitality. I also remember asking them what they thought about the Israelis and them telling me, with a kind of nervous smile which at the time made me think they did not really believe it themselves, that 'the Jews should go and live in the sea'.

I also have fleeting memories of one day going to the Al-Aqsa mosque, sitting down in that serene courtyard outside it with a young Palestinian man and talking with him for hours on everything from the Israeli occupation to his heartfelt belief that I should become a Muslim, but that if I wanted to remain a Christian that was something he would respect. I remember liking him. Like almost all subsequent meetings with ordinary Palestinians that encounter was good-natured and illuminating. I have nothing against the Palestinians on a day-to-day level. Indeed, I sympathise with their suffering as I believe anyone with an ounce of humanity must.

Looking back, then, on my formative influences, I cannot see anything which would have led to an inbuilt bias since I have met many people with broadly similar backgrounds who hold very different views from my own. In sum, I have no personal, emotional, family, religious or identity-based reasons for holding the views on the Israel–Palestine conflict that I do. Those views have evolved over many years and in response to a multitude of different influences from all sides of the debate.

INTRODUCTION

The moral and civilisational integrity of Europe is now being called into question. Europe's opinion-forming classes – its journalists, academics, analysts, student organisations, trade unions, churches, people of influence generally – stand accused in large numbers of reawakening the centuries-old beast of anti-Semitic bigotry, rebranding it for the modern world and sending it charging at full speed against the world's only Jewish state.

It hardly seems possible that the accusation could be justified, or that serious people could level it in good faith. Even today, more than six decades after it took place, the systematic murder of six million Jews in the Nazi Holocaust remains deeply engraved in Europe's collective memory. The uniquely disturbing images of emaciated corpses piled up inside the muddy death pits of German concentration camps, of the gas chambers and crematoria at Auschwitz, and of the Nazi propaganda films likening Jews to vermin in order to dehumanise them sear into Europe's conscience, and its consciousness. For post-war Europe, no charge could be more serious than that the past has been forgotten, its lessons unlearned. The specific allegation that Europe is now reverting to old form in its treatment of the Jews is like a dagger thrust at the heart of everything its opinion formers say they stand for.

The fact remains that in its treatment of Israel Europe is charged with a deliberate and malicious bias which at the very least contains anti-Semitic undertones. It is berated for dishonouring the memory of the Holocaust, for making common cause with tyranny against democracy, for lacking moral compass or the backbone to follow its directions, for hypocrisy, wickedness and appeasement. It is accused of succumbing to an obsession, of giving in to irrationalism and anti-intellectualism, of hatred, scorn and contempt.

The broader critique is no less damning. It posits a European civilisation enervated by the legacy of its momentous and terrible past; devoid of believable ideals; racked by self-loathing; fatally deficient in the will even to defend itself; hedonistic, materialistic, relativistic, pacifistic; puffed up, and lazy; complacent, and defeatist. It is an image of a continent bereft of the ability to make serious judgements about matters of consequence. Faced with the moral, political and strategic implications of Israel's predicament in the Middle East it is cast as a whining and pampered child among men: unable to empathise; unwilling to sympathise; unworthy of respect for its views.

From the United States to Israel, through Jewish communities around the world and even among minority voices supportive of Israel in Europe, these charges are now delivered with such frequency that they have acquired the status of a received wisdom. It is as if no more discussion were required.

To put it mildly, this does not sit easily with the continent's self-image. Europe's intellectual and opinion-forming elites see themselves as nothing less than the richest repository of enlightened values the Western world has to offer, and certainly superior to the 'uncouth'[1] Americans. The world, in a sense, lies beneath them. They occupy a higher ground, formed from the accumulated wisdom of the continent's long and turbulent history. Chauvinism is indeed a thing of their past but it is a past that they have learned from. It is they who now do the accusations of barbarism. It is they who do the judging.

Far from feeling a sense of inhibition about criticism of Israel, many among Europe's opinion formers see it as a moral imperative. They oppose Zionism as they opposed apartheid in yesteryear's South Africa or even Nazism itself. It is in the name of human rights and the basic dignity of the 'long-oppressed'

Palestinian people that they ply their wares against the State of Israel. As for accusations of bigotry, they constitute a cowardly, deeply insulting and thoroughly disreputable manner in which to conduct debate. If the best defence that Israel's supporters can muster is to launch into accusations of anti-Semitism this in itself is evidence of the weakness of their case.

It would be disingenuous at this stage to say that the purpose of this book is to adjudicate between these competing narratives. I am quite openly motivated by a belief that there is something profoundly troubling about the way Israel is being treated these days. This does not mean that what needs to be argued for is merely assumed. The book is packed full of evidence, and argument built upon that evidence, which proves beyond any doubt that Israel is indeed getting a raw deal in Europe. That is the easy part. The puzzle here is not 'whether' but 'why?' Why exactly is it that Europe has such a problem with the State of Israel? Why is it that so many influential people and institutions on the continent now seem motivated by a reflexive hostility to the Jewish state? Why among all the nations of the world has Israel been singled out and where precisely does all this come from?

This, of course, is the conflict that never goes away. Periods of calm always seem, with hindsight, to have been the calm before a new storm. As one threat recedes another takes its place. Moderates become hardliners as often as hardliners become moderates, making a nonsense of both terms. Peace efforts bring Israelis and Palestinians within a hair's breadth of an agreement only, as in 2000 and 2001, for the whole sorry situation to descend into worse chaos and bloodshed than before. Hope sometimes seems to be on the horizon, as when Israel unilaterally ended its occupation of Gaza in 2005, only for Israeli forces to be drawn back into fierce fighting in that benighted strip of land at the end of 2008 and the beginning of 2009.

And then there are the game changers: the entry into the fray of factors which complicate matters, for good or ill, in a novel or unexpected way. The election of Barack Obama in November 2008 was one, raising hopes that a fresh perspective from Washington could bring the two sides together to form a lasting peace. But with the looming threat of a nuclear-armed Iran, another potential game changer, who now are Israel's most dangerous opponents?

To be sure, the lot of both Israelis and Palestinians might be significantly improved if long-standing hopes for a peace agreement could be realised. But even if that monumental task were to be accomplished, it could still amount to little in terms of a wider Middle East peace. The situation, as ever, is precarious and unpredictable. Everything, it seems, is in a state of flux.

And yet there is one factor related to this conflict which does not change, or at least does not change as rapidly or as dramatically as the facts on the ground. As the news reports tell us of the latest suicide bombing or Israeli raid, the latest diatribe against the 'Zionist entity' from Iran or Hezbollah, or the latest pledge for a renewal of the peace process from inside or outside the region, we in the West survey the scene from a position of relative stability. We are the constant factor in this conflict.

Israel and its predicament in the Middle East can therefore tell us a lot about ourselves. For the judgements we make about day-to-day events proceed from values and historical contexts which are home-grown. As Frenchmen, Germans, Britons, Dutchmen, Italians, Spaniards, Swedes, Poles or indeed Americans, we come to the question of Israel and the Middle East with assumptions which are quintessentially Western. And, as anyone who follows this conflict in even the most cursory way knows, mere mention of Israel opens up a schism in the mind of the West like no other. America and Europe do not agree, and that disagreement is fraught with tension and rancour.

This book is designed to illustrate and explain the various strands of thought which make up the anti-Israeli narrative and to offer reasons as to why that narrative has achieved a kind of hegemony over mainstream European discourse. It also asks whether America could follow in Europe's footsteps. Crucially, it deals squarely with the question of whether this anti-Israeli discourse can truly be said to represent a new wave of anti-Semitism as so many now contend.

But before coming to a sketch of the issues dealt with in the chapters which follow, there are a number of preliminary matters which need to be addressed first. If left unattended for long, they have the habit of intruding upon a meaningful discussion of the core issues whenever the Israel–Palestine conflict is broached. First among them are questions relating to one's reading of the conflict as a whole.

It is inevitable, after all, that a writer looking at questions of bias must have some sense of what a fair and reasonable reading of the conflict would look like. In any case, no one comes to this subject from a *tabula rasa*. The Israel–Palestine conflict takes place over one of the great ideological and civilisational fault lines of the modern world. It matters to everyone who takes global affairs seriously. Not to have a view on it, not even to take an interest, is to remove oneself from one of the most important political conversations of our time.

I outline below eight broad points relating to both the history of the conflict and some of the most heated discussions surrounding it, past and present. This is not a history book. These points do not represent an exhaustive list. But they do touch upon most of the themes surfacing in the debate as it is commonly conducted in Europe and, indeed, the United States. I reintroduce and expand upon several of these themes later in the book.

I am fully aware that what follows will, for some at least, jar with received wisdoms. In so far as it does, I say this: first, I am not claiming that my reading of the Israel–Palestine conflict must remain set in stone for all time. This is not scripture. It is an honest, factually based appraisal made in good faith. It is practically definitional of a good-faith approach to political debate that one will allow for the possibility that new evidence or better argumentation could alter one's thinking. As long as it is conducted in good faith, I am open to debate and fair-minded discussion on everything connected with the Israel–Palestine conflict. This does not mean that I shirk from putting my case robustly. But it does mean that in making that case I reject entirely the dogmatic and intransigent frame of mind that stands behind much of the anti-Israeli thinking outlined throughout this book. Second, all of the above notwithstanding, I believe that what follows does in fact represent the best and fairest reading of the history and contemporary realities of the conflict. My approach is not intended to please one side or the other or to find the lazy man's middle ground in order to avoid causing offence. It is impossible to please everyone, and foolish to try. I submit that anyone who cannot at least accept that this is *one* reasoned and honourable way of looking at the Israel–Palestine conflict should reflect upon their reactions.

Historical overview, current controversies: eight points

1. Israel has the same fundamental right to exist as any other state in the world. The country's foundational legitimacy, through the aspirations of both the British Mandate under the League of Nations as well as United Nations resolution 181 (which offered a two-state solution as far back as 1947), is as impressive as for most 'new' states formed in the last one hundred years or so. Also, Israel's right to exist as a specifically Jewish state is no less (or more) defensible than the right of any other state to exist within the moral, political, legal and historical framework of national self-determination. Just as France has a right to exist as a state for French people, China for Chinese people, Egypt for Egyptian people and so on, Israel has a right to exist as a state for Israeli people. That right is complemented, indeed it is made real, by a corollary:

Israel, a liberal democracy, has the same right as other states to define the essence of its own constitutionality. Just as dozens of states define themselves as Christian or Muslim, so Israel has a right to define itself as Jewish.

Clearly, the condition of the Jewish people prior to the establishment of Israel, their dispersal throughout the world in the Diaspora, has meant that national self-determination has proceeded along unusual lines. In most cases, the assertion of this right has not involved mass migration from other parts of the world. Consider the subject nations of the empires of the Habsburgs, the Ottomans, the British, the French, and the Russians and Soviets. The standard model, as we experienced it in the twentieth century, involved peoples which had long inhabited a particular piece of land and who were united by a single ethnic and linguistic identity throwing off the yoke of a foreign oppressor, seeing that oppressor forced out by war, or negotiating a peaceable withdrawal. Emigrés, exiles and refugees may subsequently return home but usually after a relatively brief period of absence from the motherland, and generally in relatively small numbers.

Set against this sort of scenario, the Israeli/Jewish case is indeed unusual. Though Jews have lived in the lands of Israel/Palestine for millennia and have been in a plurality or an outright majority in Jerusalem since at least the 1840s, the fact remains that national self-determination in this case has overwhelmingly proceeded through migration. And, moreover, that migration has been to a land ruled by Jews only in the dim and distant past.

Does that affect the legitimacy of the Jewish claim to national determination in the State of Israel? There are two important reasons why it does not. First, due to the dispersal of the Jewish people in dozens of different countries, migration was the *only* way in which Jewish national self-determination could possibly have been effected. To deny

Jews the right to national self-determination because it was exercised through migration is, therefore, merely another way of saying that Jews had no right to self-determination at all. It uses the dispersal of the Jewish people, itself a product of anti-Semitism, as a reason to deny to Jews the same rights accorded to other peoples. Past anti-Semitism is thus used as a justification for subsequent anti-Semitism. Second, there are no sound legal or moral reasons why Jews should not have chosen to emigrate to the land of their forefathers. The geographical space to which the early Zionists aspired to move in the nineteenth century was extremely sparsely populated (around 500,000 people in total compared with more than 11 million today), being an underdeveloped backwater of the Ottoman Empire. Jewish immigration proceeded via land purchases under the Ottomans and the British. It was usually legal, and it led directly to a dramatic improvement in the social and economic conditions of everyone in the area.

By the time that the United Nations voted for the establishment of Israel in 1947, Jews were in a clear majority in the areas designated for their state. Contrary to some of the more bizarre assumptions now current in the debate about Israel's foundational legitimacy there was, of course, no Palestinian state in that or any other part of the Middle East. Nor, in the main, did the various Arab communities scattered around the area entertain ideas of creating one. That idea grew in importance from very small beginnings and did not gain wide currency until very much later – very much later, one might add, than the sense of national consciousness among the Jews which led to the establishment of Israel. In terms of national self-determination, the Jews made the prior claim.

As for the Holocaust, it brought home (at least for a while) to the civilised nations of the world a deep understanding that anti-Semitism was no longer acceptable and that

Jews must be given the same rights, including to self-determination, as other peoples. It also created a large pool of Jewish refugees who needed a place to live.

In the aftermath of World War II all of the factors sketched out above came together to provide the basis on which the State of Israel was constructed. The basic legitimacy of the Jewish state of Israel – a question quite separate from the debate about the borders of that state – is thus underpinned by an impressively powerful set of moral, political, historical and legal arguments.

2. The Palestinians also have a right to national self-determination. I understand, but do not want to accept, the argument that the Palestinians have lost the moral right to statehood because of their long-standing rejectionist views of the Jewish state, or because of terrorism. However, this does not alter the fact that the key reason for their inability to exercise their right to self-determination has been a decades-long refusal by Israel's enemies, the Palestinians themselves included, to accept a division of the land involving the existence of a specifically Jewish state.

Plans for partition – two-state solutions – mooted in 1937 according to the terms of the British commission headed by Lord Peel and, more importantly, by the United Nations a decade later, were flatly rejected by the Palestinian and wider Arab leaderships. True, the Jewish side was unhappy with some of the Peel Commission's conclusions but it agreed to keep talking. Crucially, the Jewish side did, of course, accept the UN plan for two states while the other side opted for violence.

Everyone involved in the debate about Israel and the Palestinians knows how central this point is to the question of culpability for the wider conflict and all that it has entailed. Israel's fiercest opponents are painfully aware that widespread knowledge and acceptance of these basic historical realities would seriously undermine key elements of their case. If, after all, the international community in the first half of the twenty-first century is attempting to forge a peace on the basis of a two-state principle that was accepted by the Jewish/Israeli side but rejected by the Palestinian/Arab side in the first half of the twentieth century it is clear which side must bear underlying responsibility for the conflict as a whole.

It needs to be stressed that this does not mean for one moment that the Israelis emerge as guiltless about every event, major and minor, which has unfolded since the inception of the state. But it does mean that the Palestinian/Arab side must bear primary responsibility for Palestinian statelessness and for much that that has implied. As occupiers of the West Bank and the Gaza Strip until 1967, the Arab states of Egypt and Jordan could have established an independent Palestinian state in the manner now demanded of Israel. They did not, and that tells us a lot.

Knowing what is at stake here, Israel's detractors have brought forward a number of counter-arguments which need to be understood. There have been several lines of attack. Most have amounted to a rejection of the idea that there should have been a Jewish state in the first place: the United Nations was in the grip of 'colonial powers', as was the League of Nations before it; the partition proposals were thus tainted by institutional bias and injustice.

The argument is, of course, self-defeating since it merely underlines the reality of Palestinian rejectionism and its centrality to the conflict. Subsets of this argument focus on the percentages of Jews and Arabs in the region which purport to show that Arabs were in the majority and Jews the minority. Again, this is self-defeating since the point of the partition proposals was to delineate out of a land with no state the borders of two states: one with a Jewish majority; the other with an Arab majority. That is exactly what they did. The

Jewish/Israeli side accepted this. The Arab/Palestinian side rejected it.

A final stand is often made on the following lines: the Jewish leaders may have accepted a two-state solution in 1947, the argument goes, but they did not really mean it. In other words, although it cannot be denied that the Jews *formally* accepted the two-state solution there is reason to believe that they did not intend to honour the attendant agreements in practice. To back up their argument, its proponents then usually proceed to parade selective quotations from David Ben-Gurion, the most important Jewish leader at the relevant time and subsequently Israel's first prime minister, suggesting that his long-term ambitions were to expand the borders of the Jewish state beyond the terms of the partition proposals and to transfer in more Jews and to transfer out more Arabs. Here are two examples of the kinds of quotations used. They are taken from the pro-Palestinian website, palestineremembered.com, which readers can refer to for a more extensive rendition of the argument. The first relates to Ben-Gurion's reaction to the 1947 partition resolution of the UN and shows the conflicting emotions that he felt at the time:

'In my heart, there was joy mixed with sadness: joy that the nations at last acknowledged that we are a nation with a state, and sadness that we lost half of the country, Judea and Samaria, and, in addition, that we [would] have [in our state] 400,000 [Palestinian] Arabs.'[2]

In another comment a month later, in December 1947, Ben-Gurion spoke to leaders of the Histadrut, the Israeli trade union movement. To his concerns about the geographical size and extent of the Jewish state granted by the UN, he added and expanded upon his concerns about the relatively small Jewish majority that it contained:

'In the area allocated to the Jewish State there are not more than 520,000 Jews and about 350,000 non-Jews, mostly

Arabs. Together with the Jews of Jerusalem, the total population of the Jewish state at the time of its establishment, will
be about one million, including almost 40% non-Jews. Such
a [population] composition does not provide a stable basis
for a Jewish State. This [demographic] fact must be viewed
in all its clarity and acuteness. With such a [population]
composition, there cannot even be absolute certainty that
control will remain in the hands of the Jewish majority ...
There can be no stable and strong Jewish state so long as it
has a Jewish majority of only 60%.'[3]

There are plenty of other quotations which can be found
to back up the view that Ben-Gurion and other Jewish leaders
were not happy with the deal they had been offered by the
UN in 1947 and even that they would seek to improve upon
it if they could. This does nothing to alter the basic facts.
Moreover, there is nothing shocking in the notion that Ben-
Gurion had dreams of a bigger state with more of his own
people inside it. Unsurprisingly, in talking to his own constituencies, he would wax lyrical about his grandest designs.
Of course he wanted a better deal. When people enter into
negotiations they attempt to extract the maximum for themselves that they can. When they come out of those negotiations the deal they have struck may in some respects
disappoint them. It is quite normal for them to hope that
they can improve upon what they have got at a later date.
Again, though, the incontrovertible fact is that the
Jewish/Israeli side accepted the 1947 UN deal for two states
while the Arab/Palestinian side did not.

The argument is flawed for another reason. The
Palestinian/Arab side did not reject the two-state proposals
because of concerns that the Jews might not honour its terms.
They rejected it because they opposed the idea of a Jewish
state, period. If anyone had cause to worry about the underlying motivations of the other side during the inter-war
period and beyond it was surely the Jews. In contemplating

the attitudes and motivations of the Palestinians, they had had to contend with the likes of Mohammed Amin al Husseini, Grand Mufti of Jerusalem, chairman of the Arab Higher Committee (the main Palestinian political organisation, founded in 1936) and president of the Supreme Muslim Council (the leading Muslim affairs body in the British Mandate of Palestine).

During World War II he assumed a prominent role in Nazi Germany, enthusiastically helping to prosecute the Holocaust. I submit that in an argument aimed at proving Jewish perfidy and duplicity and Arab/Palestinian innocence this is an unhelpful entry on the curriculum vitae of the Palestinian side's leading man. Husseini, an admirer of Adolf Hitler, worked closely with the Nazis in German-occupied Europe broadcasting anti-Semitic propaganda on Berlin Radio and playing a leading role in setting up Bosnian Muslim divisions of the Waffen SS which participated in genocide in Yugoslavia. He was a wanted war criminal after 1945 but escaped to Egypt. In his memoirs he made clear what his intentions were for the Jews of Palestine:

'Our fundamental condition for cooperating with Germany was a free hand to eradicate every last Jew from Palestine and the Arab world. I asked Hitler for an explicit undertaking to allow us to solve the Jewish problem in a manner befitting our national and racial aspirations and according to the scientific methods innovated by Germany in the handling of its Jews. The answer I got was: "The Jews are yours."'[4]

Attempts to slur ordinary Palestinians as Nazis are unworthy of serious debate, though the Nazi influence on aspects of modern-day Palestinian and Arab anti-Semitism is a depressing reality. Nor should it be assumed that Husseini spoke for all Palestinians or that his words and actions in the past should be laid at the door of Palestinians today, though he was in fact revered by the late Yasser Arafat.

What is important is simply to recognise that the most important Palestinian leader of his day became an active (and prolific) Nazi during World War II and that he was a thoroughgoing anti-Semite with murderous intentions towards the Jews. This tells us something highly significant about the Palestinian political culture of which Husseini was the leading light. It tells us about the depths of the rejectionism of the Jewish state inside that culture. It tells us quite how justified were the concerns of Jewish leaders as they accepted a two-state solution in full knowledge of the possibility that Husseini or someone like him could emerge as the leader of the very Palestinian state that they had agreed to. And yet, just two years after the Holocaust, they still accepted it.

In summary then, it cannot sensibly be denied that Palestinian/Arab rejectionism forms the historical root cause of the conflict with the State of Israel.

Unfortunately for all concerned, that rejectionism proved to be a durable feature of Palestinian politics. The long-standing failure to achieve a comprehensive peace agreement in later years proceeded from the same problem as evidenced, among many other examples that could be quoted, by Yasser Arafat's rejection of the initiatives sponsored by former US president Bill Clinton from 2000 to the end of his term of office. Again, recognising what is at stake here, there have been desperate efforts to paint a different picture. Again, none of them can be considered convincing. As close observers of the negotiations know, the most impressive counter-argument to this analysis was made by Robert Malley, Special Assistant for Arab-Israeli Affairs under President Clinton from 1998 to 2001.

Malley has argued that blame for the failure of the negotiations must be shared between all three parties to the negotiations: the Israeli Prime Minister Ehud Barak and his team, the Palestinians and even the Americans. But even if one accepts, as Malley has argued, that in addition to problems with Arafat, Israeli negotiating tactics and American preparations and timing also played a part, it is still not possible to shake the fact that peace proposals involving a two-state solution were accepted by the Israelis and rejected by the Palestinians.[5]

As Dennis Ross, Malley's boss at the time and Clinton's chief official heading the US negotiating team, has said: 'Both Barak and Clinton were prepared to do what was necessary to reach agreement. Both were up to the challenge. Neither shied away from the risks inherent in confronting history and mythology. Can one say the same about Arafat? Unfortunately, not . . .'[6]

And, he goes on: 'Consider Arafat's performance at Camp David. It is not just that he had, in the words of President Clinton, "been here fourteen days and said no to everything." It is that all he did at Camp David was to repeat old mythologies and invent new ones, like, for example, that the Temple was not in Jerusalem but in Nablus. Denying the core of the other side's faith is not the act of someone preparing himself to end a conflict.'

As one of the most experienced and knowledgeable Western figures involved in the Middle East, Ross's observations have been invaluable. Widening his argument from the person of Yasser Arafat to the problem with the Palestinian leadership generally, he adds: 'It is not, as Abba Eban said, that the Palestinians never miss an opportunity to miss an opportunity. It is that in always feeling victimized they fall back on blaming everyone else for their predicament. It is never their fault. History may not have been kind or fair to the Palestinians. They have suffered and been betrayed by others. They are, surely, the weakest player with the fewest cards to play. But by always blaming others, they never have to focus on their own mistakes. And that perpetuates the avoidance of responsibility, not its assumption.'

The public statements of some moderate Palestinian leaders to the international community (including those connected with the Oslo Accords) recognising the right of Israel to exist may be genuine in individual cases. However, the broader Palestinian elite remains opposed to the fundamental right of Israel to exist as a *Jewish state*, as shown by public statements from leading Palestinian officials and the consistent policy of virulent propaganda against the very existence of Israel through Palestinian media, schooling and religious authorities. Some polls now show the Palestinian people to be willing to accept Israel out of a pragmatic recognition that it is not going away. There is evidence to suggest that a majority of them might accept a two-state solution in some form. Unfortunately, much of this is undercut by their simultaneous preference for allowing the millions of descendants of the refugees of the war of 1947–8 (see below) to flood 'back' into Israel, thus destroying its character as a majority Jewish state. In other words, their preference for a pragmatic acceptance of Israel, grudging as it is, is shown to be contradicted by other of their preferences and thus to be lacking in seriousness.

As ever, though, it is important to keep in mind that the real problems lie not so much with ordinary Palestinians as with their leaders. In response to a call from Israeli Prime Minister Ehud Olmert in November 2007 for the Palestinians to recognise Israel as a Jewish state, a slew of senior figures aggressively and publicly refused. Salam Fayad, the Prime Minister of the Palestinian Authority, said emphatically: 'Israel can define itself as it likes, but the Palestinians will not recognize it as a Jewish state.'[7] Chief Palestinian negotiator Ahmed Qurei said: 'This [demand] is absolutely refused.'[8] Another very prominent Palestinian negotiator, Saab Erekat, added: 'The Palestinians will never acknowledge Israel's Jewish identity. ... There is no country in the world where religious and national identities are intertwined.'⁹ As the analyst Daniel Pipes said of Erekat's words in the second half of that quotation: 'Erekat's generalization is both curious and revealing. Not only do 56 states and the PLO belong to the Organization of the Islamic Conference, but most of them, including the PLO, make the sharia (Islamic law) their main or only source of legislation. Saudi Arabia even requires that every subject be a Muslim.'¹⁰

There is yet another layer to Palestinian rejectionism and it has its supporters in the West. Tellingly, every now and then senior Palestinian officials raise the prospect of eschewing a two-state solution in favour of a one-state solution.¹¹

It is a transparent attempt to destroy Israel's Jewish character by suggesting a bi-national state in which Jews and Palestinians live side by side in 'peace and harmony'. At face value, the argument is about as convincing as suggesting that the best solution to the ethnic divisiveness of the Balkans would be to recreate the old Yugoslavia. It is not a serious proposition and there is not the slightest chance of the Israelis ever agreeing to it. But that is not the point. Whenever Palestinian leaders talk in this manner they are once again demonstrating to anyone who is watching and listening that their commitment to a two-state solution is tenuous. It is still possible that they could be pushed into it. Ultimately, though, their hearts are not in it.

The underlying thinking of the Palestinian leadership on this question has shown remarkable continuity over time. While the so-called Greater Israel movement – a movement dedicated to annexing historic Jewish lands in the West Bank and elsewhere – did enjoy a certain popularity following the 1967 and 1973 wars, when accommodation with the Palestinians seemed impossible, it has since retreated as a serious proposition and is now being pushed only by a small, though vociferous, minority. Despite popular misconceptions, most of the actual settlers are neither religious zealots nor ideologically motivated. The single most important incentive for the majority of them is economic. The settlements simply offer them a better standard of living.

Overall, the bulk of the Jewish/Israeli side has tended to accept the principle of dividing land in order to accommodate the national aspirations of two distinct peoples rather than just one. The bulk of the Palestinian and Arab/Muslim side has tended to reject that principle in both word and deed. For those interested in peace, this is deeply problematic. But that is no reason for pretending that the problem does not exist.

3. My third core proposition is that, even though Palestinian/Arab rejectionism forms the root cause of the conflict, this does not mean that Palestinian suffering is any less real. Just because a man is the author of his own misfortune this does not mean that his misfortune can be discounted. Nor does it mean that in authoring his misfortune in a general sense he cannot fall victim to subsequent injustice. In the face of Palestinian and Arab violence and rejectionism, Israel has made certain moves which have made peace agreements more difficult to achieve and which have increased the sense of despair among the Palestinians. First among these is settlement policy on the West Bank. This is a contentious issue and it needs a little time and effort to understand.

If Israel's enemies had not started a war in 1967 there would be no settlements and the whole problem would not have arisen. In the immediate aftermath of that war the Arab states made it clear that they had not been chastened by their defeat and that their rejectionism remained as implacable as ever. The infamous Khartoum Resolution of 1 September 1967 issued the so-called 'Three Nos': 'No peace', 'No recognition' and 'No negotiation' with Israel.[12] Rejectionist words became annihilationist deeds six years later when Arab states launched the Yom Kippur War, yet another attempt to destroy the State of Israel by violent means. It is against this background that the occupation of the West Bank and the settlement issue must be judged. If it is not being judged in this manner I submit that it is not being judged in good faith.

The fact is that nobody has full sovereign rights to the land currently occupied by Israel. Supporters and opponents of Israel often expend much energy debating whether the territories should be described as 'occupied' or 'disputed'. In fact, both terms are correct: the land is occupied and it is also disputed. A better, more neutral way of describing the status of the occupied and disputed territories might be to call them 'unallocated territories'. They exist in a kind of limbo which will endure until final status agreements precisely define how much of the land is given to whom. Nonetheless, this is not to absolve Israel of responsibility on a technicality. Basic common sense suggests that a two-state solution to the conflict will be harder to achieve if the area which is going to form the Palestinian state is compromised to the extent that it no longer forms a meaningful whole.

Discussion of the settlement issue in particular and the West Bank in general is plagued by misunderstandings. It may be helpful at this stage to add a few correctives.

First, although the settlements are indeed problematic the problem is not insurmountable. Settlements have been evacuated in the past – in the Sinai in 1982 and in Gaza in 2005. In the context of an overall peace agreement – and perhaps even in the absence of one – settlers could be moved from the West Bank while land transfers to a Palestinian state could be made as compensation for settlements that remain. In other words, a deal involving compromise on the settlers can be done in the future as it has been done in the past. By contrast, a compromise deal cannot be done on the question of Israel's right to exist as a Jewish state. The former is an important and complex problem. The latter is formative of the conflict as a whole.

Second, in so far as one attaches significance to the murky machinations of international law as enunciated by the United Nations, it is not reasonable to ask, nor, despite widespread misunderstandings, is it demanded by the key resolutions, that Israel withdraw from any of the territories until Israel's enemies agree to make peace. No state can be expected to make itself more vulnerable to attack by conceding strategically important territory to self-declared enemies. Thousands of rocket attacks on Israel following withdrawal from Gaza provide clear evidence that Israel's concerns in this regard are justified. On the question of a state's right to defend itself, Israel is not an exception nor should an exception be made for Israel.

There are also multiple confusions in the public debate about United Nations Security Council Resolution 242. This famous resolution was passed on 22 November 1967 in the aftermath of the Six Day War. In most readings of the Israel–Palestine conflict, Resolution 242 is seen as the principal expression in international law of the so-called 'land-for-peace' formula: Israel gives up territory in exchange for durable and credible peace agreements. Despite the fact that it was long rejected by the Palestinian leadership (until 1988) it is frequently seen as an embarrassment to Israel. It is also referred to as though it makes a clear call for Israel to withdraw to the precise borders which existed before the 1967 war.

On the contrary, Israel is *not* required to withdraw from all of the territories occupied in 1967 by Resolution 242. The so-called 'Green Line' representing the armistice lines drawn between Israel and Jordan at the formal end of hostilities in 1949 is no basis for permanent borders as the drafters of the resolution itself have made clear and as all of the members of the Security Council well understood in passing it. Resolution 242 called on Israel to withdraw from 'territories occupied' (meaning most of them), but it emphatically did not call on Israel to withdraw from 'all territories'.

In the *American Journal of International Law*, Eugene V. Rostow – US Undersecretary of State at the time, a drafter of the resolution and a prominent professor of law – said of Resolution 242:

'... the absence of the definite article in paragraph 1 (i) of Resolution 242 was fully and carefully considered – and fully understood – in the debates of the Council. As Lord George-Brown, who was the British Foreign Minister in 1967, remarked the omission of the word "the" was deliberate. The Soviet and Indian draft resolutions were both explicit in requiring Israeli withdrawal from *all* the territories in question. They did not prevail. Many, many attempts were made to persuade Lord Caradon [the British ambassador to the UN] and the British Foreign Minister to accept language which would require withdrawal to the Armistice Demarcation Lines. They all failed. In the end the Council agreed unanimously on the British draft, knowing exactly what it meant: that is, that Resolution 242, resting on the Armistice Agreements of 1949, did permit parties to make what President Johnson called "insubstantial" changes in the Armistice Demarcation Lines of 1949 as they moved from armistice to peace.'[13]

Lord Caradon, the principal drafter of the resolution, himself said: '... the essential phrase which is not sufficiently recognized is that withdrawal should take place to secure and recognize boundaries, and these words were very carefully chosen: they have to be secure and they have to be recognized ... It was not for us to lay down exactly where the border should be. I know the 1967 border very well. It is not a satisfactory border, it is where troops had to stop in 1948, just where they happened to be that night, that is not a permanent boundary ...'[14]

Caradon's boss, British Foreign Minister George Brown, was equally emphatic. There have been attempts by Israel's detractors to counter that, since the introductory words to the resolution refer to 'the inadmissibility of the acquisition of territory by war' another interpretation is at least possible. Most international lawyers have always seen this as unconvincing since the body of a text would usually take precedence over commentary leading up to it and, more importantly, because the debate over the definite article ended up having material significance to the resolution's passing. (Arguably, it would only make sense in any case with reference to the aggressor, that is to say *not* Israel. Israel acquired territory via self-defence not via a war of aggression.) There has also even been an attempt to suggest that since the French translation of Resolution 242 effectively *includes* the definite article, it can at least be argued that Israel is required to withdraw to the Green Line. Again, the counter-argument fails: the resolution was passed according to the English-language version which therefore takes precedence.

Commenting on the broader issue of who has legal rights to the West Bank, the writer Yossi Klein Halevi has summed up a truth about the situation which is voiced all too rarely: 'Legally,' he stated in an article in 2003, 'the West Bank is extraterritorial: The international community didn't recognize Jordan's annexation, and, because Palestine isn't being restored but invented, its borders are negotiable.'[15]

In sum, what this all means is that the situation surrounding the legality or otherwise of Israeli settlements on the West Bank is much less clear-cut than one might suppose given the table thumping which so often attends discussion of them. United Nations Resolution 446 – affirming the Fourth Geneva Convention prohibiting population transfers to occupied land – is often invoked to suggest that settlements on the West Bank stand in clear violation of international law. But if, as can be argued on the basis of UN Resolution 242, some of that land will become part of Israel anyway, it does not seem reasonable to say that Israel cannot build on it. The drafters of Resolution 242 made it clear that they did not envisage that the final borders would be *substantially* different from the Green Line. But more than four decades after the event who can now define what 'substantial' might mean?

At the very least, the matter is open to debate. It seems that in the context of contemporary peace efforts the most reasonable, real-world interpretation of the key United Nations resolutions as they relate to the West Bank in general and the settlements in particular is the same as the common sense interpretation: given the mistakes on both sides since 1967, Israel should keep land and settlements on areas of strategic importance a small way into the West Bank but it may not take so much territory that a Palestinian state is impossible to construct. Broadly speaking, this approach to the matter was endorsed in the Clinton peace proposals which accepted that some of the settlements would remain, while the land on which they had been built would formally become part of Israel.

4. A fourth set of points concerns the Palestinian refugees. It is a sign of the inbuilt bias in much of the debate about Middle Eastern refugees that it all but excludes discussion of the Jewish refugees who fled Arab countries for Israel at around the same time. Most estimates put the number of Jewish refugees at around 850,000 compared with something in the order of 750,000 Palestinians. Nonetheless, the anti-Israeli polemic is what it is and it needs to be dealt with.

A fair and balanced reading of history suggests that responsibility for the Palestinian refugee problem lies in many quarters. However, in terms of the root cause of the problem, responsibility must lie with the Arab/Palestinian leadership in the late 1940s. Had the Arab/Palestinian side joined the Jewish/Israeli side in accepting the two-state solution offered by the United Nations in 1947 instead of opting for violence –

which intensified immediately after the passing of the resolution – there would have been be no Palestinian refugees.

There is no wiggle room here: no violence and war, no
refugees from violence and war. Once a war of annihilation –
for that is what it was intended to be – was launched against
the nascent Jewish state a combination of factors led to the
refugee crisis on the ground and perpetuated it.

As far as I can tell – my primary influence in this regard is
the Israeli historian Benny Morris – the most accurate
reading of what happened disproves both extremes in the
debate. Some early Zionist narratives appeared to talk as
though the Palestinians left their homes in a robotic, collective response to coordinated Arab propaganda telling them
to clear the way for their armies' onslaught. Others were
deliberately vague, seeming to suggest that the Palestinians
simply upped and left in search of more congenial climes and
that that was more or less that. For their part, extreme anti-
Zionist narratives, now fashionable in many quarters and
given the veneer of respectability by the scribblings of the
militantly anti-Zionist historian Ilan Pappé,[16] have attempted
to blame the refugee problem on an allegedly premeditated
Israeli programme of 'ethnic cleansing'.

Neither narrative will stand up to serious scrutiny. What
really seems to have happened is that in their tens and hundreds of thousands ordinary Palestinian Arabs simply fled
from the fighting and the general chaos in the hope of
returning to their homes once the business of destroying the
Jewish state had been done. They did not need to be told to
leave by anyone, Arab or Israeli. Most sympathised with the
invading Arab armies and the Palestinian fighters. Many
collaborated with them. Some joined them. But, overall,
their motivation for leaving was the same as the motivation
of people throughout history confronted with war and
seeking to get themselves out of harm's way. It is certainly
true that in a minority of cases Palestinians were driven out

by Israeli forces, notably in strategically important villages being used against the Jews on the road to Jerusalem. It is also true that Arab propaganda played a part in other cases. By and large, though, there appears to be no reason to resort to conspiracy theories of whatever description to understand the broad picture.

Having backed the aggressor, and eventually the loser in the conflict, the Palestinian refugees, not surprisingly, were not allowed back once hostilities came to an end. Why should they have been? United Nations General Assembly Resolution 194 – passed on 11 December 1948 – stated that those refugees 'wishing to return to their homes and live at peace with their neighbours should be permitted to do so at the earliest practicable date'.[17] Since Israel had every reason to believe that the refugees did *not* want to 'live at peace with their neighbours' it is at least arguable that they forfeited their right to return. Which other state in the world could reasonably be asked to welcome back hundreds of thousands of people who had been taught by their leaders to strive for that state's destruction?

The desperately harsh truth is that the Palestinian refugees found (and placed) themselves on the wrong side of history. This does not mean that their suffering – not least at the hands of Arab governments who have used them ruthlessly as pawns – has not been real. But it does mean, surely, that Israel's response to the refugee problem was understandable. A war that Israel did not start, and which, if it had lost, could quite possibly have resulted in the massacre of large sections of the Jewish population, ended up with a situation in which Israel had more land and a more favourable demographic mix. The Israelis pressed home their advantage. Under the circumstances, who could really blame them? Certainly not the European Union or most of the nations of Europe which have long accepted the reality of the almost contemporaneous German refugee problem following World War II. The millions of ethnic Germans who, in contrast with the Palestinians, were expelled systematically from the Czech lands following the defeat of the Nazis (see pp. 124–5) do not have many champions inside the European commentariat. Why the double standard? We need an answer.

5. A fifth guiding assumption, bringing the discussion up to the present day, is that Israel is a vibrant, liberal democracy with an independent judiciary and a free press. It is governed through a parliamentary system made up of freely organised parties elected via free and fair elections. These characteristics make it the only mature democracy in the region and one of only a minority of such states in the world. In my view, this makes Israel a natural ally for Europe and the United States. Others may disagree. It all depends on the premium one attaches to democratic rule.

Of course, Israeli democracy is far from perfect. Israel's Arab minority, representing 20 per cent of the population, has political rights but its civil rights are certainly restricted. Many of these civil right issues arise from land disputes made all the more heated because of the conflict between Arabs and Jews across the region. Other problems arise in the same manner that they arise in other Western democracies where minorities encounter serious discrimination in such matters as job opportunities and integration with the majority community generally.

Palestinians in the West Bank, of course, do not live in a liberal-democratic environment at all. They are subject to myriad restrictions on their daily lives including check points, travel restrictions generally and many other consequences of the Israeli military occupation. Problems, for some, have become more acute since the construction of Israel's security barrier. It is nonetheless obvious that the vast majority of these restrictions have been put in place in order to combat terrorism. They would not exist at all if Palestinian leaders had accepted rather than rejected peace offers and if terrorism had been renounced once and for all.

More generally, in contrast with other countries, such as Russia in Chechnya, Israel has not responded to the mass terrorism of recent years through large-scale atrocities such as carpet bombing, the burning or razing of entire villages or mass disappearances. It is a great mistake, and an all too common one, to address the question of Israeli treatment of the Palestinians through the human rights paradigm. The situation can only be correctly understood through the paradigm of security and anti-terrorism policy. This does not mean that the Palestinians do not suffer or that they do not live in a restrictive environment. What it means is that Israeli restrictions do not proceed from an oppressive or authoritarian political culture. Israel is a democracy under fire. Palestinian suffering is primarily the consequence of Palestinian violence.

6. A sixth point concerns Israeli military attacks on the terrorist infrastructure. I reject as wrong-headed all moral parallels between Israel's use of force to defend itself and Palestinian attacks on Israeli civilians. Israel does kill civilians during attempts to strike at militants, but it never intends to kill them. Palestinian terror attacks are deliberately aimed at maximising civilian casualties. Civilians, in other words, are not seen as unfortunate victims killed instead of, or alongside, the real targets. They *are* the targets. Disgracefully, but tellingly, the deliberate targeting of civilians is conducted with the support of large sections of the Palestinian population, as opinion polls consistently show. Where Israel is reckless or negligent in its pre-emptive or retaliatory attacks on the Palestinian terrorist infrastructure – and there are cases where it clearly has been – its government is rightly criticised. Israel's problem in avoiding loss of life among Palestinian civilians, however, is compounded by the systematically

employed strategy among terrorist groups of embedding themselves inside the civilian population thus using civilians as human shields. Israel, by contrast, attempts to minimise its own civilian casualties by taking civil defence measures and by putting its soldiers, rather than its civilians, in the front line. The fact that more Palestinian civilians die than Israeli civilians is the inevitable consequence of all of the above factors as any reasonable and objective appraisal must inevitably conclude.

7. Israel's security concerns vis-à-vis the Palestinians are compounded by Israel's security concerns in the wider region. There is emerging evidence that some Arab states in the Middle East now take a more pragmatic approach towards Israel, not in the sense that they accept Israel as an equal partner on the international stage but in the sense that they now acknowledge the reality that Israel does in fact exist and is likely to do so in the long term. This new pragmatism has been bolstered by a recognition that the very real threat from an increasingly powerful Iran may have to take precedence over elemental hatred of Israel. While it would be naïve to talk about alliances between Arab states and Israel, both sides recognise that they have a common enemy.

Nevertheless, it is not reasonable to ask a state in Israel's position to give the benefit of the doubt to Arab and Muslim nations as long as they continue to use official media to pump hate-filled propaganda against Jews and the Jewish state into the minds of their people (see pp. 78–81). Israel would still have no choice but to see its security situation in existential terms even in the absence of Iranian leader Mahmoud Ahmadinejad's declared aim of destroying the Jewish state. One may retort that with an impressively modern and equipped military and with the fallback option of nuclear weapons, Israel is strong enough to inflict massive retaliation on any regime or group foolish enough to attack it. Nonetheless, in the Middle Eastern neighbourhood there are constant reminders that the will to harm Israel continues to exist. An attempt to destroy Israel may fail, but it could still cost vast numbers of lives in the process. There is no cause for complacency.

Constant attempts in Europe to draw analogies between Israel's situation and localised conflicts on the continent and in the United Kingdom, such as Spain's problems with the Basque separatist group ETA and Britain's former conflict with nationalists in Northern Ireland, indicate a complete intellectual and moral failure to understand the true nature of Israel's conflict with the Palestinians, the Arabs and the wider Muslim world.

8. Due to the duration and intensity of the conflict the Israeli psyche often approximates to a kind of siege mentality. After more than six decades of conflict it would be extraordinary if it did not. This has a number of negative consequences including, on occasion, a tendency to push policies that are self-destructive, such as excessive settlement policy, or to conduct poorly conceived operations, such as the response to Hezbollah aggression in Lebanon in 2006 which was criticised around the world and more especially in Israel itself. More broadly, constant reminders to the Israeli people that they cannot trust the motives of their adversaries has given hardliners in Israel who are not disposed to do a peace deal far greater power in the political process than they might otherwise have had. This problem has been compounded by Israel's extraordinarily inclusive democracy. The country's proportional representation system sets a threshold for parliamentary representation of just 2 per cent. Germany and many European states, by contrast, have thresholds of 5 per cent. This means that people representing the far extremes of Israeli public opinion can find themselves as kingmakers in the Israeli parliament. It is not a healthy situation.

Like all other countries in the world, Israel makes mistakes and gets things wrong, sometimes badly wrong. Whenever it does so it deserves to be called to account. Reasoned criticism of Israel is perfectly legitimate and is built into the structure of Israeli society just as it is built into the structure of any fully functioning democracy.

These eight points come together to form a core narrative which is obviously very different from the one under whose terms Israel's most vociferous enemies in the West now operate. Of course, there is much more that could be, and will be, said on these matters. There is a vast and easily available literature to provide a full picture of the history of the conflict to anyone who is sufficiently interested. However, the above list captures many of the key issues which usually cause controversy.

As I suggested in introducing this section, there is plenty of room for debate. At the very least, though, I submit that whether or not one accepts all of my conclusions they need to be taken into account by anyone interested in a fair-minded discussion of this conflict. When they are, criticism of Israel remains possible and reasonable; demonisation does not.

Do Israel's detractors matter?

At this point, let me restate the purpose of this book in order to preclude misunderstandings. This is not a survey or analysis of inter-state, governmental-level relations between Israel and the countries of Europe or the European Union. Its central focus is on the way in which Israel is talked about and written about by the opinion formers – people and institutions aiming to influence public perceptions.

Of course, governmental leaders themselves have an influence on public perceptions. They are not excluded from the discussion and they are referred to in some detail in Chapter 6 in considering the way in which aspects of international diplomacy can have a negative impact on Israel. But I believe there is a special value in placing emphasis on non-governmental actors since, in the main, their commentary is an unalloyed expression of what they really believe. Unlike top-level political leaders they are not usually engaged in a political balancing act in which every statement made on sensitive matters has to be carefully crafted to suit a variety of different audiences. This is not to say that top politicians are inherently dishonest. It is simply to recognise that the business of politics is different from the business of political commentary. When prime ministers and presidents address the public we can never really be sure whether what they are saying is reflective of what they, in their personal and private capacities, truly believe. Commentary on Israel from writers, Nobel Prize winners, columnists and the like provides us with a window into the European soul. It gives us an indication about what's down there. It tells us something about fundamental values and the capacity for moral judgement of the collective mind. If for no other reason than that, I believe that the task is worthwhile. But there are other reasons as well and they do in fact relate to the sphere of high politics.

Contrary to the preconceptions of some, relations between Israel and Europe at the governmental level are not all bad. To the horror of anti-Israeli groups, for example, the European Union again upgraded its relations with Israel in June 2008 reflecting increasing cooperation in the fields of trade and technology and giving Israel the best formal-diplomatic relationship with the EU of any country in the Middle East. Commenting on the move, the centre-right *Jerusalem Post* celebrated it in an editorial and placed it in some useful perspective:

'The EU'S move – and the deepening ties it heralds – is a welcome one for several reasons. First, at an auspicious time, it braces and reinforces a growing friendship. Israel has started to enjoy stronger ties with France under Nicolas Sarkozy, Britain under Gordon Brown, Germany under Angela Merkel, and Italy under Silvio Berlusconi ... The announcement is welcome, too, in light of the fact that the EU remains the financial backer of the PA [Palestinian Authority] and the United Nations Relief and Works Agency. The EU's engagement with the region, after all, has not always been judicious. It has a history of allocating millions of Euros to NGOs based in the PA and Israel, some of which pursue partisan activities that have a less than benign influence on the conflict ... The upgrade is also welcome for the economic fruits it promises to bring to an already robust partnership ... But the upgrade of relations perhaps takes on its deepest significance in light of the EU's role as a Quartet member, and the increased leverage with which Israel can now encourage the Europeans to take a firm stand against Hamas and Iran, while coaxing Palestinian relative moderates to temper their demands so as to increase chances of a bargaining breakthrough. For all these reasons, the EU announcement, and the far-reaching effects it betokens, represent a step in the right direction.'[18]

On the other hand, there are still good reasons to be worried. Ideas matter. They frame the context in which political decisions are made, legitimising some courses of action, delegitimising others. Politicians do not belong to a different species. Like the rest of us, they are influenced and, to a degree, formed by the people and ideas which surround them. In democracies, their jobs depend on an acute awareness of how things are portrayed in the media, which sections of their constituencies believe what, and how things will play to the people. The leaders of Europe's most important countries may, relative to the past and relative to the majority of the opinion formers, be exhibiting a more reasoned attitude to Israel. But this is no guarantee for the future. Nor does an improving relationship dominated by trade and technology mean that European leaders can be relied upon to back Israel when it really matters, as it does when Israel is involved in conflicts. During the Lebanon war of 2006, for example, support for Israel in Europe all but evaporated. During Israel's Operation Cast Lead in Gaza in

December 2008 and January 2009, it was mixed and often contradictory.

The fact is that from a large proportion of contemporary Europe's opinion formers we are now experiencing a tidal wave of hysteria, deception and distortion against the Jewish state which has not only brought resurgent anti-Semitism in its wake but also risks becoming a stain on the continent's entire political culture. In light of what is now going on inside the newspapers, television stations, trade unions, universities and non-governmental organisations of Europe, as well as inside the continent's growing Muslim minorities, governments and political establishments are already under intense pressure. The danger is very real.

As important, it is vital to recognise that there is now a serious risk of anti-Israeli contagion (see Chapter 8) spreading from Europe to the United States, just as a hateful discourse has spread from the Middle East itself into Europe. America, of course, has always had a vocal, anti-Israeli constituency of its own. But recently, febrile hostility to Israel has started to find its way out of the humanities departments of the universities and into the mainstream. It is possible, as I will argue, that the boldness of Mearsheimer and Walt, authors of *The Israel Lobby and U.S. Foreign Policy*, as well as of former President Jimmy Carter, author of *Palestine: Peace not Apartheid*, is at least partly explained by the way an extreme anti-Israeli discourse has been legitimised in Europe. In an age of instant communication, ideas flow freely back and forth across the Atlantic. It is as easy for a Briton or a Frenchman to read online editions of the *New York Times* as it is for an American to read the *Guardian* or the English-language edition of *Le Monde Diplomatique*. It may be more than coincidental that Mearsheimer and Walt's book was first mooted in essay form in the *London Review of Books*.

Finally, in assessing the extent to which anti-Israeli discourse really matters, it is important to recognise the dangers that it poses to Europe's Jewish communities. More than at any time in recent memory, European Jews feel threatened and isolated. The anti-Israeli atmosphere appears to be generating a feeling of alienation. It has also led to an upsurge in anti-Semitic attacks in Europe, as Jewish leaders were at pains to point out during the 2008–9 Gaza campaign.[19] At that time major news organisations outlined a catalogue of anti-Semitic outrages. The Associated Press noted that: 'Molotov cocktails have been hurled toward synagogues in France, Sweden and Belgium. Jews have been beaten in England and Norway, and an Italian union endorsed a boycott of Jewish-owned shops in Rome. In Amsterdam, a Dutch lawmaker marched in a demonstration where the crowd hollered 'Hamas, Hamas, Jews to the Gas'.[20]

For all of these reasons, what is now going on in Europe is a matter of profound importance to Jews and non-Jews, Europeans and Americans and anyone anywhere who believes in reason and decency.

Jews against Israel

One other set of preliminary matters needs to be touched upon before coming to the main body of arguments since it tends to get in the way of clear-headed discussion of the issues. Israel's sharpest detractors believe they have a defence that they can roll out to parry accusations of bias, distortion and, especially, anti-Semitism. Some of their most prominent allies are themselves Jews. And this, they believe, is significant. In a way it is, but not for the reasons they think. Another favourite cleverness among many of Israel's detractors is the related strategy of arguing as if Israel and the Jews belonged to entirely different categories, categories so distinct that when one is talking about Israel one is not necessarily talking about Jews. These are important matters for other arguments in this book. But they are also vital to an understanding of the proper setting in which European discourse about Israel is taking place.

Now, it is of course true that not every Jew is an Israeli (nor even that every Israeli is a Jew). Among the world's thirteen million Jews, less than half of the total live in the Jewish state. It is also true that not all Jews support Israel. There are (very small) sections of the ultra-Orthodox Jewish community which have always opposed the right of Israel to exist on religious grounds: Israel should have been founded by the Messiah; Ben-Gurion jumped the gun.

Apart from this special case, there are also varied attitudes to Israel in the Diaspora and even in Israel itself. These range from the deeply and passionately attached, the quietly but firmly supportive, through the lukewarm and indifferent to the outright hostile. It is that latter group, though by far the smallest, that is seized upon by those who wish to detach conceptually Israel from the Jews. It is an attempt to de-Judaise the question of Israel, to liberate anti-Israeli discourse from the charge of anti-Semitism and to remove from the entire discussion the context in which it has traditionally taken place. It is a slick strategy employed with increasing frequency. It is fundamentally misconceived and it is important to understand why.

The first point to recognise is that the large majority of the world's Jews – inside and outside Israel – do in fact feel a sense of identity with the Jewish state at some level or another. It does appear that there are generational factors at play: younger Jews may have less of an affinity than older Jews.[21] There are differences in emphasis on the ultimate significance of Israel between Diaspora Jews and Israeli Jews. Michael Oren, for example, has written eloquently on competing 'American Jewish and Israeli utopias', whereby many American Jews see America as as much of a home for the Jewish people as Israel.[22] There also appear to be differences of emphasis in different parts of the Diaspora: American Jews do not necessarily see things quite the same way as European or Latin American Jews. Nonetheless, the importance of Israel to most of the world's Jews is not in doubt.

The question of why so many Jews support Israel and share

such a strong affinity with it is not easy to answer precisely. On the simplest level, most Jews perhaps feel a loyalty to the Jewish state in the same kind of way that, for instance, most Australians, whether they live in Australia or not, feel a loyalty to Australia. It's their state. End of story. On a more complicated level, a deeper understanding of the relationship between Diaspora Jews and the State of Israel can only be gained through an appreciation of sociological trends observable across the Western world and especially in Europe.

Most significant among them for the purposes of this discussion is increasing secularisation. Religious observance has collapsed, especially among the young. Jews, like their Christian (but not Muslim) counterparts, are now far less likely to feel a bond of identity with their fellows through the faith into which they were born than their parents and grandparents. Of course, Jews understand themselves as a people as well as a religious group. It is also true that secularisation for Jews, as for Christians, does not mean that the cultural symbols and traditions deriving from the religion have ceased to be relevant or important. But it does mean that the decline in the faith-based, scriptural part of Jewish identity for many Jews has left a gap which needs to be filled if Jewish identity is to retain its vitality. What could fill the gap?

The question raises a multitude of immensely complex issues. But perhaps the most powerful answer is: Israeli nationalism. For many secular Jews, the State of Israel itself has become the abiding symbol of modern Jewishness. What religion can no longer provide as a convincing locus of identity, the State of Israel can. It is impossible to rise completely above the level of enlightened speculation here. But this, ultimately, may be the reason why Israel looms so large in the lives of so many Diaspora Jews and why virulent and irrational criticism of the Jewish state is taken so personally. The most potent symbol of their very identity is under attack. This they cannot ignore. Evidence showing less of an affinity with Israel among Diaspora Jews in the younger generations reinforces the point since the same people also show a decreasing affinity with their Jewishness *per se*. Indifference to one implies indifference to the other.

Whatever the ultimate reason for Jewish affinity with Israel, it is important to recognise how unrepresentative some of the Jewish opponents of Israel really are. It is also important to understand the general point that there is nothing remotely surprising about movements with ill intent against a particular group finding small numbers of willing recruits from within that very group to help promote their aims. In its most common incarnation this practice can be seen all over the democratic world when parliamentary parties proudly parade new recruits from the ranks of their political opponents. The propaganda value is clear and those that can be lured to the other side can expect to be richly rewarded. The practice has been no less common in racial and national contexts. Russian leader Vladimir Putin has always found it easy to recruit Chechens to support, and indeed to execute, his oppressive policies in Chechnya. President P. W. Botha's South Africa found blacks to defend apartheid. Prior to the American Civil War, there were more than three thousand black slave owners,[23] a fact ruthlessly exploited by leading apologists for slavery as a way of diverting attention from the reality of their utterly reprehensible cause. The list could go on and on. All national groups contain small minorities which stand in opposition to the overwhelming majority in terms of their loyalties and the way they define their identity. The phenomenon, that is to say, is normal.

There are also a number of very particular issues which need some explaining in the Jewish case. Throughout much of Jewish history there have been Jews who have been prepared to break ranks decisively with the majority of their community. The extent to which this has been possible has depended on historical circumstances. As Bernard Lewis has put it:

In anti-Semitism's first stage, when the hostility was based in religion and expressed in religious terms, the Jew always had the option of changing sides. During the medieval and early modern periods, Jews persecuted by Christians could convert. Not only could they escape the persecution; they could join the persecutors if they so wished, and some indeed rose to high rank in the church and in the Inquisition. Racial anti-Semitism removed that option. The present-day ideological anti-Semitism has restored it, and now as in the Middle Ages, there seem to be some who are willing to avail themselves of this option.[24]

In terms of the motives for rejecting one's own Jewish identity this has, in some cases, been a predictable consequence of the battle of identities that Diaspora Jews have fought through the centuries and which continues to this day. Sometimes it has taken the form of a desperate attempt to escape anti-Semitism and the social ostracism that goes with it. At other times it has been entirely voluntary and taken the form of a genuine belief that another form of identity is more appropriate – conversion to French Catholicism, for example. In still other cases, the reasons are much more mundane. Jews deeply assimilated inside their host community simply lose touch with their Jewishness. Perhaps they marry out, perhaps not. But the fact of their being Jewish, through having Jewish parents, ceases to have relevance to their lives as they become imbued with the social, political and cultural priorities of the majority community in which they are now firmly embedded. If those priorities include virulent hostility to Israel it is not surprising that some people who are Jewish by birth will also absorb such feelings.

But there is another category which needs to be added to this list and which goes beyond a merely passive absorption of anti-Israeli prejudices. For it is often suggested that some Jews actively and aggressively turn against the majority view of Israel inside their community due to the much discussed problem of self-hatred. They, like their predecessors in the centuries before them, internalise the anti-Semitic mantras of their oppressors, yield to them and eventually propagate those mantras with the passion of the convert in an attempt to ingratiate themselves. Within the Jewish world today the accusation that Jews who publicly turn against Israel are motivated by self-hatred is commonplace. This may be part of the story. But there is another explanation, running parallel and sometimes overlapping with it, that could well be more convincing in most cases. It is an explanation which touches on one of the core arguments in this book.

Almost without exception, Israel's Jewish opponents have one overwhelmingly important characteristic in common. They are almost all identified with the political Left. More precisely, many of the most vociferous of Israel's Jewish critics are identified with that particular brand of left-wing politics now referred to as the 'radical' Left, the 'socialist' Left or just the 'Old' Left.

It is this Left that during the Cold War could not decide whether it backed the West or its Soviet, totalitarian opponent. It is this Left which still rails against the inequities of capitalism, which scorns the virtues of Western society, which still hankers after something fundamentally different, though it is now hard pressed to define what that alternative society would look like. It is this Left which despises the United States and supports its enemies at every turn. It is this Left which despises Israel and which, for a whole variety of reasons, has played the key role in spreading hostility to the Jewish state from the fringes right into the mainstream of European political discourse. It has attempted to do the same in the United States.

This phenomenon will be discussed in detail and refined and expanded upon at other junctures in the book At this stage it is important to understand two points. Firstly, since Jews find themselves dispersed across the political spectrum as widely as other groups, it should be no surprise that some among their number find themselves inside the ranks of the ideological community just described. Since hatred of Israel is now part and parcel of the radical Left's ideological world view it is quite predictable that Jews of this political persuasion should end up among Israel's harshest critics.

The second point is more difficult to grasp, but it is important. The radical Left is not merely defined by a set of policies, principles or ideas which its adherents may pick and choose at will. To think of it this way would be to misunderstand the tradition in which it rightfully belongs. It is better understood – indeed it can only be properly understood – as a kind of identity in its own right. Moreover, it is an identity which for many of its adherents trumps all others, something more like a secular religion than a political philosophy. It is a place where one goes to seek the truth, to find friends and, of course, to designate enemies. For some it may even define the way they dress, what they eat, where they go on vacation, the music they listen to, the books they read and the newspapers they subscribe to. It is something holistic and all-embracing. It may be hard to define, but we all recognise it when we see it. No other political ideology in the Western tradition is quite like this. One may be conservative or liberal and hold one's views with passion. One may even join a political party espousing such views or run for public office. But, usually, it is only inside the ranks of the radical Left that one encounters a degree of commitment and adherence which reaches such identity-forming levels.[25]

The key point here is that for Jews imbued with this radical Left identity – and over the decades there have been many of them – it is, or at least can come to be, an identity of far greater importance than the one that, by virtue of their parents' origins, they were born into. When the radical identity and the Jewish identity conflict there is every chance that the Leftist identity will win through, especially when other of the factors discussed above are also thrown into the mix. It makes no significant difference whether the individual in question is an American Jew like Noam Chomsky or an Israeli-born Jew like Ilan Pappé.

There is no need to invoke the charge of self-hatred. The fact that they are Jews has simply been superseded by the extreme ideological-based identity which now more properly defines them.

To summarise, the following four points should be borne in mind whenever anti-Israeli groups seek to thrust Jews into the front line of their attack. Firstly, they represent only a small and unrepresentative minority of the overall Jewish population. Israel is a state for Jews, by Jews, of Jews which is supported by the vast majority of Jews around the world. (The fact that not all Israelis are Jews – since 20 per cent of the population of Israel is Arab – is neither here nor there for the purposes of this argument. None of Israel's critics direct their vitriol against the country's Arab minority. It is always and exclusively directed against Jewish Israelis and the Jewish nature of the Israeli state.)

Secondly, hateful discourse against Israel is hateful discourse against Jews regardless of who is involved in it. No amount of squirming, no rhetorical gymnastics can alter that basic and unyielding reality. The presence of Jews among the ranks of those who oppose Israel – the most important Jewish enterprise of our time – is a normal and predictable phenomenon. It has happened before and it will happen again.

Thirdly, since most Jews who despise Israel are drawn from the radical Left – itself a political ideology wrapped around a particular form of identity – the contemporary manifestation of this phenomenon is easily explained.

Fourthly, and finally, it doesn't matter anyway. The case for Israel is based on historical realities and moral imperatives which stand or fall on their own merits regardless of ethnic, religious or indeed any other identity-forming affiliations.

The chapters that follow

History, for much of this book, begins in 2000. Although I set contemporary events in a broader historical context, the discussion revolves around attitudes to Israel from the beginning of this century and the ten years thereafter. Partly this is because the second Intifada, which followed the breakdown of peace efforts led by former President Bill Clinton in 2000, inaugurated a new era in the Israel–Palestine conflict, and of commentary and analysis about it. Also, in looking at trends in the political culture across Europe the dangers of generalisation are great enough without compounding them by extending the time-frame unduly. In any event, the first decade of the twenty-first century – marked indelibly by the terror attacks on September 11 2001–brought together a sufficient number of new factors to make reappraisal of big-picture issues a worthwhile endeavour. If that is true in the general sense, I submit that it is also true of the particular subject at hand.

There are many issues confronted in this book. But the central question threading its way through all of it is this: in what ways and why has Israel become such an object of disdain for so many influential people in Europe and to a lesser extent in the United States and the wider West? Not everybody in Europe is anti-Israeli, of course. I am living proof of that. I am also aware that there are those who would dispute the validity of my underlying premises. Some would say that Israel is getting everything it deserves, others that if bias does exist it is not especially egregious or particularly representative. I do not see how such defences could seriously be sustained, certainly not in the first case which bespeaks an anti-Israeli hostility so deeply internalised that it has become invisible to those purveying it. In the second case, too, it suggests a state of affairs where mainstream bias against Israel has come to seem more or less 'normal'. Those engaged in it are simply unaware of what they are doing or that there is anything unusual about it – something like institutionalised racism. It may be thought, then, that there are simply not enough shared assumptions for such people to feel comfortable joining the conversation.

Risks of this kind are ever-present when dealing with issues where opinions are sharply polarised. I accept that from the outset. But I still believe that, apart from the most extreme anti-Israeli polemicists, most people who are unsure about whether they can accept all of my arguments can still accept that there is enough going wrong in Europe to make the discussion worthwhile. They might at least accept that there is a case for thinking again. Most people, I hope, can be persuaded that there is something quite abhorrent at work in attempts to associate Israel with the Nazis. To anyone who can accept something as basic as that, I would rephrase the central question, in the hope of drawing them in, as follows: in so far as virulent hostility to Israel exists at all in the mainstream in Europe where might it be coming from and why has it not remained at the fringes? I suggest that anyone who refuses to engage in the discussion even on those terms is, by that very fact, a part of the general problem I am describing and, effectively, inaccessible to reasoned debate.

It is also important to recognise that, while allowing for digressions, I have kept a reasonably tight focus throughout this book. This is not a book about the relationship between anti-Semitism and hostility to Israel along the lines of Bernard Harrison's excellent study on the subject in his book *The Resurgence of Anti-Semitism*.[26] I have a chapter on the subject and it is an important one. In trying to understand why Israel is being subjected to such a battering a discussion of this nature is essential. But since I do not believe that traditional anti-Semitism lies at the heart of what is going on in Europe I do not devote the bulk of my time to it. Nor is this a book along the lines of *The Case for Israel*[27] by Alan Dershowitz or *Why Blame Israel?* by Neill Lochery.[28] For what it is worth, I recommend both of them highly. But my own purpose is different.

The chapters that follow break down in the following manner:

Chapter 1, Talking Israel down, taking Israel down

This chapter surveys the nature and extent of hostility to Israel in contemporary Europe by outlining the kinds of discourse that are commonly used by Israel's opponents. It attempts to delineate the different ways in which hostility towards Israel is commonly expressed in an active sense, and also in the passive sense in which the delegitimisation of Israel takes place via an absence of crucial context. It also provides some opinion poll evidence of the extent and manner in which all this has fed through into public perceptions. This chapter is mainly descriptive and is intimately related to Chapter 3 where the forms of discourse described are assessed in terms of whether they constitute anti-Semitism or some other form of bigotry on the one hand or fair comment on the other.

Chapter 2, Of Jews and Israel

This part of the book deals directly with the charge that European hostility to Israel is a product of anti-Semitism. It argues that anti-Semitism is indeed an important part of the picture but not for the reasons commonly asserted. It argues that, in most cases, there is no clear and direct, causal relationship between traditional anti-Semitic starting points and anti-Zionist or anti-Israeli conclusions but that irrational and hateful discourse about Israel does nonetheless represent a fully modernised form of anti-Semitism.

Chapter 3, Fair comment?

As stated above, this chapter is the interpretive counterpart to the largely descriptive essay in Chapter 1. It draws on the interpretive framework constructed in Chapter 2 in order to make judgements about the forms of discourse described in the first chapter. The first three chapters, therefore, need to be read consecutively in order to get a full understanding of my arguments.

Chapter 4, Europe's broken back

This chapter deals more broadly with Europe's ability to overcome the tragedies of its own past and the effect that that past is having on the way the continent's opinion formers come to terms with Israeli and Middle Eastern realities. It addresses issues such as post-colonial guilt, moral relativism, post-nationalism, multiculturalism and pacifism, and points to how this makes for an awkward fit in terms of the way Europe relates to a state in Israel's predicament.

Chapter 5, Muslims in Europe

This section of the book deals with the question of virulent hostility to Israel among Europe's increasingly large and well-organised Muslim minority. It argues that since Muslims are becoming electorally significant, and will become much more significant as time goes by, their influence on the debate should not be underestimated. Politicians and opinion formers will inevitably be affected and there is plenty of evidence that they already are.

Chapter 6, The diplomats' dilemma

This chapter surveys the extent to which hostility to Israel is driven by the basic mathematics of international relations. For many Western governments, Israel is seen as a thorn in the side of better relations with dozens of Arab and Muslim countries. There is only one Israel and it has no oil or gas. There are inbuilt disincentives to supporting Israel in the international system and I look at the extent to which this may be influencing the way Israel is being talked about.

Chapter 7, Ideology against Israel

The ideology chapter examines the reasons why it is the old, ideological Left which has been leading the charge against Israel and how and why its thinking about Israel has spread into important sections of the more modernised, liberal Left. It seeks to explain why the traditionalist Right has also jumped on board the anti-Israeli bandwagon. In addition, it looks at the counter-cases of the mainstream American and central east European Left which are not, in the main, anti-Israeli.

Chapter 8, Contagion: Is America next?

This chapter looks at whether the terms of debate in Europe could now be exported to the United States. As America looks to rebuild its popularity in Europe after eight turbulent years of the Bush administration, there is a danger that Israel may end up being one of the first casualties. European discourse on Israel may already be helping to legitimise the opinions of Israel's enemies in the United States.

Conclusion

A short summary of the key arguments in the book.

CHAPTER 1

Talking Israel down, taking Israel down

Consider the words and images with which Israel has in recent years been associated: 'shitty', 'Nazi', 'racist', 'apartheid', 'ethnic cleanser', 'occupier', 'war criminal', 'violator of international law', 'user of disproportionate force', 'liability'. In its cumulative effect, the consequences for Israel's reputation have been devastating. No other state in the world is talked about in such terms.

But it is not simply the kind of discourse about Israel that matters. It is also its intensity, its relentlessness and, above all, the kind of people and institutions who are engaged in it. There is little purchase, after all, in the rantings of extremists or cranks. Nor is there particular significance in polemics emanating from more substantial individuals if they are tucked away in university departments or non-governmental organisations remote from mainstream society. Such people may take *themselves* seriously. They may even have a following of sorts. But if their voices are drowned out by a mainstream discourse telling a different, more reasonable, story they will remain marginal.

The greatest difference between the way Israel is talked about in Europe from the way it is talked about in the United States does not lie in the substance of what is said. The likes of Noam Chomsky, Norman Finkelstein and David Duke have, in their different ways, been demonising Israel in America for decades. Europeans have little to teach them. The difference lies in the fact that aggressive anti-Israeli discourse in Europe has a substantial presence right inside the mainstream.

It involves commentators and reporters of the highest repute.

It involves people of courage and vision who have been recognised around the world. It involves novelists and artists of the highest calibre. It involves Church leaders and trade unionists, politicians from the centre ground, high-ranking diplomats, charities, and newspapers of record. Such people and institutions are listened to and accorded respect.

The cases of former President Jimmy Carter and professors Walt and Mearsheimer do suggest that virulent anti-Israeli sentiment may now be making inroads in the United States as well. Apart from an elucidation of the main currents of anti-Israeli discourse in Europe, what follows, therefore, should be seen as a warning. Europe, in its treatment of Israel, holds up an image to the United States of one of its possible futures. Though alarmism would be misplaced, Barack Obama's America is also at risk.

In assessing matters of this kind, perspective is everything. Among those who participate in negative discourse about Israel not everyone does so in all its aspects. Equally, not every element of that discourse can simply be dismissed as unfair. The essence of the problem for Israel, and indeed for Israel's more reasoned critics, is that moderate and extreme narratives have, to a great extent, morphed into each other. The whole has become greater than the sum of its parts. It has become an agenda. While it should be possible to see a world of difference between attempts to characterise Israel as a modern-day equivalent of Nazi Germany and constructive criticism of settlement activity on the West Bank, the distinction has become increasingly blurred. Good cop goes for the settlements; bad cop slams Jews as Nazis. One form of criticism feeds off the other.

All of the examples I provide here are from western Europe. The formerly communist countries of central and eastern Europe do not feature, and with good cause. Anti-Israeli polemicists can certainly be located in the region but not – and this is crucial – to any significant degree inside the mainstream.

There are important reasons for this which will be explained later in the book.

Finally, neither in this chapter nor in the rest of the book do I place great store on the differences *between* west European countries in their opinion formers' attitudes to Israel. This is not because differences do not exist at all but because, I believe, it is more about emphasis and tone than content. Andrei S. Markovits has made similar observations about anti-Semitism and anti-Americanism in his book *Uncouth Nation: Why Europe Dislikes America*.[1] At some level I believe anti-Zionism, anti-Semitism and anti-Americanism in Europe are conceptually related. We are witnessing something civilisational, something which goes to the core of what Europe is all about.[2]

This inventory is illustrative and impressionistic rather than exhaustive. Each subsection begins with brief biographical details to show just how prominent some of the purveyors of anti-Israeli sentiment actually are. It is ordered, roughly, in terms of the most egregious and extreme categories at the top with more commonplace cases laid out further down. That said, the aim at this stage is mainly to describe rather than to interpret.[3]

All of the following subsections, many of which overlap, are discussed individually in Chapter 3 in terms of whether they represent one form or another of anti-Semitism or generalised bigotry or whether, by contrast, they can constitute fair and reasonable comment. This and the following two chapters need to be read together in order to get a full appreciation of my arguments. More broadly, this inventory serves as a platform for discussion and interpretation throughout the book.

Talking Israel down: Israel and excrement, Israel as a 'shitty' country

In the world of British journalism, long thought of as a standard setter for reliability, accuracy, elegance and fair comment,

Johann Hari is one of the country's brightest young prospects. Born in Scotland in 1979, he was educated in England at Cambridge University. He characterises himself as a European-style social democrat. He has written for newspapers across Europe and the United States. In 2007, he won the Newspaper Journalist of the Year award from Amnesty International. In April 2008 he was awarded the Orwell Prize for political journalism which is given out, its trustees say, on the basis of writing which reflects George Orwell's 'courageous independence of mind, steely analysis and beautiful writing'. A few weeks after winning the Orwell Prize he penned a column in the *Independent*, the newspaper for which he writes, outlining his thoughts ahead of the 60th anniversary of Israel's declaration of independence. He said:

I would love to be able to crash the birthday party with words of reassurance. Israel has given us great novelists like Amos Oz and A. B. Yehoshua, great film-makers like Joseph Cedar, great scientific research into Alzheimer's, and great dissident journalists like Amira Hass, Tom Segev and Gideon Levy to expose her own crimes. She has provided the one lonely spot in the Middle East where gay people are not hounded and hanged, and where women can approach equality.

But I can't do it. Whenever I try to mouth these words, a remembered smell fills my nostrils. It is the smell of shit. Across the occupied West Bank, raw untreated sewage is pumped every day out of the Jewish settlements, along large metal pipes, straight onto Palestinian land. From there, it can enter the groundwater and the reservoirs, and become a poison.[4]

And then, concluding his piece with a flourish, he opined: 'Israel, as she gazes at her grey hairs and discreetly ignores the smell of her own stale shit pumped across Palestine, needs to ask what kind of country she wants to be in the next 60 years.'

Consider also a different kind of example from Daniel Bernard, a distinguished figure in the French foreign ministry who served, among other roles, as French foreign ministry spokesman, French ambassador to the United Nations and French ambassador to London. In 2001, at a dinner party hosted in London by media tycoon Conrad Black, Bernard said Israel was a 'shitty little country' and asked rhetorically: 'Why should we be in danger of World War Three because of these people?'[5] His remarks were then widely reported.

In support of his comments, the British newspaper columnist Deborah Orr published a piece in December of that year in which she said: 'Ever since I went to Israel on holiday, I've considered it to be a shitty little country too.' Later in the same piece she said it was her 'honest view that in my experience Israel is shitty and little'.[6] In the course of her article the word 'shitty' to describe Israel appeared no fewer than five times.

Israel and Nazi Germany

Mairead Corrigan Maguire won the Nobel Peace Prize in 1977 in recognition of her efforts to end violence between Catholic and Protestant communities in Northern Ireland. Born in 1944, she comes from a Catholic family and was drawn into the peace movement after three of her sister's children were killed at the ages of eight, two and six weeks as a car driven by a gunman from the Irish Republican Army (IRA) rammed into them following a firefight with British soldiers. Maguire has long campaigned against Israeli policies and in September 2007 she secured an apology from the Israeli government after having been hit by a rubber bullet earlier that year in a demonstration against the extension of the security barrier in the West Bank village of Bil'in.

In April 2004, she was at the prison gates to welcome the release of Israeli nuclear whistle-blower Mordechai Vanunu who served eighteen years in jail after revealing secrets about Israel's nuclear programme. Later that year, on another trip to Israel, she reflected on Israel's nuclear programme in the following terms: 'When I think about nuclear weapons, I've been to Auschwitz concentration camp ... Nuclear weapons are only gas chambers perfected ... and for a people who know what gas chambers are, how can you even think of building perfect gas chambers?'[7]

The use in Europe of the greatest crime against the Jewish people as a rhetorical weapon against the Jewish state appears to have originated in Soviet anti-Zionist propaganda (see Chapter 7) and is now a staple of Arab, Palestinian, Islamist and far-Left invective with a serious presence across the internet. However, it has increasingly made its way into the European mainstream. Nobel Laureate Maguire is no exception.

In March 2007, a delegation of German bishops made a trip to Israel, stopping at the Holocaust Museum, Yad Vashem, and also Palestinian areas such as Ramallah. Two among the delegation sought to compare Israel's treatment of the Palestinians with Nazi Germany in comments that were widely reported in the German and international media. Bishop Gregor Maria Hanke of Eichstaett said: 'Photos of the inhuman Warsaw ghetto at Yad Vashem in the morning, in the evening we go to the ghetto in Ramallah – that blows your lid off.'[8] Walter Mixa, Bishop of Augsburg, described conditions on the West Bank as 'Ghetto-like'.[9]

In 2001, Erkki Tuomioja, the Foreign Minister of Finland, lambasted Israeli policies in an interview in the Finnish magazine *Suomen Kuvalehti*: 'I am appalled that Israel's policy is to crush, humiliate, subjugate and impoverish the Palestinians,' he was quoted as saying. 'What else could arise from that other than endless hate? It is rather shocking that some people advocate towards the Palestinians the same kind of policy as they themselves were victim to in the 1930s.'[10] (After a huge row involving then Israeli Foreign Minister Shimon Peres, Tuomioja sought to back away from an interpretation of his remarks that implied a direct comparison of Israeli government policies and Nazism. But the damage had already been done.)

In January 2009, a senior Norwegian diplomat in Saudi Arabia was publicly exposed for sending out emails making direct comparisons with Israel's behaviour in Gaza and Nazi Germany. The email, sent from a Norwegian foreign ministry account, said: 'The grandchildren of Holocaust survivors from World War II are doing to the Palestinians exactly what was done to them by Nazi Germany.'[11] The email contained more than forty pictorial attachments, including comparisons between Nazis and Israelis.

In the same month, British Labour MP Gerald Kaufman accused Israel of exploiting gentile guilt over the Holocaust 'as justification for their murder of Palestinians'.[12] He also said of Israel's arguments about the difficulties of rooting out Hamas terrorists in the Gaza Strip and the attendant loss of life: 'I suppose the Jews fighting for their lives in the Warsaw ghetto could have been dismissed as militants.'[13]

In 2006, during the war in Lebanon, veteran British Conservative MP Sir Peter Tapsell threw in his own two cents accusing then British Prime Minister Tony Blair of working with President George W. Bush to allow Israel to commit war crimes in Lebanon. He said Israel's policies were 'gravely reminiscent of the Nazi atrocity on the Jewish quarter of Warsaw'.[14] In 2002, a one-time labour minister for the German Christian Democrats, Norbert Blum, used the word 'Vernichtungskrieg', Nazi-type term for 'war of extermination', in a letter to the Israeli ambassador in Germany condemning Israel's actions against Palestinian militants.[15]

In 2001, the poet, Oxford academic and broadcaster Tom Paulin wrote a poem in the *Observer*, one of Britain's leading Sunday newspapers. With a preamble from the anti-Zionist, Jewish-born diarist Victor Klemperer, it is entitled 'Killed in Crossfire':

'To me the Zionists, who want to go back to the Jewish state of
70 AD (destruction of Jerusalem by Titus), are just as offensive as
the Nazis. With their nosing after blood, their ancient "cultural
roots", their partly canting, partly obtuse winding back of the
world, they are altogether a match for the National Socialists' –
Victor Klemperer, 13 June 1934.

> We're fed this inert
> this lying phrase
> like comfort food
> as another little Palestinian boy
> in trainers jeans and a white teeshirt
> is gunned down by the Zionist SS
> whose initials we should
> – but we don't – dumb goys –
> clock in that weasel word *crossfire*.[16]

There are many examples from the mainstream of the use of
the Nazi comparison in cartoon form. To quote just one, in
April 2002 the Left-leaning Greek daily newspaper *Ethnos*
portrayed two Israeli soldiers, with huge noses, wearing helmets
emblazoned with the Star of David and Nazi-style uniforms
stabbing two helpless Arabs to death. The caption had one
Israeli soldier saying to the other: 'Don't feel guilty, brother, we
were not in Auschwitz and Dachau to suffer but to learn.'[17]

Somewhat more oblique references, which may or may not
be direct comparisons with Nazi policies but could certainly be
interpreted as such, are also common. In 2009, the Vatican's
Justice and Peace Minister Cardinal Renato Martino decried
the Israeli attack on Hamas in Gaza saying: 'Defenceless populations are always the ones who pay. Look at the conditions in
Gaza: more and more, it resembles a big concentration camp.'[18]
Israel responded by blasting the Cardinal for parroting 'Hamas
propaganda'.[19] As a sign of how dangerous loose talk can be,
Martino's remarks were seized upon by anti-Israeli constituencies. Writing in the *Dar Al Hayat* newspaper, one Jihad

El-Khazen opined: 'For years, I have been saying that Israel turned the Gaza Strip into a Nazi concentration camp. But I am a supporter of Gaza's inhabitants. Now a prominent Christian cleric says what we know to be the truth about Israel.'[20]

There are also plenty of instances in which defenders of Israel are compared in one way or another to Nazi officials. In January 2009, Aengus O'Snodaigh of Ireland's Sinn Fein party condemned fellow parliamentarian Alan Shatter (the only Jewish member of the Irish parliament) and Israel's ambassador to Ireland for defending the operation in Gaza. O'Snodaigh said: 'Goebbels would have been proud' of their 'twisted logic and half-truths'.[21]

And then there is a litany of instances in which it is suggested that discussion or commemoration of the unique Jewish experience of the Holocaust is inappropriate at a given moment due to the actions of the State of Israel. Quite apart from the prevalence of this kind of thinking among Muslim groups (see pp. 176–7), it can crop up more or less anywhere. Thus it was in January 2009 that the municipal and Church authorities in the northern Swedish town of Lulea decided not to hold a torchlight march for Holocaust Memorial Day. The official reason cited for the cancellation was 'safety concerns'. Bo Nordin, a spokesman for the Church, gave a different version of events to Swedish National Radio. 'It feels uneasy to have a torchlight procession to remember the victims of the Holocaust at this time,' he was quoted as saying. 'We have been preoccupied and grief-stricken by the war in Gaza and it would just feel odd with a large ceremony about the Holocaust.'[22]

Cultural references to the Holocaust can be treated in a similar manner. In a review in the *Observer* of Edward Zwick's movie *Defiance* (also in January 2009), film critic Philip French struggled with the implications of the subject matter and the timing of its release. The movie portrays a group of Jewish partisans and families taking refuge in the forests of Belarus whose survival depends on ruthlessly cutting down Nazis and collaborators alike. Writing at the time of Israel's offensive in Gaza, French could not resist concluding his review in the following manner: 'It took the American cinema quite a time to make pictures like *Exodus* and *Cast a Giant Shadow*, which presented Jews fighting for the creation of Israel, but this week is not, I think, the best moment for a picture celebrating them in ruthless, take-no-prisoners mode.'[23]

Israel as a racist or 'apartheid' state

José Saramago is one of the most talented writers his country has ever produced. In 1998, the Portuguese novelist was awarded the Nobel Prize for Literature. Born in 1922, he is also one of Europe's most celebrated artistic figures with a vast presence across the media. In 2008, the movie *Blindness*, based on one of Saramago's novels, opened the Cannes Film Festival. He has openly compared Israel to Nazi Germany.[24] But in a 2002 article in the Spanish newspaper *El País* he also proffered a lurid explanation of why, in his view, Israel was a racist state:

Intoxicated mentally by the messianic dream of a Greater Israel which will finally achieve the expansionist dreams of the most radical Zionism; contaminated by the monstrous and rooted 'certitude' that in this catastrophic and absurd world there exists a people chosen by God and that, consequently, all the actions of an obsessive, psychological and pathologically exclusivist racism are justified; educated and trained in the idea that any suffering that has been inflicted, or is being inflicted, or will be inflicted on everyone else, especially the Palestinians, will always be inferior to that which they themselves suffered in the Holocaust, the Jews endlessly scratch their own wound to keep it bleeding, to make it incurable, and they show it to the world as if it were a banner. Israel seizes hold of the terrible words of God in Deuteronomy: 'Vengeance is mine, and I will be repaid.' Israel wants all of us to feel guilty, directly or indirectly, for the horrors of the Holocaust; Israel wants us to renounce the most elemental critical judgment and for us to transform ourselves into a docile echo of its will.[25]

As Paul Berman, the translator of this passage, put it, 'Saramago must have been ablaze, writing those lines.' The generalised accusation of racism against Israel is frequently complemented by the particular charge that Israel is the modern-day equivalent of apartheid South Africa. Many prominent individuals, charities, trade unions, student bodies and even Church leaders have been pushing hard for several years now to turn such comparisons into an accepted part of the mainstream discourse. The battle still rages. But its purveyors have scored notable successes across the continent and show no sign of giving up.

In an attempt to stop a Davis Cup match between Sweden and Israel in Malmö in March 2009, a prominent member of the country's Social Democratic party was widely quoted calling for a boycott of Israel using the kind of incendiary rhetoric which has now become typical. Worked up into such a frenzy that she appeared quite unable to decide whether Israel should be condemned in terms of apartheid or Nazism, Ingalill Bjarten, deputy head of the social democratic women's organisation in southern Sweden, spat: 'Israel is an apartheid state. I think Gaza is comparable to the Warsaw ghetto.'[26]

In July 2007, Luisa Morgantini, a vice-president of the European Parliament from Italy, denounced in the Italian newspaper *Liberazione* a decision in the Knesset on the allocation of land controlled by the Jewish National Fund (JNF) which aimed at entrenching in law the JNF's ability to sell land to Jews according to a mandate going back to before the establishment of Israel. Considering an immensely complex subject where right and wrong are not easily distinguished, Morgantini did not miss the opportunity to slam Israel in terms that are now all too familiar: 'In this way Israel strikes another blow against democracy, fuelling discrimination and apartheid,' she was quoted as saying.[27]

In January 2009, Eamonn McCann, a columnist for Northern Ireland's *Belfast Telegraph*, said: 'During the second intifada, from 2000 to 2005, four Palestinians were killed for every Israeli. In 2006 the ratio rocketed to 30 to one. In 2007 it reached 40 to one. Now it is running at around 100 to one. The steeply declining relative value of Palestinian lives indicates an institutionalised racism reminiscent of apartheid.'[28]

In March 2008, the UK Charity Commission said in a letter that it had warned the charity War on Want about possible violations of its charitable status over its vitriolic campaign against Israel's security barrier which included production of a pamphlet entitled 'Together we can knock down Israel's Apartheid Wall'. The letter said the Commission had received assurances from the charity's trustees that its strategy would be reviewed and the issue appeared to have been resolved to the satisfaction of both parties.[29] At the time of writing, however, the charity's website was still peppered with references to 'apartheid'. In one press release, the word 'apartheid' was used in the context of the security barrier no fewer than seven times.[30]

In 2006, Britain's *Guardian* newspaper, which has readers across Europe and beyond, put out a purportedly serious and considered comparative analysis of apartheid South Africa and Israel by Chris McGreal, who had extensive experience reporting from both countries. Among other things, McGreal said: 'There are few places in the world where governments construct a web of nationality and residency laws designed for use by one section of the population against another. Apartheid South Africa was one. So is Israel.'[31]

In 2003, the European Parliament hosted an exhibition entitled: 'The New Doors of Jerusalem: Apartheid Israel'.[32]

Israel and ethnic cleansing: Nakba abuse

Eric Rouleau is a former French ambassador to Tunisia and Turkey. He also undertook important diplomatic missions for former French President François Mitterrand. Born in 1926, he writes for France's prestigious *Le Monde Diplomatique*, a monthly publication aiming at a high-level and influential audience. Its circulation in France is around 350,000 but its total sales are dramatically augmented to around 2.5 million by its international editions, of which there are more than seventy in twenty-six different languages. Between 1955 and 1985 Rouleau was a correspondent holding senior positions for *Le Monde*, France's most celebrated daily newspaper. He is thus a prodigious opinion former with important connections in the mainstream French political and journalistic establishment.

In May 2008 he wrote a commentary for *Le Monde Diplomatique* entitled 'The "ethnic cleansing" of Palestine; Israel faces up to its past'. The piece focused on Israel's 'new historians' who took a fresh look in the 1980s at the events of 1947 and 1948 and found that Israel bore some responsibility for the exodus of the approximately 750,000 Palestinians who subsequently became refugees. Rouleau is aware of the problem he faces with the Israeli historian Benny Morris – the most respected and conscientious among the new historians – whose research has shown that the refugee problem did not derive from a master plan to ethnically cleanse but was a by-product of war and violence begun by the Palestinians and the Arabs. He therefore proceeds to discredit him as a member of the 'far right', which he is not. Rouleau then devotes the substantial portion of his piece to glowing references to Ilan Pappé, who as a thorough-going post-modernist has himself openly admitted that he is not objective and that he is ideologically motivated.[33]

These facts about Pappé, who now teaches history at the University of Exeter in Britain, can be found and verified in a moment's search on the internet. This does not stop Rouleau referring to Pappé's writings as though they were objective and to Pappé himself as a kind of hunted hero:

Pappé is not the first dissident intellectual (nor is he likely to be the last) to leave his country to escape the suffocating atmosphere reserved for 'lepers' such as him. But unlike his predecessors, it is much harder to dispute his versions of events, because they are so much more detailed. Pappé has had access to documents from 60 years of Israeli archives (unlike most of his colleagues who only had access to 40 years' worth).

Pappé has also made use of the work of Palestinian historians in his writing, often for eyewitness accounts. He has collected the testimony of survivors of ethnic cleansing, a source thus far studiously avoided by his fellow historians, either through an instinctive rejection of such material or through mistrust, or more prosaically because of their ignorance of the Arabic language.[34]

The use and abuse of Israel's 'new historians' to promote the systematic 'ethnic cleansing' charge is a stock in trade of anti-Israeli opinion formers across Europe. Seumas Milne, associate editor of the *Guardian*, wrote the following in an opinion piece also published in May 2008. Milne is also aware of the Benny Morris problem, but this does not stop him lumping him together with Pappé as though they represented a united front on the context in which the events transpired. He says:

... ethnic cleansing began months before the end of British rule, as has been meticulously documented by Israeli historians such as Benny Morris and Ilan Pappé, and before the arrival of the Arab armies, who mostly fought in areas earmarked by the UN for an Arab state. Sixty years ago, Arab Jaffa, now part of Tel Aviv, had just fallen to the forces of the embryonic Israeli state and tens of thousands of Palestinians had fled or been driven out, some of them literally into the sea.[35]

Milne says Morris now regards the 'expulsions' as justified. But he simply fails to add that Morris also shows they were precipitated by Arab and Palestinian violence.

The case of Jostein Gaarder, the celebrated Norwegian intellectual and novelist, whose book *Sophie's World* has sold more than thirty million copies and has been translated into fifty-three languages, is also highly illustrative of the mentality that deals in accusations of ethnic cleansing. In 2006 he wrote an article in a top Norwegian newspaper, *Aftenposten*, under the headline: 'God's chosen people'. In it he compares Israel to the Taliban in Afghanistan and to apartheid South Africa. While also criticising terror groups, he lambasts Israel, saying, 'shame on ethnic cleansing' and adds: 'It is the State of Israel that fails to recognize, respect or defer to the internationally lawful Israeli state of 1948. Israel wants more; more water and more villages. To obtain this, there are those who want, with God's assistance, a final solution to the Palestinian problem.'[36]

Israel as brutal and illegal occupier, terrorism as an understandable response

From 1997 to 2006, Karl Gustav Hammar was head of the (Lutheran) Church of Sweden, the country's pre-eminent religious institution. Born in 1943, he has written widely on theological issues. He is known as a liberal who has offered non-literal interpretations of biblical accounts such as the Virgin Birth and who has sought to open up the Church to a more inclusive attitude to women and homosexuals. Hammar also used his position to lead a campaign of vilification against the State of Israel. In January 2003, he was one of the leading figures among a group of seventy-three prominent Swedes calling for a boycott of Israeli goods produced on the West Bank and in Gaza, as well as a suspension of the European Union's free trade agreement with Israel. The call came in the form of a commentary in a leading Swedish newspaper, *Dagens Nyheter*. It said: 'To buy and sell goods from the occupied territories is to actively support the illegal Israeli occupation . . . It is also a crime against international law.'[37]

The Israeli occupation of the West Bank and Gaza Strip

represented, 'a permanent violence and a crime against international law that has continued for more than three decades'. It added: 'The occupation is the root cause that triggered the Palestinian intifada.'

The description of Israel's occupation of the West Bank and (formerly) the Gaza Strip in terms of a criminal enterprise involving deliberate or gratuitous brutality is a standard part of the anti-Israeli narrative.

It often mutates into the notion that whatever actions Israel takes to root out terrorists it only succeeds in inflaming passions further and 'radicalising' people. Commenting on Operation Cast Lead in Gaza in 2009, former Italian Prime Minister Massimo D'Alema opined that: 'War against Hamas is a partisan expression on the part of the Israeli army. It is an outright punitive expedition in which around 300 children have already been killed. How can fundamentalism be fought? With the massacre of children, fundamentalism is bolstered.'[38]

A related part of the discourse posits Israel's occupation as a 'root cause' of Palestinian terrorism, and Palestinian terrorism, therefore, as in some sense forgivable. In 2004, Jenny Tonge, a prominent MP for the Liberal Democrats and subsequently a member of the British House of Lords, made a set of widely publicised remarks on suicide bombers centring on the 'desperation' of the Palestinians. She even went so far as to say: 'I think if I had to live in that situation . . . I might just consider becoming one myself.'[39]

In an attempt to explain that this did not mean that she actually supported suicide bombing, she said that all she was saying was that: '. . . having seen the violence and the humiliation and the provocation that the Palestinian people live under every day and have done since their land was occupied by Israel, I could understand and was trying to understand where [suicide bombers] were coming from.'[40]

Tonge was subsequently fired for her remarks as her party's spokesperson on children's affairs. The *Independent* newspaper, one of the harshest critics of Israel in the British media, described her sacking as a 'terrible mistake',[41] saying that the Liberal Democrat leader, Charles Kennedy, should not have disciplined her but should rather have 'defended to the last her right to speak her mind'.

In 2003, the Greek artist Alexandros Psychoulis unveiled a painting of a woman Palestinian suicide bomber self-detonating in a crowded Israeli market. In the same year he was quoted as saying: 'I personally feel that the experiment of Israel has failed … and I understand the desperation of a girl who carries out a suicide bombing having nothing to lose.'[42] In 2007, the Belgian Member of the European Parliament Véronique De Keyser waxed philosophical about oppression of the Palestinians under occupation and expressed deep anger that Israeli officials tried to explain restrictions in terms of the dangers from terrorists: 'If the Israeli ambassador comes in the future to speak of Israel's security,' she said, 'I feel like I want to strangle him.'[43]

Israelis as war criminals

Belgium is the host country for the European Union, NATO and a whole set of related international organisations. A small country of 10.6 million people, it thus punches above its weight in terms of its influence and the impact of what emanates from that country in Europe and the wider world. In 1993 Belgium passed a law on 'universal jurisdiction' which allowed war crimes charges to be brought regardless of whether there was any relation to Belgium. Predictably, the law was turned against Israel and the United States, among others. In 2001 a case was brought against Israeli Prime Minister Ariel Sharon over the massacres of Palestinian civilians in 1982 in the Lebanese refugee camps of Sabra and Shatila. It was eventually quashed in 2003 amid changes to the law and due to immense pressure on Belgium from the United States (which threatened to move NATO headquarters out of Brussels) and Israel (which temporarily withdrew its ambassador). By this time, though, events had acquired a momentum of their own. The proceedings both perpetuated and helped legitimise a form of anti-Israeli discourse which has flooded the mainstream.

A BBC documentary called *The Accused* was timed to coincide with the proceedings against Sharon in the Belgian courts. It was aired for the first time the day before the action began and was broadcast across Europe at later dates. The documentary brought no new information about the Sabra and Shatila massacres but featured a host of luminaries arguing that Sharon could or should be indicted for war crimes. This was despite the fact that the massacres were perpetrated by an Arab militia allied with Israel and not by Israeli forces themselves.

The 'war crimes' accusation against Israel is now routine. In January 2009, Amnesty International researcher Donatella Rovera was quoted by the French news agency Agence France-Presse as saying of the alleged use of white phosphorus weapons during the Israeli offensive in Gaza: 'Such extensive use of this weapon in Gaza's densely-populated residential neighbourhoods is inherently indiscriminate ... Its repeated use in this manner, despite evidence of its indiscriminate effects and its toll on civilians, is a war crime.'[44]

In March 2008, the General Secretary of Unison, one of Britain's largest trade unions, wrote to British Foreign Secretary David Miliband calling Israeli strikes against rocket makers in Gaza a 'war crime'.[45] In 2006, a Danish parliamentarian, Frank Aaen, from the country's Leftist Red-Green Alliance, called for the detention of Israeli Foreign Minister Tzipi Livni during a trip to the country in order to establish the extent to which she bore responsibility as a member of the Israeli cabinet for 'Israeli war crimes' during the war against Hezbollah in Lebanon.[46] Aaen's charge was itself based on a report issued by Amnesty International. The group said: 'Many of the violations examined in this report are war crimes that give rise to individual criminal responsibility. They include directly attacking civilian objects and carrying out indiscriminate or disproportionate attacks. People against whom there is prima facie evidence of responsibility for the commission of these crimes are subject to criminal accountability anywhere in the world through the exercise of universal jurisdiction . . .'[47]

Israel as a violator of international law

The *Financial Times*, like the BBC, is a British-based media outlet with enormous influence all over the world. It is read by governments, functionaries and businessmen and businesswomen across the continent. It has a particularly important position in Brussels where officials of the European Union closely read its reporting and commentary, often writing to the letters page or appearing on its comment pages themselves. More generally, it has a reputation for being a high-level media outlet which stands above the fray and takes a sober and considered stance where others are quick to take sides or make sweeping statements. That reputation has frequently been called into question, however, over the paper's stance on Israel.

In the wake of tens of thousands of Gazans breaking into Egypt in January 2008 after the border barrier was blown up by militants, the paper took the opportunity to produce an editorial article condemning Israel's actions in Gaza in the following terms: ' . . . Israel's tactic of "collective punishment" is illegal. Targeting a civilian population is prohibited by international law: *there is no debate to be had about it.*'[48] (My italics.)

In 2006, the government of Switzerland, the depositary nation of the Geneva Conventions, had also chipped in about 'collective punishment' and international law. The Swiss foreign ministry said in a statement: 'A number of actions by the Israeli defense forces in their offensive against the Gaza Strip have violated the principle of proportionality and are to be seen as forms of collective punishment, which is forbidden.'[49]

And, it went on: '*There is no doubt* that Israel has not taken the precautions required of it in international law to protect the civilian population and infrastructure.' (My italics.)

The Swiss have a habit of invoking international law against Israel. In January 2009, the country's foreign ministry slammed Israel's actions in Gaza saying, 'attacks against humanitarian organisations, hospitals and medical staff amount to a violation of international humanitarian law'.[50]

In the same month of the same year a group of charities from Belgium, France, Britain, Ireland, Denmark, Sweden, the Czech Republic, Germany, Switzerland and the Netherlands called on the European Union to suspend further upgrades to its relationship with Israel due to its alleged violations of international law in Gaza. In the joint communiqué, Daleep Mukarji, director of Christian Aid for the UK and Ireland, spoke for the group in saying: 'The EU's credibility is now at stake. It is inconceivable that we should extend further benefits of European partnership to a government that violates inter-national humanitarian law and refuses negotiation in favour of continued violence.'[51]

Similarly uncompromising denunciations have flown freely over Israel's construction of its security barrier usually (and wrongly) referred to as a 'wall' – the vast majority of the barrier is a fence. Criticisms of this type went into hyperdrive after the International Court of Justice (ICJ), based in the Dutch city The Hague, issued an advisory ruling in July 2004 saying the route of the barrier, part of which goes beyond the 1967 borders, was illegal and that those parts of it crossing the 1967 borders should be torn down. German and other European judges sup-ported the ruling, with only the American judge rejecting it. The United Nations General Assembly voted overwhelmingly to support the ICJ ruling by a margin of 150–6, with ten abstentions.

The British-based international charity group Oxfam issued a statement in 2004 welcoming the ICJ ruling in the following terms: 'Oxfam International recognises the right of Israelis and Palestinians to live in peace and security, free from the threat of violence. However, Oxfam International's experience shows that the barrier is preventing nearly one million Palestinians from reaching their workplaces, schools, hospitals and relatives. It undermines the economy, erodes livelihoods and increases suffering in a population of which half already live below the poverty line of two dollars a day.'[52]

Accusations of criminality have also been common in reference to Israel's policy of targeted assassination of terrorist leaders. After Israel's assassination of Hamas leader Abdelaziz Rantissi in April 2004, the French foreign ministry released a statement saying: 'France condemns the attack perpetrated against the head of Hamas, Abdelaziz al-Rantassi, which caused his death ... It states once again that extra-judicial executions are contrary to international law and unacceptable. Each state in the [Middle East] region has the right to protect its citizens, but not with contempt of the law.'[53] Similarly worded condemnations followed the assassination of wheelchair-bound Hamas leader Sheik Ahmed Yassin in March of the same year. European Union foreign ministers issued a statement acknowledging that Hamas was guilty of perpetrating 'atrocities' but said: 'Israel is not, however, entitled to carry out extra-judicial killings.'[54]

References to the alleged illegality of Jewish settlements (see pp. 24–7) on the West Bank are also commonplace in Europe as elsewhere. As one example from many in the European Union, the formal conclusions of the meeting of heads of government in Copenhagen in 2002 included a statement on the following lines:

The expansion of settlements and related construction, as widely documented including by the European Union's Settlement Watch, violates international law, inflames an already volatile situation, and reinforces the fear of Palestinians that Israel is not genuinely committed to end the occupation. It is an obstacle to peace. The European Council urges the Government of Israel to reverse its settlement policy and as a first step immediately apply a full and effective freeze on all settlement activities. It calls for an end to further land confiscation for the construction of the *so-called* security fence.[55] (My italics.)

Israeli responses to attacks as 'disproportionate'

At the time of writing, Heidemarie Wieczorek-Zeul was the longest serving minister in German Chancellor Angela Merkel's government. Indeed, she had held her post since being appointed by Merkel's predecessor, Gerhard Schroeder, after he assumed the chancellorship in 1998 and had been a member of the German parliament for more than twenty years. Born in 1942, she is known as 'Red Heidi' for her left-wing views. She is one of the most prominent social democrats in Germany. During the Lebanon war of 2006 she provoked a furore in Germany, particularly among the country's Jewish community, after harshly worded criticism of Israel's attacks on Hezbollah and related targets. She called for the UN to investigate allegations of Israeli carpet-bombing and said: 'The fact that civilian targets and civilians in another state are being bombarded is against international law and completely unacceptable.'[56]

The word 'disproportionate' (along with conceptually related allegations) has become a buzzword in public discussion about Israeli responses to aggression and terrorism. It is a particular favourite in the institutions of the European Union which is usually also careful to issue references to the unacceptability of attacks on Israel.

In December 2008, after the start of the Gaza campaign, French President Nicolas Sarkozy – whose country at the time held the rotating presidency of the EU – said that he 'firmly condemns the irresponsible provocations [by Hamas] that have led to this situation, as well as the disproportionate use of force [by Israel]'.[57]

The *Financial Times* chipped in at the same time with an editorial lambasting 'the disproportionate scale of Israeli air strikes' in response to what it called 'the pinprick provocations of the home-made rockets fired from Gaza at southern Israeli towns'.[58]

In November 2006, all five main political groupings in the European Parliament – spanning conservatives, greens, liberals, social democrats and Leftists – passed a joint resolution expressing 'deep indignation' at Israeli actions in Beit Hanoun and in Gaza generally, condemning the 'Israeli army's use of disproportionate action'.[59]

In August of the same year, the president of the European Parliament, Josep Borrell of Spain, issued a statement on behalf of the Euro-Mediterranean Parliamentary Assembly (an influential group inside the Parliament) condemning 'the disproportionate Israeli military actions in Lebanon ... the systematic destruction of Lebanese infrastructure and the forced departure of hundreds of thousands of persons'.[60] In April 2001, Sweden, which then held the EU presidency, issued a sharp denunciation of an Israeli attack on a Syrian radar station in Lebanon. It said: 'The Israeli attack on Syrian objectives in Lebanon, the first in many years, as a retaliation for the Hizbollah attacks on the Shebaa Farms, was an excessive and disproportionate reply.'[61]

In March 2008, Slovenia, taking its own turn as holder of the EU's rotating presidency, issued another denunciation of Israel, this time over Gaza. The wording was hardly unfamiliar. Speaking for the EU, it said: 'The Presidency condemns the recent disproportionate use of force by the Israeli Defense Forces (IDF) against Palestinian population in Gaza and urges Israel to exercise maximum restraint and refrain from all activities that endanger civilians. Such activities are contrary to international law. The Presidency at the same time reiterates condemnation of continued firing of rockets into Israeli territory and calls for its immediate end.'[62]

Israel as a liability

The sense in which Israel is condemned as a strategic liability was amply demonstrated by the remarks in the first sub-section in this inventory with former French ambassador Daniel Bernard's question referring to Israel thus: 'Why should we be in danger of World War Three because of these people?'

Since many of Israel's enemies are vital suppliers to Europe of oil and natural gas, Europeans do not usually need to be reminded of the price they may pay for adopting a supportive, or at least non-hostile, attitude to Israel. The message is sometimes delivered nonetheless. Ibrahim Mohamad, senior editor for the Arabic website of influential German media outlet Deutsche Welle, said in an opinion slot for Deutsche Welle in 2006 that German Chancellor Merkel's refusal to lambast Israel during the Lebanon crisis risked 'damaging Germany's good reputation in the Arab world and putting the country's interests at risk'.[63]

It is an ever-present theme in the sphere of international diplomacy (see Chapter 6). Muslim leaders in Europe (see Chapter 5) also constantly warn European governments that Israel is a liability to them and that support for Israel may harm their interests with Muslim countries around the world and with Muslim communities back home.

Finally, the Israel-as-a-liability argument frequently comes wrapped in some familiar packaging. The high-ranking and widely respected British MP Tam Dalyell, famous for talking about a 'cabal' of influential Jews surrounding Prime Minister Tony Blair, told the Arabic television station Al-Jazeera in 2003 that Zionist Jews in the United States were even influencing British policy: 'I believe that the US government wields great influence on Tony Blair. I cannot say that the Jewish lobby's influence on the British government is direct influence, but it is influence resulting from the extremist Zionist lobby's pressure on President Bush, and then by Bush on the British government.'[64] Dalyell avers that he has nothing against Jews, rather he is opposed to the closeness of some Jews to Israel and the effect this may be having on British interests.

Nothing would have been easier in writing this section than to round up the usual suspects: to compile an extensive anthology of anti-Israeli commentary from lobby groups such as the Palestine Solidarity Campaign, from far Left and far Right political parties, from Islamist groups, from mavericks or from well-known anti-Israeli polemicists. Their influence should not be underestimated. But lobbyists and extremists are easily seen for what they are. Mainstream media outlets do sometimes give them a platform, but their credentials are usually flagged up clearly. The impact of what they say is reduced accordingly. All of the above has been designed to give a sense of the main lines of attack against the Jewish state from people and institutions that operate right inside the mainstream. Each subsection represents an important element of the broad assault on Israel's integrity as a member of the community of nations. Taken together, this is how a reputation is destroyed. And this is how the world's only Jewish state is being talked about these days in Europe.

From the active to the passive

The way in which we should interpret the various aspects of the anti-Israeli discourse is dealt with in Chapter 3. But this is only part of the picture. Active hostility to Israel is complemented by a passive hostility in which relevant context and history are either completely absent from the discussion or are manipulated in such a way that Israel's behaviour is rendered incomprehensible except with reference to the most negative interpretation possible. It is arguable that lack of context, especially in media reporting, is even more damaging than the active side of the assault on Israel. When presented with the full picture most people are quite capable of drawing intelligent and reasoned conclusions even in the face of a sustained attack from individuals and institutions with an agenda. Not only is lack of context possibly more damaging, it is also more insidious since it is harder to expose. It is difficult to prove a negative. Holding a newspaper or television station to account for the *absence* of what is said requires vast analysis, involving large amounts of time and money, in order to establish consistent patterns rather than one-off shortcomings. (Some studies have in fact been conducted including a particularly devastating analysis of reporting patterns in the BBC, one of the two or three most influential news networks in the world. There are also several reputable institutions monitoring such trends closely.[65])

What follows is a concise elucidation of one of the most important elements of the context and history which is frequently absent from news reports and commentary about Israel, with some explanation as to why it matters.

Partners for peace in a hostile political culture

It is surely impossible to adjudicate on the question of whether Israeli responses to the Palestinians, neighbouring states and militant groups are reasonable or not without reference to the ideas and attitudes which motivate these opposing forces. Of course, rounded analysis does not mean going to extremes and focusing solely on the negative. It is not necessary, indeed it would itself be unreasonable, simply to dismiss all thinking about Israel in the Middle East as the product of fanatical, annihilationist underpinnings. There are important figures, such as Mahmud Abbas and King Abdullah of Jordan, whose political ambitions have appeared to centre on the construction of an independent Palestinian state living in peace with Israel and on the basis of good neighbourliness.

Jordan and Egypt have both signed peace treaties with Israel. The Saudi-sponsored peace plan, first mooted in 2002 and revived at an Arab League summit in Riyadh in 2007, opened up the prospect of a normalisation of relations with much of the region if Israel were to agree to a settlement on the basis of the 1967 borders. In an interview in 2008, Prince Turki al-Faisal, an adviser to the Saudi King said: 'The Arab world, by the Arab peace initiative, has crossed the Rubicon from hostility towards Israel to peace with Israel and has extended the hand of peace to Israel, and we await the Israelis picking up our hand and joining us in what inevitably will be beneficial for Israel and for the Arab world.'[66]

He added: 'One can imagine not just economic, political and diplomatic relations between Arabs and Israelis but also issues of education, scientific research, combating mutual threats to the inhabitants of this vast geographic area.'

It is fair and reasonable that these strands of thinking are brought out. What is unfair, unreasonable and a travesty of honest, even intelligent, commentary on the Middle East is to downplay or ignore other key aspects of Palestinian and Mid-East political culture to such an extent that someone coming to this subject for the first time could have no proper under-standing of Israeli suspicions and concerns. Without a full picture of the political culture which Israel faces in the Pal-estinian, Arab and wider Muslim world, Israel's actions and attitudes inevitably seem unreasonable, intransigent or driven by ulterior motives.

What is the real basis for Israeli suspicions? First among them is public anti-Semitism, much of which is sponsored (or approved) on a daily basis by governments which say they are serious about peace. Evidence for this is ubiquitous though it rarely features in the reporting. Consider the findings of a Pew Global Attitudes survey published in 2006.[67] Pew asked respondents in a set of countries to describe their feelings towards Jews as either '*very favourable*', '*somewhat favourable*', '*very unfavourable*', or '*somewhat unfavourable*'. In terms of polit-ical relations the two friendliest countries in the Middle East are unquestionably Egypt and Jordan. As pointed out above, both countries have signed formal peace treaties with Israel. They therefore provide an important test case. Pew surveyed both countries.

The results could hardly have been more emphatic. In Egypt 0 per cent (that's zero) said they had a very favourable opinion of Jews, with 2 per cent describing their opinions as somewhat favourable. On the other side of the equation, 82 per cent said they had a very unfavourable opinion of Jews, with 15 per cent holding a somewhat unfavourable opinion. Thus, the biggest Arab country, and the first Arab country to sign a peace agreement with Israel, contains a population among which a mere 2 per cent of those who expressed a preference have positive feelings towards Jews, and among which 97 per cent admit to having negative feelings. In Jordan, the proportion of the population with a very favourable view towards Jews was also 0 per cent (zero) with 1 per cent professing a somewhat favourable view. On the flip side, 96 per cent said they had a very unfavourable opinion of Jews, with 2 per cent having a somewhat unfavourable opinion. In total, only 1 per cent of Jordanians have positive feelings to Jews, while 98 per cent have negative feelings.

Significant numbers of Egyptians and Jordanians are also prepared to believe things about Israel's role on the world which can only properly be described as deranged. In a poll by WorldPublicOpinion.org in September 2008, for example, 43 per cent of Egyptians and 31 per cent of Jordanians said they believed that Israel carried out the terror attacks on the United States on September 11, 2001.[68]

It is surely impossible to understand the strategic challenges faced by Israel without an awareness of such realities. And these are merely the most generalised reflections of political cultures which also contain relentless attacks in the media and in the mosques on Jews and Israel which are truly reminiscent of Nazi and medieval Christian anti-Semitism. Such attacks take the form of writing and imagery portraying Jews as bloodsuckers, as sacrificers of non-Jewish children, as butchers, as poisoners of the wells, as subhuman monsters perpetrating innumerable acts of bestiality. Holocaust denial is routine. The notorious anti-Semitic forgery alleging a worldwide Jewish conspiracy, *The Protocols of the Elders of Zion*, is a bestseller across the Arab world.

The extent of what is going on is truly extraordinary. Sometimes anti-Semitic bigotry appears from the most unexpected quarters indicating how deep it goes in society and how casual it can be. On 11 July 2008, Egyptian TV broadcast what was presumably intended to be a light-hearted segment with the eccentric but loveable-sounding Egyptian Unique Moustache Association. Members of the group talked proudly about different kinds of moustaches, one of which was discussed in particularly glowing terms. Asked about Adolf Hitler's moustache, one Captain Sayyed Shahada said: 'By the way, I respect the moustache of this Hitler, because he humiliated the most despicable sect in the world. He subdued the people who subdued the whole world – him with his "11" moustache. By the way, that kind of moustache is called "11". The generation of this Hitler ... When I was little, my father, may he rest in peace, grew that kind of moustache, and so did all his classmates. They all had this "11" moustache ...'[69]

Old-style blood libels are also common. On 30 January 2007 Lebanon's TeleLiban TV broadcast an interview with the Lebanese poet Marwan Chamoun who told viewers about an alleged incident in Syria in 1840 in which a Christian priest was murdered in the presence of two rabbis and the head of the Damascus Jewish community (whom Chamoun described as a close friend of the priest, presumably as a warning about what can happen if one is foolish enough to befriend a Jew). 'After he was slaughtered,' Chamoun said, 'his blood was collected, and the two rabbis took it. Why? So they could worship their God, because by drinking human blood they can get closer to God.'[70]

As for the mantra that the Jews descended from apes and pigs, it is more or less ubiquitous and is repeated endlessly.

Other animals are sometimes thrown in for good measure. On 21 July 2006 Syrian TV broadcast an interview with the country's Deputy Minister of Religious Endowment, Dr Muhammad 'Abd Al-Sattar. Speaking of the Jews, he said: 'The Koran used terms that are closer to animals than to humans only with regard to those people. Look at the bestiality they demonstrate in the destruction of the Arab, Lebanese, and Palestinian people. This is why the people who were given the Torah were likened to a donkey carrying books. They were also likened to apes and pigs, and they are, indeed, the descendants of apes and pigs, as the Koran teaches us.'[71]

In December 2008, Egyptian cleric Safwat Higazi appeared on Hamas TV with an uncompromising, but hardly unfamiliar, New Year's Eve message. 'We say to you: despatch those sons of apes and pigs to the hellfire on the wings of the Qassam rockets.'[72]

In April 2002, Saudi Sheik Abd Al Rahman Al-Sudayyis, an imam at the revered Al Haraam mosque in Mecca, remonstrated with those (such as members of the Saudi government) talking of Arab peace initiatives with Israel since the Jews, he opined, were 'the scum of the human race, the rats of the world, the violators of pacts and agreements, the murderers of the prophets and the offspring of apes and pigs'.[73]

These sorts of comments are being broadcast to millions across the Middle East. No Israeli government has the luxury of ignoring their significance let alone of concluding, in the casual words of the BBC's Cairo correspondent in 2003, that: 'The use of anti-Semitic imagery in the Egyptian media may seem bizarre, racist and anachronistic to outsiders. But it is not based on any historical hatred of Jews as a race. It has more to do with the need to be seen supporting the Palestinians, even if only in a purely symbolic way. That means that if and when real peace comes, the Egyptian media are likely to quickly forget their anti-Semitic line.'[74]

In other words, it is all due to the conflict with Israel so it matters little. We can quickly move on. One doubts whether the BBC would draw such gentle conclusions if Arab media were launching similar tirades against blacks. The reporter has failed to understand that there is always an ostensible 'reason' for anti-Semitism. Not even the Nazis said they simply hated Jews and left it that. Anti-Semites always accuse the Jews of doing, or having done, something which explains and therefore legitimises anti-Semitism: if the Jews could only be better, no one would hate them.

Given the depths that have been plumbed in the Arab and Muslim world it would be naïve to say the least to believe that hatred of Jews has not now become a core feature of the political culture. But conjecture is, in any case, unnecessary. We merely need to listen to what some in the region are openly announcing to us. As the Egyptian cleric Muhammad Hussein Ya'qoub told Al-Rahma Television in January 2009: 'If the Jews left Palestine to us, would we start loving them? Of course not. We will never love them. Absolutely not. The Jews are infidels ... You must believe that we will fight, defeat, and annihilate them, until not a single Jew remains on the face of the Earth.' And, he added with a familiar flourish: 'Allah, we pray that you transform them again, and make the Muslims rejoice again in seeing them as apes and pigs. You pigs of the earth! You pigs of the earth! You kill the Muslims with that cold pig [blood] of yours.'[75]

There is nothing wrong, and much to be commended, in encouraging Israel to explore the possibilities for peace with its neighbours. But neither Israel nor the rest of us can afford to ignore the fragile foundations on which any peace in the region would be founded as long as hatred for the Jews continues. Peace agreements that have already been signed, peace offers on the table, could evaporate completely with a simple change of regime or if existing governments decided that it was in their interests to draw on elemental hatreds with such widespread public approval.[76]

Similar issues apply in dealing with the Palestinians.[77] Quite apart from the reality that Palestinian leaders have rejected peace deals with Israel since the inception of the state (and before), and quite apart from the avowedly rejectionist position of groups such as Hamas, it takes a leap of faith to take would-be Palestinian peacemakers such as Mahmoud Abbas seriously when the Palestinian media, education system and religious authorities consistently demonise Israel and Jews in the most abominable and violent terms. (Abbas himself wrote a doctoral thesis denying the extent of the Holocaust.) Attempts to indoctrinate children are particularly worrying. Summer 2007 provided a rare occasion when the media did pick up on aspects of this. Stories broke in media across Europe and America about a Mickey Mouse lookalike on a Hamas television station urging children to kill Israelis. As controversy raged and the bad publicity became an embarrassment, the character, a puppet called Farfur, was killed off by being beaten to death by an Israeli soldier. It was undoubtedly a touching final episode for the children.

But this was merely a single illustration of a daily reality in which Israel's right to exist is systematically denied, in which suicide bombing and violence generally have been glorified on television by both Hamas and Fatah (Abbas's own party) and in which hatred of everything to do with the Jews and Israel is more or less routine.

Far from preparing their people for peace, the leaders and opinion formers in Palestinian society do everything they can to sew hatred and contempt. The Israelis know this because it is taking place right in front of them. Since Western, and especially, European media all but ignore these crucial parts of the context, audiences have little prospect of properly understanding the Israeli point of view.

It is precisely the absence of all of this background and context about Middle Eastern political culture which makes the active forms of discourse outlined in the first part of this chapter such an easy sell. Even people of goodwill are understandably perplexed by Israeli behaviour because they are simply not being informed about the environment in which Israel operates. Consciously or unconsciously, the European media is effectively engaged in mass censorship about key regional realities. I say 'consciously or unconsciously' but sometimes denial of the core realities appears all too contrived. There is good evidence for this from the manner in which some editors have sought to assault the integrity of one of the most valuable sources for translation and dissemination of Arab and Muslim commentaries and broadcasts: the Middle East Media Research Institute (MEMRI) whose regularly updated archives can be found at www.memri.org.

This has come in a number of forms. First there is sometimes an attempt to dispute the validity of the organisation's translations. Unsurprisingly, MEMRI has made mistakes in the course of translating from thousands of articles and broadcasts. But in all but the tiniest minority of cases even critics have had to accept that the translations are sound. More commonly, MEMRI has been attacked because some of its senior staff have had past employment with Israeli state intelligence organs. This also falls flat since it blatantly plays the man rather than the ball. The MEMRI translations are either right or they are wrong. Who makes them is irrelevant.

For the *Guardian*'s Middle East editor Brian Whitaker in 2002, however, the fact that MEMRI officials have worked for the Israeli security apparatus made him 'uneasy' about the selection of material to translate. In an attempted demolition job on MEMRI, Whitaker made it quite plain why he was really so afraid of the organisation in words that should serve as a reminder to everyone of the mindset we are dealing with. 'The second thing that makes me uneasy,' he said in his article, 'is that the stories selected by Memri for translation follow a familiar pattern: either they reflect badly on the character of Arabs or they in some way further the political agenda of Israel.'[78]

The truth about Arab political culture is painful. Worse, it shows Israel in a different, more positive light. At all costs, therefore, it must be denied.

This applies in more concentrated form when it comes to the context in which Israel is forced to deal with groups like Hamas and Hezbollah. Both are, of course, avowedly anti-Israeli and, while sometimes making reference to the possibility that Jews, Christians and Muslims could live together (though not in Palestine except under Muslim rule), their anti-Semitism is thoroughgoing.

The Hamas charter is easily available in translation. As well as giving explicit approval of the notorious Tsarist forgery, *The Protocols of the Elders of Zion*, it is riddled with statements such as the following:

For a long time, the enemies have been planning, skilfully and with precision, for the achievement of what they have attained. They took into consideration the causes affecting the current of events. They strived to amass great and substantive material wealth which they devoted to the realisation of their dream. With their money, they took control of the world media, news agencies, the press, publishing houses, broadcasting stations, and others. With their money they stirred revolutions in various parts of the world with the purpose of achieving their interests and reaping the fruit therein. They were behind the French Revolution, the Communist revolution and most of the revolutions we heard and hear about, here and there. With their money they formed secret societies, such as Freemasons, Rotary Clubs, the Lions and others in different parts of the world for the purpose of sabotaging societies and achieving Zionist interests. With their money they were able to control imperialistic countries and instigate them to colonize many countries in order to enable them to exploit their resources and spread corruption there.

You may speak as much as you want about regional and world wars. They were behind World War I, when they were able to destroy the Islamic Caliphate, making financial gains and controlling resources. They obtained the Balfour Declaration, formed the League of Nations through which they could rule the world. They were behind World War II, through which they made huge financial gains by trading in armaments, and paved the way for the establishment of their state. It was they who instigated the replacement of the League of Nations with the United Nations and the Security Council to enable them to rule the world through them. There is no war going on anywhere, without having their finger in it.[79]

Such statements represent a serious problem for Hamas apologists and dissemblers about the group's true nature. Hamas itself is also aware of the potential public relations disaster it could imply for the Palestinian cause in the West. Hamas spokespeople have therefore occasionally sought to downplay their anti-Semitism for Western consumption operating on the (reasonable) assumptions that gullibility on the part of some and wilful blindness on the part of others might help sanitise their image at least in some quarters. Hamas Prime Minister Ismail Haniyeh thus told a *Washington Post/Newsweek* reporter in an interview in 2006 that: 'We do not have any feelings of animosity toward Jews. We do not wish to throw them into the sea. All we seek is to be given our land back, not to harm anybody.'[80]

Quite why Hamas should go to such lengths given that media outlets usually ignore the basic facts is, nonetheless, a mystery. The BBC website, for example, carries a lengthy description of Hamas entitled 'Who are Hamas?' which, although it says that Hamas has been designated a terrorist body by the EU and US, is committed to the destruction of Israel and has carried out suicide attacks in Israel, makes no reference whatsoever to the group's anti-Semitism.[81]

The reality is that virulent anti-Semitism remains an ever-present feature of Hamas discourse. It is a central and defining part of the organisation's character. Indeed, the charter merely represents one among myriad instances of its viciously anti-

Semitic agenda. The global banking crisis in 2008 provided yet more evidence of the nature of what Israel has to contend with. In a statement in October of that year, Hamas spokesman Fawzi Barhum blamed the crisis on 'a bad banking system put into place and controlled by the Jewish lobby'.[82]

And Hamas is not just anti-Semitic. It can be virulently racist against blacks, too. On 15 June 2008, in an interview on Al-Aqsa TV, the group's Minister of Culture, Atallah Abu Al-Subh, described US Secretary of State Condoleezza Rice as a 'black scorpion with a cobra's head'. He went on to say: 'Every proud Palestinian views you as a murderer, and sees the blood of the children of Palestine between your lips and on your fangs. I pray to Allah that you will soon slither away, along with your master who is more Zionist than the Zionists . . .'[83] (Given the nature of anti-Israeli Islamist groups, racist rhetoric should not be surprising. Following Barack Obama's victory in the US elections, Al-Qaeda's second-in-command, Ayman al-Zawahiri, wasted no time in slamming Obama (along with Rice and Colin Powell) as a 'house negro' for allegedly sucking up to the American political establishment as well as to Israel and the Jews.[84])

Hate speech is also a staple of Hezbollah propaganda. In December 2004, French Prime Minister Jean-Pierre Raffarin, to his credit, described the programming of Hezbollah's television station Al-Manar as 'incompatible' with French values.[85] The previous month, Al-Manar had broadcast a programme in which 'Zionists' were charged with spreading AIDS around the Arab world.[86]

The fundamentally fanatical and hateful character of groups such as Hezbollah and Hamas, as well as numerous other militant organisations, ineluctably translates into the pitiless manner in which they conduct their terrorist attacks on Israel. From such beginnings, which dehumanise Israelis and Jews, it is in no way surprising that the primary focus of their attacks is on civilians. Nor is it surprising that when massive civilian destruction is achieved, through suicide bombing for example, it is greeted by widespread (and literal) public applause. The dire living conditions of the Palestinians could never explain this. There are large numbers of people on the planet whose condition is, and has been, much worse than the Palestinians but who do not attack civilians. Public approval for such wanton destruction of human lives, even the lives of the enemy, does not arise without a political culture which has been programmed to see the enemy as sub-human.

The difference between the political culture of Israel and its enemies was demonstrated in stark terms by the way in which the Hezbollah child killer Samir Kuntar was feted as a hero by vast crowds in Lebanon upon his release by Israel in the summer of 2008. Contrast that with the survivor of one of his rampages describing some years earlier what happened to her husband, Danny, and her daughters, Einat, four, and Yael, two, at their home in April 1979. These are the words of Smadar Haran Kaiser:

I will never forget the joy and the hatred in their voices as they swaggered about hunting for us, firing their guns and throwing grenades. I knew that if Yael cried out, the terrorists would toss a grenade into the crawl space and we would be killed. So I kept my hand over her mouth, hoping she could breathe [which she could not; she suffocated] ... As police began to arrive, the terrorists took Danny and Einat down to the beach. There, according to eyewitnesses, one of them shot Danny in front of Einat so that his death would be the last sight she would ever see. Then he smashed my little girl's skull in against a rock with his rifle butt. That terrorist was Samir Kuntar.[87]

For that terrorist, Samir Kuntar, Hezbollah supporters in their tens and hundreds of thousands cheered and wept for joy in images that were broadcast around the world. That is what it means to have a degraded political culture. Smadar Haran Kaiser's words on the subject of revenge are also instructive: 'One hears the terrorists and their excusers say that they are driven to kill out of desperation. But there is always a choice.

Even when you have suffered, you can choose whether to kill and ruin another's life, or whether to go on and rebuild. Even after my family was murdered, I never dreamed of taking revenge on any Arab.'[88]

It is only when one understands the brutal ideological under-pinnings of anti-Israeli terror groups and the popular approval they enjoy that one can understand why Israel finds it so hard to defend itself against them, and how collateral damage to civilians is so difficult to avoid. Just as such groups use civilians as offensive weapons in the form of suicide bombers, for pre-cisely the same reasons they have no qualms about using civilians as human shields to protect themselves. The political culture has been so degraded that it appears acceptable to do anything to anyone in furtherance of the ultimate goal. And 'anyone' in this regard applies just as much to their own people as it does to the Israelis. They also know that civilian deaths will play well for their cause on international media outlets that are effectively in a state of denial about such groups' real nature.

It bears repeating that the totality of Arab and Palestinian political culture cannot be reduced to its annihilationism vis-à-vis Israel, its anti-Semitism and its glorification of violence. Social and economic factors also play their part in legitimising and sustaining groups such as Hamas and Hezbollah. (This was also true of the Nazis.) There are pragmatists, of a kind, inside and outside such groups. There are many in the Arab world for whom Israel and the Palestinians are simply not a priority.

But while it is important to see the bigger picture, it is also vital that the part of the picture which explains why Israel acts and feels the way it does is not simply airbrushed from history.

Feeding the European mind

When the active and the passive elements are put together, how has this fed into the public mind? There have been numerous surveys of European attitudes to Israel in recent years. Like all opinion polls, the answers can depend greatly on the question that is asked. They may also depend on when the questions are posed. Hostility to Israel tends to spike in periods of conflict and to be more subdued during periods of calm. This book is not, in any case, about public opinion as such. It is about the people who attempt to lead it. Nonetheless, the surveys that have been taken offer some interesting pointers.

For example, the German Marshall Fund of the United States (GMF) conducted polls over five years (from 2004 to 2008) among nine European countries asking a very generalised question about warmth or coolness of feeling on a thermometer scale of 0 (the coolest) to 100 (the warmest).[89] On average over the five years there was no great difference between feelings towards Israelis or Palestinians, with Israel getting a rating of 42 out of 100 compared to 40 for the Palestinians. Opinions of both are slightly on the cool side – a rating of 50 would indicate that feelings are neither warm nor cool – but there is nothing much to choose between sympathies for either. The comparison with the United States, however, is dramatic. Over the same five-year period, Americans gave Israel a rating of 61 compared with 38 for the Palestinians.

This tells us much about societal attitudes to Israel and the Palestinians on either side of the Atlantic and is therefore valuable. It is also interesting that even in Europe such very generalised questions do not elicit any obvious relative hostility to the Israelis as compared to the Palestinians. But that is because the question is not directly political. It does not ask respondents to be judgemental. They are merely invited to give a generalised opinion about a matter they may not follow very closely.

When we go beyond questions about general feelings and ask respondents to express their preferences for one side or the other we push them back towards the places where their preference have been 'learnt' – the newspapers, the columnists within them, the people whom they respect, the opinion formers generally. When pushed in such a manner, the shift in public opinion against Israel in Europe can be dramatic.

A survey commissioned by the Anti-Defamation League in 2005 of sympathies among twelve European countries to the Palestinians and the Israelis was typical of many.[90] When pressed to say which side they sympathised with more, the Palestinians came out on top by a margin of almost 2:1, with 13 per cent sympathising with the Israelis against 25 per cent with the Palestinians.

Interestingly, there has also been some highly significant polling data which indicates that the closer people get to Europe's opinion-forming classes the more hostile to Israel they become. Since more educated sections of the population are more likely to read top newspapers, follow the news generally and take an interest in the views of influential people in society we would, in view of the evidence laid out in this chapter, expect them to exhibit a stronger bias against Israel or a stronger bias in favour of the Palestinians than the general population.

This is precisely what we find. In a survey by Pew in April 2002 the propensity of respondents to express sympathy for the Palestinians in Europe's four largest countries – France, Germany, Italy and Britain – was measured among the population as a whole, among highly educated sections of the population and among less well educated sections of the population.[91] In every case, sympathy for the Palestinians rose among more educated groups in the population and fell among the less educated. In France, sympathy for the Palestinians rose to 51 per cent among the highly educated from 36 per cent in the general population. In Germany it rose to 40 per cent from 26. In Italy it rose to 34 per cent from 30. In Britain it rose to 36 per cent from 28 per cent.

With the population as a whole, the harder one pushes, the more concrete the question gets, the worse it is for Israel.

In a survey of countries around the world conducted by GlobeScan and the Program on International Policy Attitudes at the University of Maryland for BBC World Service in 2007, European views on Israel's influence in the world were emphatic.[92]

In Germany, 77 per cent of respondents expressed a negative view, a figure which was actually higher than the 73 per cent having a negative view in the United Arab Emirates and only 1 percentage point below the figure for Egypt. Very high negative ratings in France (66 per cent), in Britain (65 per cent), in Italy (58 per cent), in Greece (68 per cent) and in Portugal (60 per cent) paint a depressing picture. The contrast with the United States, the only surveyed Western country where positive views (41 per cent) outweighed negative views (33 per cent), was clear.

With the above poll showing the German people leading the pack in Europe in terms of hostility to Israel, one inevitably turns one's attention to the specific question of Germany's Nazi past. Are Germans, perhaps through a desire to exculpate their nation's past sins via false equivalence, particularly susceptible to the Nazi analogy being put about by European opinion formers? An extensive survey conducted by the University of Bielefeld suggested they might be. In a poll of three thousand German citizens conducted in 2004, 51 per cent of respondents who expressed an opinion said that Israeli treatment of the Palestinians was similar to Nazi treatment of the Jews.[93] An astounding 68 per cent said that Israel was conducting a 'war of extermination' against the Palestinians. Influential and respected people in Europe are validating a discourse which equates Israel with Nazism. We should not be surprised to see it trickling down to the masses.

Bearing in mind everything that has been said in this chapter, it should not be difficult to understand how Israel's reputation has suffered so badly. A full-scale assault on the country's integrity has taken place in the context of denial and unawareness about the political culture that Israel is confronted with. Aggression partners with ignorance. For the Jewish state, the combination has been devastating.

CHAPTER 2

Of Jews and Israel

Is there an overlap between anti-Zionism and anti-Semitism? If so, is there a large or a small overlap? Do most people who oppose Israel oppose it because it is a Jewish state? Do they begin by hating Jews and end up hating Israel? Is the relationship the other way round? Is it possible to be profoundly hostile to Israel without simultaneously being hostile to Jews?

Everyone involved in the debate about Israel, whatever their loyalties and assumptions, instantly sees the relevance of such questions. Here, or somewhere like it, is where the debate about Israel and anti-Semitism always starts. But it is important to understand that, in so doing, the debate starts in the wrong place. These questions are good questions. They are relevant questions. And they will be seriously addressed as this chapter proceeds.

But in embarking upon a discussion of this subject in this manner even those motivated by good faith risk falling into a trap. For the deepest and most worrying problem in the way this debate is conducted is that it is done so under the shadow of a false dichotomy: a spurious distinction between a supposedly acceptable position described as anti-Israeli (or anti-Zionist) and an unacceptable position described as anti-Semitic. It is symptomatic of how serious the situation has become that this false dichotomy is so poorly understood and so widely indulged.

To clarify the point, it may be helpful to perform a thought experiment. Consider an imaginary example of a virulent critic of Israel defending himself against the charge of anti-Semitism after asserting that the Jewish state is comparable to Nazi Germany. (It is a sad reflection of the state of the debate about Israel that no great leap of the imagination is necessary here.) How might such a man defending himself against such a charge mount his defence? He might choose from a number of options. He might say that he is himself Jewish and that he cannot therefore be an anti-Semite. He might say that his assertion is justified: Israel is indeed like Nazi Germany and that it plans to exterminate the Palestinians. He might say that he has no problem with Jews as such, merely with the Jewish state. He might even back down a little and confess that the comparison with Nazi Germany was excessive and that apartheid South Africa would have been a better analogy. He might say a hundred things to defend himself.

The trap that has been laid here is in the risk of believing that his moral probity and his intellectual credibility rest on his ability to defend himself solely against the charge of anti-Semitism. The great mistake is precisely the assumption that, when talking about Israel, the only serious error, the only moral crevasse that one could fall into, is irrational hostility to the Jews *per se*. It is to accept before the debate has begun that anti-intellectual and hateful discourse about Israel is somehow reasonable, somehow excusable, if only the charge of anti-Semitism can be parried.

It is as if one were to hear and be satisfied by a defence from our protagonist on the following lines: 'You slander me by calling me an anti-Semite. You hurt me by calling me an anti-Semite. I support Jews. I respect Jews. My hatred is not for them. My hatred is reserved for Israel. Yes, I have cast aside rational argument in favour of emotionalism. Yes, I am deliberately distorting both the past and the present via gross and false analogies. Yes, in other words, I am a bigot. But I am not a bigot of the type you describe. I am an anti-Zionist bigot and an anti-Israeli bigot. I am innocent of the charge made against me.'

To stake everything in this discussion on whether the charge of anti-Semitism can or cannot be pinned on people and institutions who make a fetish of demonising Israel is a common mistake. But it is to introduce the kind of ethical *modus operandi* which would be immediately rejected in any other discussion. It is to allow at the outset as a defence against the charge of one form of bigotry that the accused can be absolved, his integrity restored, if he is in fact found guilty of another form of bigotry. To argue thus is to cast aside a core principle of enlightened discourse – the principle that bigotry is unacceptable whatever its object and that truthful, contextualised, reason-based discourse is the standard that all intellectually honest, decent men and women must aspire to.

For all sorts of reasons, it matters whether the demonisation of Israel amounts to a new version of an age-old hostility to Jews. More on that in a moment. But even if it is not, this does not mean that we should somehow forget that Israel is a nation, a collective enterprise of millions of men and women, like all the others. Like all the others, it and its people have a right to be treated with respect. Israel has a right to expect that criticism visited against it is factual and balanced. It has a right to expect that the good sides of its national life are brought to public view along with the darker sides. It has a right to expect that opinion formers, international bodies and politicians around the world relate to it according to the same standards by which they relate to every other state in the world. When these basic principles are violated or disregarded, moral and intellectual integrity demands that we do not to shirk from describing this as bigotry. Bigotry is a state of mind not an object of attack. It is not softened or hardened by the adjectives which precede it. There is no 'good bigotry' and there is no 'bad bigotry'. There is no 'acceptable bigotry', no 'unacceptable bigotry'. All bigotry is wrong. There are no exceptions. Irrational, hateful, dishonest discourse against Israel is bigotry pure and simple, whether it is anti-Semitism or whether it is not.

The importance of beginning the discussion with such a preamble should be obvious. We will not get clear analysis of the underlying problem if we feel duty bound at the outset to come to one conclusion or another because of the heat packed into the discussion by the term 'anti-Semitism'. We are that much less likely to come to fair and reasonable conclusions if the debate is conducted between one set of people who, come what may, will never accept that their discourse could be anti-Semitic, and another set of people who believe that the case for a reasoned and balanced approach to Israel is doomed unless the anti-Israeli narrative can be squeezed into the category of anti-Semitism.

That said, the question of whether anti-Semitism in traditional garb or in some more modernised formulation is at the root of this or maybe a part of this does indeed matter. It matters to Jews because anti-Semitism has haunted the Jewish people for centuries. They need to know whether or to what extent their condition has improved in the world since the Holocaust. It matters to everyone else of goodwill, especially in Europe, whether the single greatest stain on the integrity of Western civilisation has finally been removed. It matters for pragmatic as well as moral reasons. As the writer Christopher Hitchens, in typically flamboyant fashion, has put it: '... only a moral cretin thinks that anti-Semitism is a threat only to Jews. The memory of the Third Reich is very vivid in Europe precisely because a racist German regime also succeeded in slaughtering millions of non-Jews, including countless Germans, under the demented pretext of extirpating a nonexistent Jewish conspiracy.'[1]

If there are convincing reasons to believe that anti-Semitism is back, pure self-interest, if nothing else, should be enough to convince European elites that concerted action needs to be taken.

Defining anti-Semitic discourse

In 2004, the European Monitoring Centre on Racism and Xenophobia (EUMC) attempted to establish some ground rules on the subject by elaborating on forms of anti-Semitism that reflect traditional hostility to Jews as individuals which 'could also target the state of Israel conceived as a Jewish collectivity'.[2] The 'working definition' the group produced said:

Examples of the ways in which anti-Semitism manifests itself with regard to the state of Israel taking into account the overall context could include:

- Denying the Jewish people their right to self-determination (e.g., by claiming that the existence of a State of Israel is a racist endeavour).
- Applying double standards by requiring of it a behaviour not expected or demanded of any other democratic nation.
- Using the symbols and images associated with classic anti-Semitism (e.g., claims of Jews killing Jesus or blood libel) to characterize Israel or Israelis.
- Drawing comparisons of contemporary Israeli policy to that of the Nazis.
- Holding Jews collectively responsible for actions of the State of Israel.

However, criticism of Israel similar to that levelled against any other country cannot be regarded as anti-Semitic.[3]

It requires effort to understand the validity of the EUMC's points of reference. And no serious discussion of this subject can be undertaken without building up to such an understanding from the basic starting points of the discussion. So it may be worthwhile to begin with the most basic question of all: what is a Jew?

A common formulation gives primacy to the notion of matrilineal descent: a person is Jewish by virtue of having a Jewish mother. Less stringent definitions allow for a person to be considered Jewish due to having a Jewish father but not necessarily a Jewish mother, or due to having one or more Jewish grandparents. The religious and related cultural aspects of Judaism have also long been held to be central features of Jewishness. It is also possible, though difficult, for non-Jews to convert to Judaism through one or other of the recognised denominations of the Jewish faith. At this stage in the discussion there is no need to be too pedantic. If a person considers themselves to be Jewish, then that is up to them. What is much more important here is the question of the durability of Jewish identity, however defined, and the relationship between Jewish identity and the State of Israel.

I also work on the basis that anti-Semitism refers only to Jews not to people of 'Semitic' origin generally. To be anti-Semitic, therefore, is exactly the same as being anti-Jewish. These basic parameters seem broad enough to include most people who think of themselves as being Jewish while excluding red herrings from the discussion, such as the notion that anti-Semitism might also refer to Arabs in the Middle East who by archaic, philological (and, one might add, deliberately obfuscatory) definitions are sometimes referred to as Semites. According to the terms of this definition almost all of the citizens of the State of Israel minus the Arab population are Jewish, a characteristic they share with seven to eight million Jews in the Diaspora, mainly located in the United States, Canada and Europe.

What, then, does it mean to be anti-Jewish/anti-Semitic in practice? One way of answering this question is to say that it means many of the same sorts of things as it means to be racist against black people. To be sure, racism against blacks has taken different forms and resulted in different outcomes. It is also true that prejudice against black people is colour-based and is race-based in a way that prejudice against Jews is not. Blacks, like Caucasians, are a subdivision of the human race whereas Jews have a group identity which is usually formed via a combination of three related factors, namely biological ancestors, religion and culture.

Nevertheless, both have important characteristics in common. Both involve attempts by hostile actors to denigrate them through the use of derogatory words and phrases. Both involve attempts to defame them by the use of broader and more complex narratives evoking feelings of suspicion, fear, contempt or hatred. Both involve the use of visual images to complement the above kinds of words, phrases and narratives. Both are centrally concerned with discriminatory modes of thought, discourse and action where blacks and Jews are either singled out individually or defamed or otherwise harmed collectively. Both have resulted in grotesque political and social projects involving mass violence and oppression. Both have also resulted in lesser forms of violence and oppression which have nonetheless caused widespread pain, suffering and humiliation.

They have other observable characteristics in common. Anti-black racists and anti-Semites do not necessarily hate every black person or every Jew on the face of the planet. Old canards of the type 'Some of my best friends are black' or 'Some of my best friends are Jews' are not necessarily false just because many who trot them out are using them as a cover for broader, more generalised prejudices. They are quite capable of being comfortable with blacks and Jews individually or in 'acceptable' roles while still engaging in prejudiced discourse at a more general, collective level. Neither is it impossible (though it is certainly a minority pursuit) for blacks or Jews themselves to regurgitate racist or anti-Semitic mantras about their fellows. It is not unknown for blacks and Jews to legitimise or even engage in practices that are inimical to the interests of other blacks or Jews (see pp. 38–41). Black merchant and other elites in Africa were instrumental in the international slave trade. Just because they were black themselves does not alter the fact that they were participating in gross, racist practices. Similarly, the

Jew who participates in the anti-Semitism of his gentile neighbours has been an ever-present character in Jewish European
history since the Middle Ages at least. As Colin Shindler
has noted: 'On Hitler's accession to power there were even
minuscule groups of Jews such as Hans Joachim Schoeps's
Deutsche Vortrupp and Max Neumann's Verband national-
deutscher Juden which proclaimed their loyalty to the Führer
and the Fatherland.'[4]

The fact of being black or Jewish does not diminish or erase
the reality of the racism or anti-Semitism that is being indulged
in, though many superficial observers of the debate about Israel
and anti-Semitism labour under the mistaken belief that it
does.

Another related error in discussions about racism against
blacks and anti-Semitism concerns the relevance of the underlying motivation of the racist and the anti-Semite. Just as many
racists and anti-Semites mistakenly believe that if they can find
blacks or Jews to support or join in with their racism or anti-
Semitism it is miraculously transformed into reasoned and
enlightened discourse, there are many who believe they can
refer to motivations other than racism or anti-Semitism to
explain themselves. This is especially relevant to the kind of
anti-Semitism to be found inside some aspects of the polemic
against Israel where even extreme hostility is often excused by
claiming that the underlying motivation is honourable since it
is concerned with human rights in particular and the cause of
justice in general.

The flaw in the reasoning here is easy to demonstrate.
Imagine, by way of illustration, a political cartoonist at a major
newspaper designing a cartoon to bring attention to human
rights abuses in Robert Mugabe's Zimbabwe. If he did this by
portraying Mugabe as a gorilla jumping up and down on a pile
of bloodstained bananas this would clearly be a racist cartoon,
a particularly vile one at that. It would be no defence for the
cartoonist to say that his motivation was human rights and

concern for the suffering of the Zimbabwean people. Even if he was genuine in his claims, he and his cartoon would still be racist.

Unfortunately, in contemplating equivalent illustrations for anti-Semitism one does not need to deal in imaginary constructs. There are many real-world examples of political cartoons in contemporary Europe which have used blatantly anti-Semitic imagery to lambast Israel. In 2002, one of Italy's most celebrated political cartoonists, Giorgio Forattini, drew a cartoon for the Italian newspaper *La Stampa* depicting Jesus in the manger in Bethlehem faced by an Israeli tank. The caption read: 'They don't want to kill me again, do they?' The use of one of the most enduring and obnoxious anti-Semitic tropes – the deicide charge which posits Jews as Christ killers and which has encouraged massacres and pogroms through the centuries – is not, of course, made any less real by the context in which it is used. Rather failing to see the point, Forattini said of the controversy his cartoon had aroused that undoubtedly he had touched 'rather a delicate chord, but on the other hand that is my job'.[5]

The core distinction that needs to be made here is between what might be called 'subjective anti-Semitism' and 'objective anti-Semitism'. Subjective anti-Semitism – subjective because it relates to the person or institution engaged in it – is in evidence when a person or group starts out by despising Jews and then applies that hatred more widely in the form of a hatred for Jewish causes which may or may not include the State of Israel. Objective anti-Semitism – objective because it refers to the object of attack – is at play when different, non-anti-Semitic foundational assumptions still lead to the same irrational and bigoted conclusions as the ones drawn by the subjective anti-Semite. You do not need to hate individual Jews to end up hating Jewish causes, as I demonstrate clearly in Chapter 7 looking at the ideological underpinning of virulent hostility to Israel. Objective anti-Semitism may, as in the cartoon example above, involve the use of traditional anti-Semitic stereotypes or it may not.

A reasonable understanding of what constitutes racism generally and anti-Semitism in particular must also involve a recognition that such pathologies are at play whenever there is hateful or discriminatory discourse against matters which are constitutive of and central to group identity. One form of this might relate to history. As an example, knowledge of the history of oppression of both blacks and Jews is certainly central to both groups' identity. To deny that slavery ever happened, for example, is racist because it both seeks to remove from black people's collective memory something which is, in important respects, constitutive of their identity and because it simultaneously accuses them of inventing grievances. They are collectively libelled as liars while the crimes of their one-time oppressors are alleged not to have been crimes at all since they never took place. The same is true of attempts to deny or diminish the Holocaust and previous anti-Semitisms.

Jewish identity, Israel and anti-Semitism

But there is another sense in which matters constitutive of identity need to be understood here. The question of how to define a Jew has been briefly touched upon. But a much more profound understanding is necessary fully to appreciate why Israel is so important to the vast majority of the world's Jews and why hateful anti-Israeli discourse (something quite distinct from reasoned criticism) can constitute a new form of anti-Semitism.

Jewish identity, in common with all other comparable types of identity, has no future in the world without something to make it substantial and durable. Identity is not an empty shell. It needs to be infused with something real, something to flesh it out, something which gives it meaning. It needs a sense of a past, a present and a future. Identity is not something one can have today but lose tomorrow. It is not like a snapshot of something fleeting and ephemeral.

What, in the modern world, could give Jewish identity meaning and durability? One possibility is the obvious one: thoroughgoing adherence to the Jewish religion. If, as some groups do, Jews locate themselves in more or less closed religious communities, they have a substantial and durable Jewish identity in the present which is tied to the past via their ancestors and to the future via their friends, relatives and offspring (real or imagined) through which, by virtue of living in closed communities, they can imagine Jewish identity being perpetuated.

But what of secular Jews or of less intensely religious Jews participating more broadly in mainstream society? For secular Jews, or Jews who mainly participate in the religion in vestigial, ceremonial form the durability of their Jewish identity is far more tenuous. It is far more vulnerable to being overwhelmed by competing claims on their identity, especially over time. French Jews may, in increasing numbers, see themselves primarily as French. British Jews as British. Hungarian Jews as Hungarian. There may well be a period in which both sets of identities can happily coexist. Many Diaspora Jews today may well feel that it does. But it is surely difficult for them to see this identity as sustainable in the long term. They know that children, grandchildren and great-grandchildren will tend to marry and procreate with non-Jews. They know that attachment to the religion and the cultural practices associated with it will become ever more distant. The secularism that is a particular feature of modern Europe will affect them as it will affect everyone else. Even Diaspora Jews who make it a priority to find a Jewish spouse feel a sense of (quite justified) trepidation that their children might not.

In the Diaspora, Jewishness as a meaningful locus of identity risks disappearing almost completely in a matter of a few generations, as the historian Bernard Wasserstein has described in his portentous book, *Vanishing Diaspora*.[6] What happens to

Jewish identity, however defined, when it is one-eighth, one-sixteenth, one-thirty-second or one-sixty-fourth of the general mix? To what extent could such a person consider themselves a Jew? To what extent would they even regard the question as meaningful?

For Diaspora Jews who have left their religion behind and who live and interact with mainstream society there is one, and only one, available way to retrieve a sense of durability to their Jewish identity. And that is to locate it inside a deep and enduring affiliation with the Jewish State of Israel. Israel, for the vast majority of Diaspora Jews, is not and cannot be an incidental matter. Israeli nationalism is a central and defining feature of their Jewish identity because via no other medium can their Jewish identity be realised in concrete and durable form.

The writer Barbara Amiel has made a similar point about the centrality of Israel eloquently:

Without Israel, it is hard to see how all Jews in the Diaspora could avoid assimilation. Jews have survived more than 2,000 years in the single, unshakeable belief that one day their dislocation would end with their return to the Promised Land. This is the central underpinning of Judaism. 'Next year in Jerusalem' is the single phrase every Jew hears and remembers from the moment he can speak. If, this time, Israel is destroyed and the Jews leave, whether through progressive absorption into an Islamic state or bloody warfare, there seems little chance of a Third Temple and a return. Without the possibility of Israel, Judaism becomes pointless.[7]

This may, ultimately, mean that a long-term future for secular Jews can only be found in emigration to the Jewish state. Or it might not. A meaningful identity for Diaspora Jews might well be possible via a profound ongoing relationship with Israel without the need actually to live there. That is a matter for personal choice and forms a heated discussion among Diaspora

Jews. The paramount significance of Israel to modern, secular Jewish identity is in any case obvious.

This also sheds different light on the status of that small but vocal group of secular Jews in the Diaspora who consider themselves anti-Zionist and who therefore oppose the existence of the Jewish state. Since their secularism blocks their route to a sustainable Jewish identity through immersion in the religion and their anti-Zionism blocks their route to a sustainable Jewish identity via a deep-seated identity with Israel, they are effectively positing for themselves a state of long-term conversion away from Judaism.

Anti-Zionist Jews react to charges of this kind with a rejectionism bordering on bitterness. In a sense this is unsurprising. They are being presented with an edifice of argumentation to which there are no serious responses and which they are likely to take personally. They are therefore reduced to sophistry and denial centring on extremely vague and unconvincing definitions of Judaism – Judaism as a set of 'non-essentialised' political-philosophical ideals, for example – whose weakness they themselves must be only too well aware of. They are thrashing around in a shallow pool, and they know it.[8]

They may or may not be *self-hating* Jews but they are certainly *self-negating* Jews. They have adopted a maxim which, if adopted by all Jews, would negate absolutely the possibility of Jewish identity itself as a long-term constituent of the human race (with the exception, I repeat, of ultra-religious, closed communities). The secular, anti-Zionist Jew is a self-negating Jew because he or she lacks the ability to project a meaningful Jewish identity into the future.

From wherever it comes, hateful discourse about Israel is hateful discourse about a central facet of modern Jewish identity. For that reason it cannot be anything other than a fully modernised form of anti-Semitism.

The key point here is that it is a *fully modernised* form of anti-Semitism best described, I believe, as *neo-anti-Semitism*. It is not necessarily conceptually related to traditional forms of anti-Semitism from which many practitioners of anti-Israeli bigotry would certainly recoil.

A failure to understand this point has led to much confusion. When those who demonise Israel protest that they are not anti-Semites because they do not visit their scorn upon Jews in the manner of the Catholic Church of the Middle Ages, the Black Hundreds[9] of Tsarist Russia, the storm troopers of Nazi Germany, or even the gentleman's clubs of the British Empire they may well be right (though many writers have argued that it cannot be coincidental that so many of the same old tropes are still used). What they are missing is an understanding of how and why anti-Semitism has changed and mutated through time. They are guilty of a form of anti-Semitism but they are genuinely perplexed as to why.

There are other confusions which are related to this. Zionism itself, of course, is a term whose meaning and significance to Jewish identity has mutated over time. When Theodor Herzl, the father of Zionism, published *Der Judenstaat* (The Jewish State) in 1896 he was met with scepticism and even ridicule. At the First Zionist Congress in Basle, Switzerland, in August 1897 delegates adopted the so-called Basle Programme calling for the establishment of a Jewish state in a Palestine which at the time was little more than an Ottoman backwater.

But among the Jews of Europe, debate still raged. There were many prominent Jews who opposed the idea as unrealistic. Some opposed it on religious grounds. Others said there was no need for a Jewish state since, in one of history's worst political miscalculations, they believed conditions in Europe were improving with the emergence of liberal democratic societies. Others, such as the early Bundists from socialist and communist groupings, opposed it as 'bourgeois nationalism'. Still others opposed the idea of a Jewish state in Palestine in favour of a Jewish state in Uganda. It would be absurd, of course, to call such people anti-Semites. Zionism, at the time, was a theoretical idea. There was no guarantee that it would translate into reality in the form of a Jewish state. It was one of several possible outcomes and could not, therefore, be described as constitutive of real existing Jewish identity in the sense which it is today.

It was only after the Holocaust and the establishment of the State of Israel – two of the most significant events in the whole of Jewish history – that Zionism came to have its current meaning and significance to the vast majority of the world's Jews. In the 1940s the world changed forever for the Jewish people. Jewish identity changed in tandem. In important respects, so did the sense in which hostility to Jews would express itself.

Differences of degree, differences in kind

Disentangling different kinds of anti-Semitism is not an easy task. It is especially hard when neo-anti-Semitic (virulently anti-Israeli) discourse comes dressed in traditional anti-Semitic garb. How, after all, can we be sure of precisely what lies beneath when Israelis are slammed as Christ killers?[10] As I hinted in the opening section of this chapter, one way out of the problem might be to drop all reference to anti-Semitism and use the more general term bigotry instead. Both are accurate. The latter, it may be argued, avoids confusion.

Nevertheless, in the European and American contexts it makes sense, in most cases, to be as careful as we can be in identifying which brand of anti-Semitic discourse is at play. For it still remains true that discourses promoting hatred of Israel as a Jewish collective on the one hand and discourses promoting hatred of Jews as individuals on the other are not generally indulged in by the same people, at least in so far as the opinion formers are concerned. With the general public the lines may be more blurred. A study of public opinion by researchers Edward H. Kaplan and Charles A. Small from Yale University in 2006 showed that across ten European countries 'anti-Israel sentiment consistently predicts the probability that an individual is anti-Semitic'.[11] On the other hand, the causality question remains unresolved: do people hold hostile opinions about Israel because they hold hostile opinions about Jews, or is it the other way around? If the situation in Europe develops along the lines now evident in many Arab and Muslim countries that question may become increasingly irrelevant. As Robert Wistrich, a distinguished expert on modern anti-Semitism, has said of the discourse in that part of the world:

... Israel is today the only state on the face of the planet that such a large number of disparate people wish to see disappear – itself a chilling reminder of the Nazi propaganda of the 1930s. The most virulent expressions of this 'exterminationist' or genocidal anti-Zionism have come from the Arab-Muslim world, which is the historical heir of the earlier 20th century forms of totalitarian anti-Semitism in Hitler's Germany and the Soviet Union. Even 'moderate' Muslim statesmen such as Mahathir Mohammed [former leader of Malaysia] have publicly repeated the classic anti-Semitic belief that 'Jews rule the world' while eliciting virtually no objections in the Islamic world. The more radical Islamists from Al-Qaida to the Palestinian Hamas go much further since they fuse indiscriminate terror, suicide bombings, and a *Protocols of Zion* style of anti-Semitism with the ideology of jihad. In this case, the so called 'war against Zionism' unmistakably embraces the total demonization of the 'Jewish other': as the 'enemy of mankind,' as deadly poisonous snakes, as barbarian 'Nazis' *and* 'Holocaust manipulators' who control international finance, not to mention America, or the western mass media, while they busily instigate wars and revolutions to achieve world domination.[12]

There is, as Wistrich notes, a danger that this sort of thing is spreading into the West. On the fringes it has an established presence. In the mainstream it is making inroads. Nonetheless, we are not there yet.

So where exactly are we? With what has been said in this chapter in mind, what is the best way to interpret the kinds of discourse now prevailing in Europe?

CHAPTER 3

Fair comment?

There is a mantra much beloved of Israel's opponents. It refuses to go away. Israel's supporters, it is said, use accusations of anti-Semitism as a blanket charge to smother legitimate criticism of the Jewish state. A reading of the previous chapter should make it abundantly obvious that there is nothing casual about the way in which I handle questions about bigotry. I distinguish between different ways of talking about Israel and between different types of anti-Semitism. I have also brought forward the definitional framework worked out by Europe's leading body dealing with questions of racism and chauvinism which is broadly equivalent to my own. That definition, from the European Monitoring Centre on Racism and Xenophobia, also makes it plain that there is no suggestion whatsoever that reasoned criticism of Israel can be called anti-Semitism.

The admonishment that people calling for a more reasonable debate about Israel routinely fire off accusations of anti-Semitism is, in any case, curious. I can say in all honesty that I have never actually met anyone who behaves in such a manner (though one could undoubtedly find them on the fringes). Nor is it easy to understand why anyone would. Israeli democracy is at least as vibrant as American or European democracy. Freedom of speech in Israel is protected by law and finds its active expression in a wide variety of critical opinions available in a multiplicity of outlets. Criticism of Israel is thus built into the very fabric of Israeli society. Why and on what grounds would anyone suggest that mere criticism of Israel amounts to anti-Semitism? The frequency with which Israel's supporters are charged with casually flinging accusations of anti-Semitism is perhaps, therefore, significant in its own right. It smacks of defensiveness, of a vague awareness by the anti-Israeli constituency that at some level they are engaged in something troubling. They protest too much, and in so doing they may be revealing more about themselves than they would wish to.

It is also important to be careful in distinguishing between *anti-Semites*, for whom anti-Semitism is thoroughgoing and is constitutive of who they are as people, and the kind of unthinking indulgence in *anti-Semitic discourse* which reflects poor judgement but nothing much worse than that. Hostility to Israel is now so widespread, irrational thinking about the Jewish state has now taken such deep roots, and outright falsehoods have gained such wide currency on this subject that it is all too easy to slip into bigoted discourse about Israel without really thinking about it. This, I believe, accounts for the vast majority of people and institutions participating in virulently anti-Israeli discourse in Europe. It would not be fair or reasonable to call such people anti-Semites. True, they are engaged in anti-Semitism, but this does not speak to central features of their character.

In this chapter, I return to the forms of discourse outlined in the first section of Chapter 1. Those examples were not theoretical. Real people are involved in the defamation of the Jewish state and I have not shirked from using real-world examples. That said, I am not remotely interested in making any of this personal. If there are good grounds for suggesting that the discourse amounts to one or more forms of anti-Semitism I say so. If not, I keep my powder dry.

Inside the anti-Israeli mind

Israel as a 'shitty' country, Israel and excrement

Perhaps we should be grateful for small mercies in that forms of discourse designed to associate Israel in the popular mind with excrement are rare in the European mainstream. Still, the fact that it is possible to quote any such instances from among prominent individuals is deeply shocking. It should also serve as a warning as to how much worse the situation could yet become in Europe.

Two of the three instances quoted in Chapter 1 centred on describing Israel as 'shitty' – the first an off-the-cuff insult from a high-ranking French official and the second a more deliberate use of the same word whose force was accentuated through serial repetition by a British columnist sympathetic with the said French official.

Now, it is certainly arguable that the use of the word 'shitty' in these two instances represents nothing more (though certainly nothing less) than a desire to demean and degrade via a vulgar but everyday expletive. The two individuals using the word are not necessarily equating Israel with excrement in a conscious or literal sense. Neither would their listeners or readers take it as meant in such a way. Subconsciously, it may well be a different matter. But we cannot know this.

Taking the most generous view then, since the use of the word 'shitty' is without doubt designed to demean and degrade an entire nation, it feels like obvious bigotry. To me, it is neo-anti-Semitic since the nation in question is the modern-day Jewish state. It may also be anti-Zionist since it could be taken to delegitimise the Jewish state to such a degree that its foundational integrity is called into question. Finally, though, it is not anti-Semitic in a traditional, pre-Israeli sense since there is no evident hostility to individual Jews, *qua* individual Jews, or to the Jewish religion. Nor, to my knowledge, is the epithet 'shitty' one that is usually associated with traditional anti-Semitic discourse.

The other example quoted came from a commentary written by an influential British columnist who argued that in contemplating Israel's 60th anniversary all other sentiments which came to mind were overwhelmed by the smell of excrement. The writer, Johann Hari, meant this quite literally and went on to explain that this was because of instances in which Israeli settlers were pumping raw sewage from their settlements on to Palestinian lands, as well as how the blockade of Gaza had meant that vital equipment was not getting through, leading to the risk of serious leakage from its sewage system. He quoted environmental groups to back up his claim. Basic standards of fair dealing demand that we offer up the best defence for Hari's remarks that we can think of.

At first sight, it would seem that he could make a defence on the following lines. He could say that his claim is in fact truthful. And there is indeed *some* evidence that *some* Israeli settlers have in *some* cases pumped raw sewage on to *some* Palestinian land, though it is not at all clear whether the real fault lies with them, with the Palestinian Authority or with both. There is also evidence that there is a general problem with sewage treatment in the settlements and that this has environmental consequences for *some* Palestinians. Second, he could argue that, as a campaigning journalist, it is his duty to draw attention to such matters and that his method was merely a colourful, if somewhat extreme, way of doing that. His purpose was honourable since his aim was to draw attention to the plight of the Palestinians, perhaps also using his example as a metaphor for Israel's treatment of the Palestinians generally.

For me, these defences do not stand up to scrutiny. In the first instance, Hari has made it quite clear that the smell of excrement is the predominant sensation he encounters when he thinks of Israel in its totality. He does not just say that he thinks of raw sewage in the West Bank and then thinks of treatment of the Palestinians on the West Bank by the tiny proportion of the Israeli population that lives there. He says he thinks of raw sewage on the West Bank and then thinks of Israel generally. He is writing about Israel's 60th birthday. He uses particular instances to generalise about an entire nation.

It is an extraordinary statement about what discussion of Israel does to people these days that a writer as accomplished as Hari could not see the problem. I submit that in any other instance he would spot it in an instant. Imagine if an article were published about the black community in America celebrating a milestone in its modern history – the election of Barack Obama, for instance. And imagine if the writer had said that, although the black community had several achievements to its credit, the overwhelming sensation he experienced in contemplating that community on its day of celebration was from a recent report he had seen about gangs of black youths roaming the streets of Harlem in an orgy of mugging and murder. He had even seen an instance of it happening himself. The point does not need to be laboured. Perhaps the flagship characteristic of this style of argument is to allege or infer that isolated or small-scale instances of wrongdoing are more representative of that community's true character and worth than everything else. The fact that most of the Israeli population would be as appalled at stories of raw excrement being pumped on to Palestinian land as would the black community at stories of gang crime does not appear to concern Hari. He has his 'proof' and when you think of Israel he wants you to think of 'shit'.

That all said, there is no evidence from this or other of his writings that Hari is an anti-Semite in the sense of being motivated by a hostility to individual Jews *per se* and no one has grounds to suggest that he is. Indeed, he has at other times written passionately (though confusedly) about the dangers of traditional anti-Semitism reasserting itself.[1] All the same, his writing in this instance seems to me clearly bigoted and neo-anti-Semitic since it denigrates the State of Israel and does so in the most brutal manner imaginable.

Israel and Nazi Germany

A staple of anti-Israeli propaganda in the Arab and Muslim world, the practice of equating the Jewish state with Nazi Germany has now established a worryingly strong presence in mainstream European discourse. What kind of discourse is it?

It seems that it could fall into two categories. The first might involve the use of Nazi references as a warning to the Jews not to forget that they, above all people, should know what it is to suffer. Its use is tactical. It is an attempt to shock the Israeli people into a different way of thinking about the Palestinians by wiring the discourse into an event with powerful resonance. It does not actually say that Israel is like Nazi Germany or that its policies are Nazi. It is not a conscious effort to make an analogy in so far as it does not necessarily try to say that Palestinian suffering now is like Jewish suffering then. Rather, it takes the form of an appeal to the conscience. In this incarnation, such discourse would be crass and insensitive – Jews do not need to be reminded that six million of their brethren were exterminated in the Holocaust. It would also be indicative of shallowness since it illustrates an inability to come up with any other reference points from Jewish history to make a moral injunction to Jews. But it would usually be a passive rather than an active and aggressive form of bigotry or anti-Semitism.

The second category – direct analogies between the modern State of Israel and Nazi Germany – is very different. Most of the examples quoted in the relevant section of Chapter 1 are examples of this kind of discourse. In one form or another, they accuse Israel of doing, or preparing to do, to others what the Nazis did to Jews under the rule of the Third Reich.

To me, this is anti-Semitic in the traditional, generalised sense. The people quoted making such analogies in the relevant section of this book are not Holocaust deniers in the sense that they would ever deny that six million Jews were murdered by Nazis. The point is rather that in the rush to demonise and denigrate, they have been negligent in seeing the implications of their arguments when taken to their logical conclusion. To draw an analogy between Israeli efforts to stamp out terrorism, even if Israeli methods could be described as excessive in some cases, and the Nazi genocide is to diminish the reality of the Holocaust and thus to denigrate its significance. (The same is true of Nobel Laureate Maguire's description of Israel's nuclear weapons as 'gas chambers perfected'. She attempts to draw a comparison between a national defence strategy involving weapons of mass destruction and the most powerful symbol of the Nazi attempt to exterminate European Jewry in its entirety.) This leads directly into an anti-Zionist anti-Semitism. It assaults Israel's foundational legitimacy by drastically down-grading the significance of one of the most important historical events out of which the Jewish state was constructed. It is bigoted and neo-anti-Semitic since it is designed to heap scorn, contempt and hatred upon the most potent symbol of modern Jewry, the State of Israel.

The poet Tom Paulin may belong in a category of his own. As his poem suggests, he cannot even look at the word 'Crossfire' in the context of Israeli gun battles in the West Bank without seeing the letters 'ss' in the spelling of that word. In his mind's eye, he thus sees it written as CroSSfire. Paulin's hatred of Israel is such that it seems more like a mental condition. Taken in isolation, therefore, it may not be particularly significant. It is significant, though, that a highly respected, mainstream newspaper such as the *Observer* would publish this sort of material and thus offer it a degree of legitimacy.

Many observers have found themselves caught in the head-lights by the Nazi analogy, aware that something grotesque is at play but too stunned to work out what it all could mean. In researching this book one of the biggest surprises to me was that the attempt to associate Israel with the Nazis turned out to be far more common in the mainstream than the somewhat softer, though still anti-intellectual and deliberately insulting, apartheid analogy. Though the latter does creep into mainstream discourse it is very much more commonly used by the radical Left and its offshoots as well as the activist community. The Nazi analogy seems much more deeply embedded. Andrei S. Markovits has proffered a concise explanation as to why this might be:

Nazifying Israel makes it possible to kill three birds with one stone: The first objective achieved is the delegitimation of Israel by associating it with the symbol of evil par excellence. Second, one can attack and humiliate the Jewish people by equating it with the perpetrators of the brutal genocide that nearly succeeded in exterminating the Jews completely. Finally, this malicious analogy between Israel and Nazis frees Europeans of any remorse or shame for their history of a lethal anti-Semitism that lasted a solid millennium.[2]

Picking up on that last point, Bernard Lewis has also argued:

For more than half a century, any discussion of Jews and their problems has been overshadowed by the grim memories of the crimes of the Nazis and of the complicity, acquiescence, or indifference of so many others. But inevitably, the memory of those days is fading, and now Israel and its problems afford an opportunity to relinquish the unfamiliar and uncomfortable posture of guilt and contrition and to resume the more familiar and more comfortable position of stern reproof from an attitude of moral superiority. It is not surprising that this opportunity is widely welcomed and utilized.[3]

It is worth recalling that, among many others, two Nobel Prize winners from Europe have engaged in this kind of discourse.

Israel as a racist or 'apartheid' state

It has now become common in many quarters in Europe to describe Israel as a racist state. Nobel Laureate José Saramago based his own diatribe on a much used distortion about the meaning of the phrase 'chosen people' taken from the Bible. Saramago says the belief that Jews are a chosen people leads them to believe that they are justified in enacting 'an obsessive, psychological and pathologically exclusivist racism'.

The Jewish religion does not, of course, assert that Jews are superior to non-Jews. Like the Christian religion, it simply asserts that the Jews were chosen by God to fulfil a particular role. As a matter of observable fact, the Israeli state does not practise racism on the basis of colour or race in a systemic manner, though racist societal attitudes towards Arabs in Israel are as serious a problem as racist attitudes against blacks and Asians in Europe and America (not to mention the near ubiquitous anti-Semitism in the Arab and Muslim world). Nor does Israel stop people practising their religion whether they be Christian, Muslim or whatever. As for the apartheid analogy, Israel does not force non-Jews on to separate buses or separate beaches. It does not deny non-Jews the vote. It does not deny them political rights.

The Palestinians outside Israel, in the West Bank and Gaza Strip, do live in appalling conditions but not because Israel is constructed on a supremacist ideology of the type which underpinned apartheid. They live in such conditions because their leaders have consistently refused to come to an accommodation with the Jews in a long-running dispute over land and nationhood. As a by-product of this refusal, settlers from Israel have indeed set themselves up on land which the Palestinians claim as their own. In order to protect them from terrorism, the Israeli state has had to construct protected road networks to keep Palestinians away from Jews. But this is not because Israel believes Jews are superior to Palestinians. Rather, it has done this because of bitter experience which has shown that Palestinians will kill Jews (and will kill them because they *are* Jews) on the West Bank if such protective measures are not taken. (The same is true of the security barrier between Israel proper and the Palestinian territories.) The question of whether Israel should have allowed the settlements to be established in the first place is important in its own right. However, that question speaks to the overarching issues involved in the Israel–Palestine dispute about land, peace, self-determination and recognition. It does not affect the question of whether the Israeli state is racist or in any way comparable to apartheid South Africa. It manifestly is not.

There is also a pseudo-defence put up by Israel's opponents which needs to be dealt with at this point. One of the most enduring strategies employed by people and institutions attempting to rebut charges of bigotry generally is to find instances of people within the group they seek to defame who are indulging in the kind of discourse that they themselves indulge in. It's the 'after all, they say these sorts of things themselves' defence and I have touched upon it in my remarks in the introduction in cases where anti-Israeli Jews are thrust into the front line of the polemic against Israel, as well as in the previous chapter.

A useful example of how this works is the familiar defence offered up by racists in looking for instances in which black people have used the 'N' word (there is no need to spell it out) to each other in order to validate their own use of the term. When groups find themselves under sustained attack it is not uncommon for them to adopt the racist vocabulary of the racists themselves. Sometimes it may be ironic. Often it is simply a symptom of the oppressive atmosphere in which they live. Minority groups do not have sufficient power to control the terms of debate. Sometimes they find themselves participating in it as a defensive response to an agenda created by others. Such instances, however, are seized upon.

In a similar way, anti-Israeli contingents have seized upon, twisted and decontextualised very rare instances in which prominent Israeli figures have alluded to apartheid. The most significant example in recent times came in an interview in November 2007 by Israeli Prime Minister Ehud Olmert with Israel's *Haaretz* newspaper. In an attempt to rally support for his peace initiatives with the Palestinians, Olmert warned an Israeli population sceptical about Palestinian seriousness about peace (following the blunt rebuttals of the Clinton initiatives in 2000 and 2001) that a two-state solution was imperative for Israel's survival. A leader fully aware of the way Israel is already slammed as an 'apartheid' state drew from apartheid discourse for the purposes of domestic shock value. He did not say Israel was an apartheid state but he did say that, without an agreement, 'The day will come when the two-state solution collapses, and we face a South African-style struggle for equal voting rights ... As soon as that happens, the State of Israel is finished.'[4]

Now watch how that statement can be used against Israel. The following is taken from the *Independent* in July 2008. It is from an article whose main purpose is to parade and legitimise apartheid discourse on the back of a visit to the West Bank by a group of South African anti-apartheid veterans. In the article, entitled 'This is like apartheid', the writer ever so innocuously drops in the reference to Olmert's comment as a validation mechanism.

'Comparisons with apartheid have long been anathema to majority Israeli opinion,' the writer says halfway down the page, 'though they have been somewhat less taboo since the Israeli Prime Minister Ehud Olmert last year warned that without an early two-state agreement Israel could face a South African-style struggle for equal voting rights.'[5]

Just a twist here and a turn there and it is slipped casually into the narrative. There is no suggestion that the author is deliberately attempting to be manipulative. It is perfectly possible that he is not conscious of what he is doing. The effect, however, is devastating. Olmert's warning about a South African-style struggle in some hypothetical future turns into a kind of admission that Israel might reasonably be compared to apartheid South Africa in the here and now. No context to his remarks is provided. We are just told that a 'taboo' about apartheid discourse has been undermined by none other than the Israeli prime minister himself![6]

Returning to the broader issue, there is a danger here in taking the accusations of racism and apartheid too seriously. Neither accusation will stand up to a moment's scrutiny. The discussion is not being conducted on the basis of rational premises. I do not believe that the accusations of racism generally and apartheid in particular are usually designed to be taken seriously in any analytical sense. Their purpose is to raise the emotional temperature, to degrade and delegitimise and also, in the case of the apartheid analogy, to build a mass political movement of the kind which made apartheid South Africa a pariah and which ultimately contributed to its destruction.

As Gideon Shimoni, former head of the Hebrew University's Institute of Contemporary Jewry put it in an interview with the analyst Manfred Gerstenfeld: '... the fallacious Israel=apartheid equation is manifestly a malicious calumny used as a weapon aimed at the de-legitimization of Israel and its dissolution as a state that is Jewish in any meaningful sense. It is particularly insidious because it twists the worthy universal human rights agenda against itself.'[7]

Irrational discourse associating Israel with apartheid and labelling it as racist is clearly bigotry. Though Saramago's distortions about the 'chosen people' do constitute an anti-Semitic slur against the Jewish religion, apartheid discourse itself is not necessarily anti-Semitic in the traditional sense. (It is just possible to point to a false inversion involving subconscious references to ghettoised Jews as a precursor to apartheid: Jews were once ghettoised, this was like apartheid, and now Jews are doing the ghettoising. Maybe.) More usually, the apartheid analogy should be seen as a fully modernised line of attack. It is anti-Zionist since it seeks to undermine the foundational legitimacy of the Jewish state. It is also neo-anti-Semitic since it denigrates, via falsehoods, the State of Israel.

One other instance quoted was from an Italian Member of the European Parliament. It adds an interesting twist. Luisa Morgantini launched her own diatribe about Israel and apartheid on the back of a move in the Knesset to firm up the Jewish National Fund's ability to sell land to Jews only. The apartheid reference is absurd, and also bigoted. But can the same be said of the charge of racism in this case? Superficially, it would appear not. If Israel is discriminating in the sale of state land, giving preference to Jews over Arabs, that certainly looks like racism. If Germany, France or America sought to enact such laws we would have no hesitation in describing it as such. Surely the charge in this specific instance is fair comment? Yes and no. Yes, the practice is discriminatory and it goes beyond the kind of perfectly legitimate practice inherent in the Law of Return which gives primacy to Jews in seeking to emigrate to the Jewish state. For in this instance, the principle of equality before the law for *existing* citizens of the state is clearly being compromised. Jewish Israelis get something which Arab Israelis do not.

But it isn't quite that simple. There are some significant mitigating factors that need to be taken into account before judgement can be passed. First among them is the conflict as a whole. Above all else, of course, this is a conflict about land and who has rights to it. The tiny sliver of the Middle East that is modern-day Israel has been confronted from the first day of its existence by states and terror groups that have rejected the idea that Jews may legitimately own one square millimetre of the land inside their state. The penalty in the Palestinian territories for selling land or property to Jews, even when it is *privately* owned, is death. If Israel can be charged with discrimination in the manner in which it disposes of land, its guilt over this self-same issue is vastly outweighed by the guilt of the Palestinians. There is no suggestion that one wrong on the Palestinian side justifies another wrong on the Israeli side. But in the context of an overarching dispute over land it cannot be considered fair comment for an outsider to single out the discriminatory practices of one side in the way it approaches the land question while ignoring the much more emphatically discriminatory practices of the other. Ironically, of course, that in itself is discriminatory. Fair comment only enters into the discussion when all dimensions of the question are considered. At that point, and under that proviso, criticism of Israel in this regard is quite reasonable.

Israel and ethnic cleansing: 'Nakba abuse'

The use and abuse of Israel's 'new historians' is an increasingly common weapon in the armoury of Israel's detractors. The aim here is to delegitimise Israel by suggesting that it was founded on the basis of mass criminality involving the systematic expulsion of the Palestinian population at the inception of the state. All the relevant context is absent. (I refer to the general accusation of pre-planned ethnic cleansing as 'Nakba abuse' after the word Nakba – disaster – which Palestinians use to describe the events of 1947–8.) It seeks to argue that Palestinian and Arab opposition to Israel is entirely justified and always has been. This, by extension, can give legitimacy to the use of violence. 'How would you react,' they ask, 'if you had been kicked out of your home?'

The ethnic cleansing argument runs up against a number of insurmountable problems, some of which were touched upon in the introduction. The most obvious problem is that it is not easy to argue that Israel systematically expelled the Arab Palestinians given that a fifth of the Israeli population is made up of Arab Palestinians. It either was ethnic cleansing or it wasn't. If it was, why are there so many Arabs living in Israel? Did the Israeli 'ethnic cleansers' somehow overlook them? It is helpful to contrast the situation with a truly systematic and thoroughgoing ethnic cleansing operation such as the one which took place in post-war Czechoslovakia. Prior to World War II, fully one-third of the population of the Czech lands was ethnic German. Following the expulsion of between 2.5 million and 3 million of them under the terms of the so-called Beneš Decrees (named after Edward Beneš, Czechoslovak president at the time) the German population practically disappeared. The number of ethnic Germans living in the modern-day Czech Republic amounts to around 40,000, or less than 0.5 per cent of the population. That is what happens when a government and a people embark on a systematic policy of expelling an unwelcome ethnic group. What happened in Israel/Palestine in 1947–8 was nothing of the sort, as anyone who is aware of modern-day Israeli demographic realities must know.

As stated in Chapter 1, Nakba abuse has also run up against serious credibility problems attached to the most famous exponent of the systematic ethnic cleansing charge: the historian Ilan Pappé. Here are some examples of why from an interview with a Belgian newspaper in 1999. In Pappé's own words: 'I admit that my ideology influences my historical writings, but so what? I mean it is the same for everybody.'[8] Many historians would strongly disagree. Indeed, many would be appalled at the very suggestion. But in the same interview Pappé restated that position emphatically: 'Indeed the struggle is about ideology, not about facts. Who knows what facts are? We try to convince as many people as we can that our interpretation of the facts is the correct one, and we do it because of ideological reasons, not because we are truth seekers.' The agenda, he proudly asserts, comes before the facts.

Pappé is thus quite open in asserting the primacy in his historiography of ideology (which is militantly anti-Zionist and pro-Palestinian) over fact seeking. It is hardly surprising, therefore, that other historians such as Benny Morris have questioned the reliability of his conclusions. In a 2004 review of Pappé's book *A History of Modern Palestine*, Morris said: 'Unfortunately, much of what Pappé tries to sell his readers is complete fabrication', concluding that: 'This truly is an appalling book. Anyone interested in the real history of Palestine/Israel and the Palestinian-Israeli conflict would do well to run vigorously in the opposite direction.'[9]

Pappé later hit back at Morris, questioning his own credentials in a fiercely worded counter-attack entitled, 'Benny Morris's lies about my book', the thrust of which is self-explanatory.[10] The feud between the two continues to rage.

What matters here is not so much Pappé's reputation for accuracy. As I have said before, he himself, as a thoroughgoing postmodernist, admits that the facts of the matter do not concern him so much as the narrative which his writings can be squeezed into. What matters is that, in the full knowledge of Pappé's approach to history, so many opinion formers are pushing a ferociously anti-Israeli narrative into the public domain on the basis of his books. Pappé is quoted everywhere.

The events surrounding the genesis of the Palestinian refugee problem certainly constitute subject matter for reasoned debate and discussion. Israel did not start the train of events which led to the refugee problem. There was no plan to ethnically cleanse. Israel was not, after all, 'cleansed' of Arabs. But the demographic question was undoubtedly important and it remains so. It is also important to note that it is not so much the phrase 'ethnic cleansing' that matters here as the way in which that phrase is used and what lies behind its usage. Decent people motivated by good faith can, and should, talk about this subject. What the basic facts of the matter will not allow for is a one-dimensional, ideologically inspired assault on Israel in which the observable facts and the complexities surrounding their interpretation are simply cast aside in order to push a decontextualised charge of systematic 'ethnic cleansing'. To approach the subject in this manner is not fair comment. It is bigotry.

Israel as brutal and illegal occupier, terrorism as an understandable response

In much anti-Israeli writing the notions that the Israeli occupation is both gratuitously brutal and, thus, explanatory of Palestinian violence are simply taken for granted. The argument that Israel's occupation and all that goes with it in terms of roadblocks and other restrictions is necessary to curtail Palestinian violence, and that violence is in any case a product of ideology rather than occupation, has been largely ignored or dismissed. It was a matter of acute embarrassment for many, therefore, when Palestinian violence actually increased following Israel's withdrawal from Gaza in 2005 and the evacuation of all of the settlers. (However justified it may have been that, incidentally, was a genuine instance of systematic Israeli 'ethnic cleansing'. At the time of writing, the only Jew left in Gaza was Corporal Gilad Shalit, and he was only there because he was kidnapped by Palestinians.) With the argument about Israeli occupation as the 'root cause' of Palestinian violence in tatters, it then became necessary to attempt to save it on a legal technicality. Even though Israeli soldiers and settlers had withdrawn from Gaza, Israel remained the occupying power, the argument goes, since it controlled the movement of people and goods in and out of it.

Perhaps the first point to note is that it is manifestly clear that the only reason Israel maintains restrictions in and out of Gaza is its own security. It can hardly be denied that Hamas and other militant groups are constantly attempting to import weapons into Gaza to be used against Israel. Nor could anyone reasonably deny that such groups would attack Israel with even greater intensity if they had free access through the borders to

Israel. The Israel haters have thus constructed an iron ring around their arguments which makes them impervious to reason: even when Israel withdraws from occupied land it can still be accused of occupying that land because the measures it must take to defend itself restrict Palestinian control over borders.

When Israel is not physically occupying Gaza it is accused of legally occupying it even when it is plain for all to see that the technical/legal sense in which the occupation can be said to be continuing is itself solely the product of Palestinian violence. Whatever happens, Israel gets the blame and Palestinian violence is thus excused. It is a perfect illustration of the nature of the problem Israel faces.

The 'occupation' simply cannot explain most if not all Palestinian violence. In 2004, the Development Studies Programme of Birzeit University (a prominent Palestinian university) conducted an opinion poll among Palestinians asking whether they thought violence against Israel emanating from Gaza should stop or be continued should Israel actually withdraw from the Gaza strip.[11] More than 61 per cent said that violence should continue *from Gaza itself* even after Israeli withdrawal. The poll results distinguished between respondents in Gaza and the West Bank. But Gazans were even more emphatic than Palestinians on the West Bank in believing violence should continue after the end of occupation with support for it among them rising to 65 per cent. The Palestinians themselves are thus indicating that the direct experience of occupation is not the root cause of their own violent proclivities. There must be something more at play.

But to many in Europe, evidence must be ignored when it tells an inconvenient truth. They are driven by an emotional need to blind themselves in the face of overwhelming evidence that violence is driven by a rejectionist ideology positing the hatred of Jews and the illegitimacy of the Jewish state.

There are more general problems with the use of the occupation as a weapon against Israel. First among them is the fact that an occupation of one form or another was forced upon Israel by the 1967 war in which Arab nations attempted to destroy the Jewish state completely. The PLO was committed to the destruction of Israel even before the occupation began. Islamist groups for their part regard the whole of Israel as 'occupied territory'. That includes Tel Aviv.

As far as the broader debate in the West is concerned, there are some fairly basic historical realities whose acknowledgement would alter the terms of discussion radically. First among them is the fact that UN Resolution 242 (see pp. 24–7) was quite clearly constructed by its authors in such a way that it was not envisaged that Israel would withdraw from *all* of the territories. It also called for the: 'Termination of all claims or states of belligerency and respect for and acknowledgement of the sovereignty, territorial integrity and political independence of every state in the area and their right to live in peace within secure and recognized boundaries free from threats or acts of force.'[12]

Since only Jordan and Egypt have so far complied, and since countries such as Lebanon, Syria and Iran house or back terrorist groups which launch attacks on Israel, it is quite clear that Israel is under no legal obligation whatsoever to withdraw from the territories unilaterally. This does not at all mean that Israel is justified in building and expanding settlements wherever it wants to. But it does mean that blame for the broader occupation lies with Israel only in a secondary sense.[13] Primary responsibility rests with those states and groups that caused the occupation to exist in the first place and that have necessitated its continuation. When Israel withdraws from land claimed by the Palestinians, such as from Gaza in 2005, it is to be applauded for taking the risk of so doing. But there is no legal obligation for Israel to act in this manner. Nor is there a legal injunction on Israel against reoccupation of Gaza if the security situation requires it.

There is much that can be reasonably said about Israeli actions in the West Bank, and much that can be criticised. But it is not rational, reasonable or fair comment simply to ignore the reasons for the nature and the reality of the occupation in the first place. Nor is it rational or reasonable to dismiss the lessons of the withdrawal from Gaza. To act in this manner is to succumb to a hateful form of discourse which is entirely reflective of the neo-anti-Semitic mindset.

Israelis as war criminals

Whenever Israel engages in military action, however defensive that action may be, the suggestion that the Jewish state may be committing war crimes lurks in the background like a crouching tiger waiting to pounce on its prey. Of course, it is a welcome sign of progress in the modern world that we now pay much more regard to the way in which armies conduct themselves on the battlefield, particularly where civilians find themselves in the line of fire. But it is only a sign of progress if the new enthusiasm for closer scrutiny is applied equally as part of a commitment to the rule of law and not in a discriminatory manner suggesting the pursuit of a political agenda.

The saga of the indictments on war crimes charges against former Israeli Prime Minister Ariel Sharon in the Belgian courts clearly reflected the latter and not the former. It is worth dwelling on some of the details to understand why.

The extent to which the Belgian state bears responsibility for what happened would appear at first sight to be difficult to define. The cases were brought by private individuals – a group of twenty-eight Lebanese and Palestinians – and not by the state prosecutor. The 'universal jurisdiction' law of 1993 was not designed to single out Israel. Indeed, cases were also brought against former US President George H. W. Bush and other US officials for alleged war crimes in the first Gulf War in 1991 and against General Tommy Franks and others for alleged war crimes in the second Gulf War, which began in 2003.

Nonetheless, as the international lawyer Malvina Halberstam, who studied the situation in detail, noted at the time, Belgian political leaders and parliamentarians were quick to frustrate efforts for the law to be used against Americans but far more reluctant to do the same in the case of Ariel Sharon.[14] Moreover, the case against Sharon represented some extraordinary departures from usual legal practice: '... the killings at Sabra and Shatila that form the basis for the complaint were perpetrated by the Lebanese Christian Phalangia army, not by forces under Sharon's command. No government official has ever been convicted of war crimes for acts committed by the armed forces of another state – even an ally – not under his command. Such a rule would, for instance, make the US secretary of defense criminally responsible for atrocities committed by various Afghan factions in the war in Afghanistan.[15]

In terms of Belgium's responsibility, she added:

... it is Belgian law that makes the prosecution possible and Belgian courts that will hear the case. The U.S. Supreme Court long ago held that judicial enforcement of a racial covenant in a private contract constituted state action. In the same manner, Belgium cannot avoid responsibility for an action by its courts under its laws simply because it was instituted by private parties. Belgium has an obligation not to permit its laws and courts to be misused for political purposes. Otherwise, a law that was intended to promote the rule of law will have the opposite effect.[16]

In this, as in all cases involving accusations of war crimes against Israel, the distinction between fair comment and neo-anti-

Semitism depends on two factors, both of which must be present if the charge of bigotry is to be refuted.

First, it matters greatly whether the accusation could conceivably be truthful. Second, it must be clear that the accusation is made in good faith and not as part of a discriminatory agenda against the Jewish state. In this particular case, the defence fails on both counts. The Belgian state deserves credit for finally seeing the error of its ways. Reason eventually prevailed and the law was overhauled. But it also deserves censure for allowing years of news coverage across Europe and the wider world in which the suggestion that Israel had been guilty of war crimes over a massacre that was actually committed by Arab militiamen could be talked about as though it was a reasonable point of view. The Belgian courts had thus been turned into a platform for the legitimisation of what was effectively a neo-anti-Semitic blood libel against the Jewish state.

Accusations of war crimes in Gaza and during the Lebanon conflict in 2006 as well as any future charges (which will inevitably come) need to be addressed according to their merits. It is difficult, however, to see most of them as anything other than a crude weapon with which to beat a country faced with extraordinarily complex security challenges. Critics who can show that they have given serious attention to these challenges, that their charges have been properly thought through, and that they consistently apply the same criteria in judging all other countries in this way and not just Israel can reasonably claim to be engaged in fair comment. When Israel crosses the line it must not be immune from being held to account just because so much of the criticism it suffers is made in bad faith. At this stage, though, there is little likelihood of reason prevailing. Even organisations whose broader reputation depends on studious impartiality at all times are failing to behave rationally or reasonably.

Harvard Law Professor Alan Dershowitz usefully decon-

structed aspects of the Amnesty International report condemning Israel for war crimes in Lebanon in 2006. His words
are worth quoting at length. He said: 'Amnesty does not even
seem to understand the charges it is making. Take, for example,
this paragraph from its report:

'Israeli government spokespeople have insisted that they were
targeting Hizbullah positions and support facilities, and that
damage to civilian infrastructure was incidental or resulted from
Hizbullah using the civilian population as a "human shield".
However, the pattern and scope of the attacks, as well as the
number of civilian casualties and the amount of damage sustained,
makes the justification ring hollow.'

But, Dershowitz comments, the issue of human shields and
infrastructure are different. The first relates to civilian casualties;
the second concerns property damage. Of course Israel intentionally targeted bridges and roads. It would have been militarily
negligent not to have done so under the circumstances. But it did
not target innocent civilians. It would have given them no military
benefit to do so. The allegations become even more tenuous, as
when Amnesty writes, 'a road that can be used for military trans-
port is still primarily civilian in nature.' By this reasoning, terrorists
could commandeer any structure or road initially constructed for
civilian use, and Israel could not touch those bridges or buildings
because they were once, and still could be, used by civilians. This
is not, and should not be, the law.'[17]

And, concludes Dershowitz: 'Amnesty International's conclusions are not based on sound legal arguments. They're certainly not based on compelling moral arguments. They're
simply anti-Israel arguments.'[18]

(Amnesty's writings against Israel are sometimes breathtaking. In the Gaza crisis in January 2009 it even went so far as
to accuse the United States of being 'lopsided' in its support for
Israel. What on earth does an ostensibly objective human rights
group think it is doing in criticising US government policy on

such a complex matter? But there was worse. In the same statement it even went so far as to call on the US to impose an embargo saying that America 'must suspend the transfer of weapons to Israel immediately and conduct an investigation into whether U.S. weapons were used to commit human rights abuses'.[19])

The suspicion must be that the use of the term 'war crime' to describe Israeli military actions is usually another mantra inside a discourse of delegitimisation rather than a serious and considered attempt to promote and expand the rule of law in global conflicts. This is not always the case, but most of the time it is clear that it is. It is not difficult, after all, to see Israel's problems in confronting groups such as Hezbollah and Hamas which operate from within the civilian population. Not to see the nature of these problems requires effort. In so far as this is true, the 'war crimes' charge is merely a part of the neo-anti-Semitic agenda.

It is worth noting that in the popular mind the term 'war crime' is most commonly associated with the trials of Nazi leaders after World War II. This is unlikely to be remote from the thinking of some of those who systematically use it against Israel.

Israel as a violator of international law

The specific charge of 'war crimes' forms part of a wider discourse in which Israel is consistently accused of violating international law. Its cumulative effect is to cast Israel as a pariah. Most countries have broken international law at some level. This is not to excuse it. But there would be nothing unusual or even surprising if Israel were among them. Nor should there necessarily be anything wrong in criticising Israel on such grounds. Once again, the question of whether the accusations are made in good faith is crucial. Does the particular charge form part of a wider and considered pattern of holding nations to account? Or is it an unusually emotive and discriminatory mode of discourse which forms part of a pattern of discrimination?

The corresponding section in Chapter 1 (p. 69) began with a citation from an editorial in the *Financial Times*. In castigating Israel's assault on militant groups and the infrastructure which supports them in Gaza at the beginning of 2008, the paper said Israel was guilty of targeting the civilian population and conducting collective punishment. Having established the 'facts' of the matter the paper then said that this was a violation of international law and that there was 'no debate to be had about it'. There is, of course, no debate to be had about whether a deliberate policy of targeting civilians by using lethal force violates the law. Clearly it does. But it is Israel's opponents that target civilians in this way, not Israel. What the *Financial Times* is saying is that Israel's attempts to protect its own citizens from the lethal attacks of Palestinians in Gaza by tightly restricting movement, by targeting elements of the Hamas regime's infrastructure and by imposing economic sanctions amounts to an illegal collective punishment. But this is strange, to say the least. Does the *Financial Times* usually refer to the use of economic sanctions as 'collective punishment'? Has the *Financial Times* taken the trouble of considering the dangers to Israeli civilians if movement restrictions are lifted? And what of the complexities of dealing with terrorist groups that are deeply embedded in the civilian population? Hamas has both civilian and military wings. An impartial observer approaching such a situation without prejudice would surely recognise that Israel was faced with an immensely complicated task in dealing with terrorism without simultaneously causing hardship to civilians. Under such circumstances, if that observer were an international lawyer, one of the very few conclusions he or she might feel comfortable in stating emphatically is that questions of culpability were very difficult to answer. Anyone acting in good faith can see that this is something which would need to be discussed and debated at length. Instead we get simplistic and emotive sabre rattling on a matter of great complexity, and an attempt to foreclose on the possibility that what was going on could be the subject of reasoned discussion. To say 'there is no debate to be had about it' is a form of verbal foot stamping. It is reflective of a mindset which has been overcome by an emotional need to arrive at a particular conclusion and is angry at the idea that that conclusion might be challenged. The *Financial Times* does not habitually conduct itself in this manner. It shows every sign of having become reflexively anti-Israeli. To wit, during Israel's Operation Cast Lead in Gaza in 2008–9, the paper came out with an extraordinary assertion: 'It must be remembered that the root cause of the Israeli–Palestinian conflict is the Israeli occupation – which Israel's 2005 withdrawal from Gaza was meant to consolidate, through its subsequent expansion of Jewish settlements in the West Bank and Arab east Jerusalem.'[20] From its sheer historical illiteracy – the root cause of the conflict cannot conceivably be the occupation since the conflict with the State of Israel began two decades before the occupation took place – the interpretation of the motives behind the Gaza withdrawal is all but indistinguishable from Palestinian propaganda.

One of the most frequent senses in which Israel is lambasted for illegal behaviour concerns the settlements. Here, too, there is more than a little foot stamping going on over an issue of some complexity. As was shown in the introduction, the question of the legality of the settlements is inextricably tied up with the question of who has rights to the land on which they have been constructed. But that question can only be given a definitive answer once final status in a comprehensive peace agreement has been achieved. So far, we do not have one. Under the Clinton formulas some 'occupied' land as well as the settlements which bestride it was envisaged as becoming part of Israel. The international community has thus accepted that some of the settlements at least have some sort of claim to legitimacy.

The issue is far from clear-cut. Fair comment will reflect this. Bigotry will not.

There is a broader problem associated with discourse about Israel and international law: who makes the law and on what basis? Independent judicial systems and processes of creating laws and issuing judgements that are non-discriminatory are usually considered prerequisites for any state of affairs in which the rule of law can be said to be operating. Law, in this enlightened, Western sense is not merely the written expression of power. There must be equality before the law. There must be an important sense in which certain basic principles are being respected if law itself is to be worthy of respect. In contrast with the way domestic law is enacted in Western democracies, international law at the United Nations is not formulated on the basis of impartial decision making. In dealings between nations 'judges' are often of the same nationality as the plaintiffs. Rulings are made as a result of backroom deals. International law sounds a good deal grander than it really is. And nowhere has this been illustrated with greater clarity than in the case of Israel.

There have been dozens of United Nations General Assembly resolutions against Israel, including the notorious 'Zionism is Racism' resolution which was passed in 1975 and which was revoked under massive US-led pressure in 1991. General Assembly resolutions do not carry the same weight as Security Council resolutions but they do reflect the sentiments of the international community inside the most important institution associated with international norms. They thus give a sense of the prevailing atmosphere in which more binding injunctions on the Jewish state are made.

The inbuilt bias against Israel in the formulation of international statutes is the product of a huge Arab and Muslim bloc of countries with deeply hostile opinions of Jews and the Jewish state. The credibility of UN-associated institutions like the International Court of Justice suffers accordingly.

Alan Dershowitz has likened the ICJ in its deliberations on Israel to all-white courts in the American South in the 1930s. Israel now, like black people then, cannot get a fair hearing because of the weight of prejudices against it.[21] It is hard to disagree. Reading through the ICJ ruling in 2004, which calls on Israel to tear down a security barrier which has prevented countless suicide attacks, the extent of the anti-Israeli prejudice is breathtaking. In a wholesale adoption of the anti-Israeli agenda the ICJ simply parrots the Arab and Palestinian narrative over the routing of the barrier on 'occupied land'. The barrier itself is consistently referred to as a 'wall', despite the fact that 97 per cent of it is not in fact a wall. It is a fence.

This one small instance is indicative and illustrative of the fundamental dishonesty of the entire anti-Israeli agenda where international law is concerned. This, after all, is a court comprised of some of the most respected judges in the world. These people are used to dealing with matters of great complexity where there is a premium attached to precision and accuracy in the use of language. What on earth is going on if the International Court of Justice has debased itself to the extent that it cannot distinguish between a wall and a fence? Sadly, the answer to that question is straightforward. In order to leverage hatred against Israel and to conjure up images of ghettoisation, the Palestinians and their supporters have insisted on calling it a wall and had the strength in numbers inside the UN General Assembly to phrase the request to the ICJ to consider the matter in such terms. The fact that the ICJ decided to ape their dishonesty tells us everything we need to know about the mindset of most of its judges.

Commenting on the ruling, *Washington Post* columnist Charles Krauthammer concluded: 'Israel will rightly ignore the ICJ decision. The United States, acting honorably in a world of utter dishonor regarding Israel, will support that position. It must be noted that one of the signatories of this attempt to force Israel to tear down its most effective means of preventing the slaughter of innocent Jews was the judge from Germany.'[22]

Finally, there is also the question, hinted at above, of whether and to what extent international law is sufficiently developed to cope with mass terrorism perpetrated by non-state actors. If Israel is breaking international law when it tries to prevent terrorism by building physical barriers, if it is breaking international law by hitting terrorists that are hiding behind human shields, and if it is breaking international law by targeted assassination of terrorist leaders it is hard to see how the basic right of self-defence itself is compatible with international law in the presence of terrorist threats of this magnitude.

In sum, when Israel is accused of violating international law in a casual, reflexive or emotionally charged sense which ignores the subtleties and complexities surrounding the whole debate it is clear that we are witnessing a pandering to the neo-anti-Semitic agenda. Obviously, this does not mean that all charges against Israel for breaking legal norms constitute bigotry. Israel's own supreme court, possibly the best of its kind in the world, frequently finds against its own government. In most cases, though, it seems clear that the charges against Israel are simply not being made in good faith.

Israeli responses to attacks as 'disproportionate'

The layman's counterpart to the official-sounding denunciation of Israel as a violator of international law is the utilisation of the word 'disproportionate'. It is a near ubiquitous charge against Israeli military action aimed at terror groups such as Hamas and Hezbollah. Sometimes it is accompanied by charges that Israel, in Gaza and Lebanon, for example, is guilty of 'carpet-bombing' civilian areas. The latter accusation is either extraordinarily silly – since it is manifestly false – or, like comparisons with Nazi Germany or apartheid South Africa, it is not meant to be taken seriously in any case: it is designed to raise the emotional stakes and to heap upon Israel scorn and contempt. Israel possesses more than enough firepower to carpet-bomb Gaza and Lebanon into oblivion. It does not do so because Israel is a liberal-democratic society whose prevailing political culture would not allow such behaviour. The carpet-bombing charge is blatantly neo-anti-Semitic.

The use of the word 'disproportionate', however, is altogether more slippery. What does it actually mean? The simplest answer would be to say that it means Israel is accused of using more force in countering a threat than the amount of force actually necessary to counter that threat. Once again, what does that mean? The answer is 'nothing' until and unless the accuser has clearly defined how much force is really necessary in order to counter the threat in question. That precondition itself has a precondition: that the accuser is truly qualified to pass judgement or has at least consulted someone who is. Since people who accuse Israel of acting disproportionately are in almost all cases not qualified to pass judgement (they are not military experts and know little of the situation on the ground) and in any case almost never even attempt to define what would constitute a *proportionate* response it is clear that the accusation is usually not serious. It is devoid of meaningful content. The mystery therefore deepens. Why has this particular word become so popular?

Part of the problem could simply come down to a crude numbers game which is routinely played by comparing the levels of casualties on both sides. When Israeli casualties are lower than Palestinian and Arab casualties, Israel is accused of a disproportionate response. But this manner of thinking is perplexing. Greater casualties may be suffered by Israel's opponents because they use civilians and civilian areas as human shields. Israel, by contrast, uses its soldiers and its civil defence infrastructure to shield its civilians. One side treats its people as expendable. The other side treats its people as the top priority for protection. Under such circumstances, equal levels of military action would inevitably lead to greater casualties on the side of Israel's opponents. In any case, quoting the number of casualties suffered by one side or another still doesn't answer the question of how much force may be required to root out an opponent. It still doesn't make any sense.[23]

There may be another explanation for the popularity of the term. While largely meaningless in any substantial sense, the word 'disproportionate' when used in the Israeli context may serve a function on the field of international diplomacy. As I have said before, the word is a particular favourite of the European Union and it is widely used when European governments criticise Israel. In this sense, it is a way of giving something to both sides while still veering somewhat against Israel. To say that a response to terrorism is disproportionate, for example, is at least to imply that some sort of response was justified even if its severity is condemned. In this sense it is nothing more than a piece of diplomatic rhetoric: red meat is thrown to Israel's detractors with one hand while a few crumbs are scattered in Israel's general direction with the other. It does not offer any significant insights into what is going on since it doesn't really arise from an attempt to do so. Taken in isolation then, the usage of this terminology is neither anti-Semitic nor bigoted, nor fair comment. It is a lazy and imprecise way of expressing condemnation without actually saying anything. Perhaps it is simply shallow; nothing more and nothing less.

Israel as a liability

But there may yet be something more to be said about this; something which feeds neatly into a brief discussion of ways of treating Israel which see it as a liability. For there is undeniably a cost to supporting Israel. Israel is clearly a liability in terms of good relations with the Arab and wider Muslim world as well as in terms of good relations with Muslim communities at home.

The problem here could be described as 'agenda seepage'. In order to curry favour with dozens of states (some vital energy suppliers) whose attitudes towards Israel are characterised by unremitting hostility there may be a strong temptation to pander to elements of their agenda. Decent, mainstream politicians and commentators will usually have no truck with the kind of thoroughgoing, brute anti-Semitism which is now central to much Arab and Muslim political culture. However, they may view it as expedient to concede just enough ground to preserve friendships. But how much ground is enough? If the political culture of most Arab and Muslim states is anti-Semitic through and through as far as Israel is concerned, and it is, even seemingly small concessions may lead to the acquisition of some unpleasant ideas. It may also, in part at least, explain some of the seemingly baffling modes of discourse discussed in some sections above. People who have fallen into the trap of trying to strike a balance between hatred and decency may not, ultimately, be capable of accomplishing the task. The result is a kind of anti-Israeli discourse which is often little better than gibberish.

This agenda seepage and its implications are discussed in detail later in the book, especially in Chapters 5 and 6, but what are we to make of the general view that Israel is a liability?

While the related arguments that Western support for Israel is only explicable in terms of powerful Jewish cabals is anti-Semitic in both its traditional and modernised incarnations, discourse describing Israel as a liability probably belongs to a different category altogether.

Such discourse can easily lead into neo-anti-Semitic demonisation. That much is obvious. But what it really comes down to is a question of fundamental values and principles. There are costs and benefits associated with relationships between all states. How we assess these costs and benefits depends on what we view as valuable in the world and what we do not. Some things are straightforward in this respect. Everyone sees oil as valuable. Since Israel has no oil and many of its most implacable enemies have lots of it, cost–benefit analysis based solely on energy security will favour Israel's enemies over Israel. But what about cost–benefit analysis based on democratic values? In this case, the situation is exactly reversed. Israel's most implacable enemies have little or no democracy while Israel has it in abundance. Those who put a high premium on democratic values will tend to favour Israel over its non-democratic enemies. Those for whom democracy is unimportant will not.

And what about international security? Is Israel a cost or a benefit? The answer depends on a host of factors. On the one hand, there are those, such as the author, who will argue that long-term international security depends on the proliferation of political values which produce wealth rather than poverty, liberty rather than oppression, the rule of law rather than the rule of diktat. If that argument holds, one would inevitably want to see a Middle East (and a wider world) constructed on Israeli lines – liberal, capitalistic and democratic rather than restrictive, semi-feudal and autocratic. One would simul-taneously want 'Israeli values' to be extended to the Palestinian territories in the form of a liberal-democratic state infused with a liberal-democratic political culture.

For the sake of international security all of that would provide a strong basis for supporting the Jewish state and seeing it as a strategic asset rather than a strategic liability. Others will take a different view. This is the stuff of interesting and important debate in which the discussion tells us as much about ourselves as it does about Israel.

That last point, of course, is fundamental. The way that we talk about Israel reveals much about who we are. In current circumstances in Europe, it is certainly indicative of the extent to which we are able to think for ourselves or whether we simply default back into lazy orthodoxies. It reveals much about our commitment to truthful and reasoned discourse. But it also reflects something important about the political culture which formed us and of which we are a part. How could the political landscape of Europe influence thinking about Israel? What lies beneath?

CHAPTER 4

Europe's broken back

Europe is a wonderful place to live. But to like something and to feel an identity with something is not the same as to turn it into a religious icon. It is certainly not the same as putting Europe beyond the realm of serious and thoroughgoing criticism. Unfortunately these days too many of Europe's political and intellectual leading lights have adopted just such a disposition. The atmosphere in many quarters in Europe is depressingly anti-intellectual. There is little appetite for, and much opposition to, serious debate about first order issues relating to Europe's civilisational strengths and weaknesses. Major questions about democratic legitimacy in the European Union, demographic decline across much of the continent, the challenge from Islamism at home, and many others are addressed, if at all, in whispers. Denial is the order of the day. This matters for Europe, and it matters for Israel, too.

To be sure, Europe has cause for more than a little self-congratulation. Few parts of the modern world can claim to have been more successful over the last half-century or so in shifting the terms of everyday life towards peaceful coexistence, democratic, law-based governance and material prosperity. Above all else, the era of violent intra-European rivalry has largely passed.

From below, political parties of both Left and Right, buttressed by opinion formers across the mainstream, have expelled aggressive ethnic nationalism to the distant shores of European politics.[1] From above, hugely powerful superstructures such as the European Union and NATO have tied the continent down inside a web of duties, obligations and rights which cannot easily be tampered with. For the first time in centuries, Europe is neither a problem to itself nor to the outside world. The successes of modern Europe are remarkable; they are real; and they are there for all to see.

But there is a catch. There has been a price to pay for these successes, which may yet prove ephemeral. For in order to stop the violent practices of centuries, in order to build liberal democratic values where in most places none had flourished before, in order to rein in the potential for the kind of ideological, religious and nationalist extremism that had caused such misery for so long in Europe it has, arguably, been necessary to suck out of European political culture the energy which not only caused Europe to err but also that which caused it to excel. Political self-belief, observance of religious precepts and pride in one's nation have the potential for both good and ill. But it is not easy to remove the potential for one kind of outcome without simultaneously removing the potential for the other.

While Europe's most fervent supporters have, understandably, sought over the decades to present a picture of a continent energised by enlightened values of tolerance, pluralism and peaceful coexistence, it is possible to present a quite different picture of the underlying realities of modern Europe. This alternative picture offers up a vision of civilisational exhaustion: a continent not so much energised by tolerance, pluralism and peaceful coexistence as of one energised by nothing at all. Belief has given way to relativism; passion to apathy; resolve to appeasement. Europe has a pretty shell. But inside it is hollow.

There are all too few in contemporary Europe with the capacity to understand the point at issue or even to see that it is worth raising as a serious question. Those who have seen the point, however, have seen it with great clarity.

As Cardinal Joseph Ratzinger (now Pope Benedict XVI) put it in a 2004 article tellingly entitled 'If Europe Hates Itself':

'Europe, precisely in this its hour of maximum success, seems to have become empty inside, paralyzed in a certain sense by a crisis in its circulatory system, a crisis that puts its life at risk, resorting, as it were, to transplants that cannot but eliminate its identity.'[2]

Referring to the catastrophically low birth rates in much of Europe and painting on a broader canvas, he continued:

To this interior failure of its fundamental spiritual powers corresponds the fact that, even ethnically, Europe appears to be on the way out. There is a strange lack of desire for a future. Children, who are the future, are seen as a threat for the present; the idea is that they take something away from our life. They are not felt as a hope, but rather as a limitation of the present. We are forced to make comparisons with the Roman Empire at the time of its decline: it still worked as a great historical framework, but in practice it was already living off those who would dissolve it, since it had no more vital energy.

These are sombre words indeed. The picture thus presented does not capture everything about modern Europe, but neither can it be dismissed. Amid all the good things, Europe's political culture is beset by deep-seated pathologies which not only make for a difficult relationship with Israel (and, not coincidentally, with the United States) but also, as the current Pope in his previous role has hinted, call into question the long-term future of Europe itself. To see how anyone could be justified in talking in this way, we need to dip briefly into the past.

Reconfiguring the political culture of Europe

As far back as April 1951 leaders from Germany, Belgium, France, Italy, Luxembourg and the Netherlands signed a treaty in Paris establishing the European Coal and Steel Community – the forerunner to the European Union – with words that reflected a will to change fundamentally the fabric of European political culture. In the preamble to the treaty, the leaders agreed that they were: 'Resolved to substitute for historic rivalries a fusion of their essential interests; to establish, by creating an economic community, the foundation of a broad and independent community among peoples long divided by bloody conflicts; and to lay the bases of institutions capable of giving direction to their future common destiny . . .'[3]

These words both set the stage for the establishment of the European Union (which was founded six years later with the signing of the Treaty of Rome) and set the standard for an evolving political discourse on the continent which sought to give primacy to the supra-national over the national and to replace violent conflict with peaceful cooperation.

Note how the two core concepts in the above quoted paragraph – forging a 'common destiny' via a 'fusion of their essential interests' on the one hand and ending 'historic rivalries' and 'bloody conflicts' on the other – elide with each other. Right from the start of the European project the hints are there of an emerging ideological framework which is suspicious of the dangers of projecting political destiny through the medium of the nation-state. Writing shortly after the invasion of Iraq in 2003, the Spanish philosopher and essayist Fernando Savater made the point explicitly: '. . . two tragic world wars, begun on our continent, have convinced most Europeans of the need to seek internationally regulated formulas to prevent, avoid and, in the last resort, resolve confrontations between opposed interests, on a scale above the limits of the nation-state.'[4]

It is understandable, of course, that politicians and thinkers of the post-war era should have looked back to the very recent European past with a sense of horror and a belief that far-reaching change was the only way forward.

The British historian Mark Mazower has also picked up on the theme of Europe's latent potential for violence via grand ideological designs and brute nationalism and has seen fears of both threading their way through the post-war reconstruction right up to the present day: 'It is not surprising if today Europe is suffering from ideological exhaustion,' he has argued, 'and if politics has become a distinctly univisionary activity. As Austria's former Chancellor Franz Vranitsky once supposedly remarked: "Anyone with visions needs to see a doctor".'[5]

Continuing in this vein he says: 'The only visionaries meeting the challenge are the Europeanists clustered in Brussels, and the only vision offered that of an ever-closer European Union. Its acolytes still talk in the old way – as if history moves in one direction, leading inexorably from free trade to monetary union and eventually to political union too. The alternative they offer to this utopia is the chaos of a continent plunged back into the national rivalries of the past, dominated by Germany and threatened by war.'[6]

If nationalism in particular and political ideology in general have fallen from grace in the eyes of modern Europe's leading opinion formers, a third great pillar of the continent's past, Christianity, has also been banished from the European project in no uncertain terms. In the debates surrounding the wording and content of the European Constitution (which later became the Lisbon Treaty) in 2003, for example, European Commission spokesman Stefan de Rynck explained the EU's opposition to giving primacy to Christianity in the document in the following manner: 'When you start to mention a particular belief or tradition, you exclude traditions you don't want to exclude ... The question is whether you want to single out Christianity in your history. We all live in multicultural societies, and in a global context, in 2003, you don't want to appear as a Christian club.'[7]

Expunging Europe's Christian heritage from key statements about the continent's value system cannot simply be put down to a politically correct conspiracy emanating from the much maligned Brussels elite. While religious observance in countries such as Poland and Ireland remains strong, it has all but ceased to exist as a function of daily life for large sections of the population in countries across Europe. This has fed through into the European Union, the defining project in post-war Europe's political culture.

As suggested at the beginning of this chapter, the key question that arises from all this is whether a Europe which in order to secure peace, prosperity and democracy has had to cast aside so much of its past now has enough in the way of energising ideas to defend and promote its own civilisational integrity. And if it cannot even work up the energy to promote a meaningful vision of itself, how much less likely is it going to be able to promote Western values, embodied in the State of Israel, in the face of threats in the Middle East?

To be sure, the European project is underpinned by a set of principles. The fact that modern Europe is infused with and governed by liberal democratic values is not in question. What is in question is the extent to which Europe is really capable of defending such values. Europe likes to *consume* liberal democracy. But can it do more than simply consume? In a wish list kind of way, Europe would undoubtedly like to see such values spread further around the world and, to be fair, it has clearly demonstrated its commitment to seeing this happen in the recent waves of enlargement of the EU to bring in countries which once laboured under communist tyranny. But how much energy could Europe really summon up to defend liberal democracy if it came under sustained attack? Where is the spirit of self-sacrifice? Former Czech president, playwright and anticommunist dissident Vaclav Havel hinted at the nature of the problem at a Council of Europe Summit in Vienna as far back as 1993:

Many of the great supranational empires and alliances in history, or at least many of those that survived for long periods of time and enriched the human history of their era in some way, not only had strong central ideas that promoted intellectual and spiritual advancement, they were also remarkably determined to stand behind these ideas and willing to make great sacrifices to bring them to fruition, because it was clear to everyone that those sacrifices were worth it. This was more than just a belief in certain values; it was a deep and generally shared feeling that those values carried with them moral obligations. This, I fear, is precisely what is lacking in the Europe of today.[8]

Havel's observations about the relationship between deeply held beliefs and the spirit of sacrifice without which such beliefs cannot be sustained are supported with reference to some remarkable pieces of evidence about contemporary Europe's attitudes. Again, keep in mind how this might be of relevance to European thinking on Israel.

In a survey from the German Marshall Fund of the United States in 2004, respondents across Europe and the United States were asked to say whether they believed that under some conditions war could be justified to obtain justice.[9] That does not seem to set the bar very high in anticipation of overwhelmingly positive responses. Surely it is not hard to think of at least some circumstances in which a military campaign could be supported to secure a just outcome – a preventative war against Nazi Germany in the mid-1930s to forestall the Holocaust, for example; a hypothetical instance of a military campaign to prevent genocide somewhere else in the world, for another. Amazingly, such apparently simple thought experiments are simply lost on large sections of the contemporary European public. In Germany, the proposition was supported by a mere 31 per cent of respondents. In France it was supported by just 33 per cent; in Spain by a paltry 25 per cent; in Italy by 35 per cent. Western Europe's four leading continental countries manage nothing more than an average score of 31 per cent – less than a third of their combined populations. The only European country which even approaches the kind of results which might inspire confidence in its ability to transcend nihilism and moral relativism is Britain, where 69 per cent of respondents agreed with the proposition. (The United States topped the list with 82 per cent – a score which, leaving Britain aside, shows up a profound difference in the way in which important aspects of American and European political culture are configured.)

But even in Britain the spirit of vacuous pacifism has powerful supporters. The country's largest teachers' union, the National Union of Teachers (NUT), for instance, passed a resolution at its annual conference in 2008 condemning the way in which Britain's military seeks to recruit in the country's schools.[10] The spirit in which it was passed was well expressed by a conference delegate from east London: 'Let's just try and imagine what recruitment material would have to say were it not to be misleading,' he said. 'We would have material saying, "Join the Army and we will send you to carry out the imperialist occupation of other people's countries. Join the Army and we will send you to bomb, shoot and possibly torture fellow human beings."'[11] Further comment is surely unnecessary.

Perhaps the most influential piece of writing in recent years about Europe's political culture and its attitudes to the projection of power came with Robert Kagan's comparative analysis with the United States in his acclaimed book, *Of Paradise and Power.*

Kagan sets before his readers a grand scheme in which Americans (from Mars) are locked inside the traditional, hard-power realities that have characterised great-power efforts to fashion the world in their own image throughout the ages. Military force as an instrument for projecting power is always present – either directly in the form of military campaigns, or indirectly as a stick held over its rivals warning them of the consequences should they challenge American interests and values. As Kagan puts it, '... the United States remains mired in history, exercising power in an anarchic Hobbesian world where international laws and rules are unreliable, and where true security and the defense and promotion of a liberal order still depend on the possession and use of military might.'[12]

Europe (from Venus by contrast) is moving towards 'a self-contained world of laws and rules and transnational negotiation and cooperation. It is entering a post-historical paradise of peace and relative prosperity, the realization of Immanuel Kant's "perpetual peace."'[13]

This state of affairs, Kagan notes, is replete with irony:

Europe's rejection of power politics and its devaluing of military force as a tool of international relations have depended on the presence of American military forces on European soil. Europe's new Kantian order could flourish only under the umbrella of American power exercised according to the rules of the old Hobbesian order. American power made it possible for Europeans to believe that power was no longer important. And now, in the final irony, the fact that U.S. military power has solved the European problem, especially the 'German problem,' allows Europeans today, and Germans in particular, to believe that American military power, and the 'strategic culture' that has created and sustained it, is outmoded and dangerous. Most Europeans do not see or do not wish to see the great paradox: that their passage into post-history has depended on the United States not making the same passage. Because Europe has neither the will nor the ability to guard its own paradise and keep it from being overrun, spiritually as well as physically, by a world that has yet to accept the rule of 'moral consciousness,' it has become dependent on America's willingness to use military might to deter or defeat those around the world who still believe in power politics.[14]

Robert Cooper, once Tony Blair's top foreign policy adviser and a senior European official, summed up the problem for Europe succinctly: 'The Escape from power politics has brought great benefits to Europe. Unfortunately it has also brought illusions. Some of these were visible in the early days of the Balkans conflict, when some in Europe seemed to believe that peace and justice could be achieved by simply asking people to be reasonable.'[15]

Commenting on Europe's predilection for peaceful, law-based solutions to the world's problems he added: 'But behind every law is a policeman ready in the last resort to employ physical force. Behind every constitution stands an army ready to protect it.'[16] Modern Europe, he suggests, is suffering from a one-dimensional understanding of the responsibilities inherent in a serious engagement with the outside world: '... foreign policy is about war and peace, and countries that only do peace are missing half the story – perhaps the most important half.'[17]

No wonder the European Union has encountered so many problems in developing a credible European Security and Defence Policy (ESDP). And no wonder it has difficulties empathising with a state such as Israel where the use of force is a prerequisite to survival. Europe is a civilian and it sees the world in civilian terms.

Misreading totalitarianism

But it is not simply a question of Europe's willingness and ability to project force outwards in order to defend the values it claims to hold dear. There is also the question of Europe's willingness and ability to defend itself and its values from within or even to see threats when they are staring it in the face. Referring to the threat from Islamism, the British parliamentarian and writer Michael Gove has eloquently placed the failure of Europe's opinion formers to see and understand the true nature of the problem in the context of errors in understanding European totalitarianisms of the past. His words are worth quoting extensively:

It is a remarkable commentary on the state of analytical thinking in the West that when faced with mass-murderers who loudly proclaim the ideological basis of their actions and prophesy victory on the basis of Western weakness, Western thinkers responded by denying the ideological motivation of their attackers and instead reflexively blame the West for stoking grievances. The belief that Islamist violence can be explained by these factors is as flawed as the belief in the 1930s that Nazism could be understood as simply a response to the perceived injustices of the Versailles settlement, which could be assuaged by reuniting Sudeten Germans with their Bavarian cousins.

That response, the classic appeasers' temptation, betrays profound misunderstanding of the totalitarian mindset. The Nazis were not capable of being satisfied by the reasonable setting of border disputes. They were motivated by a totalitarian dream of a thousand-year Reich, purged of Jewish and Bolshevik influences, in which Aryan manhood could flourish. Their territorial ambitions in the 1930s were not ends in themselves but mechanisms for testing the mettle of their opponents. Hitler's success in realizing his interim territorial goals established, to his own satisfaction, the flabbiness of the West, emboldened him to go further and created a sense of forward momentum that silenced internal opposition.

Jihadists today are not conducting a series of national liberation struggles which, if each were resolved, would lead to peace on earth and good will to all infidels. They are prosecuting a total war in the service of a pitiless ideology.[18]

It is extraordinary just how determined influential people in Europe actually are to misunderstand the nature of what the world, and especially Israel, is now up against. Speaking during Israel's offensive in Gaza in January 2009, Britain's former ambassador to the United Nations, Sir Jeremy Greenstock, even sought to deny the significance of what is written in the Islamist terror group Hamas's own charter (see pp. 84–5). 'They [Hamas] are not intent on the destruction of Israel. That is a rhetorical statement of resistance,' he told the BBC. 'This is a grievance-based organisation desperate to end the occupation.'[19]

Misunderstandings about Hamas have usually been accompanied across Europe by attempts to parade its legitimacy as a 'democratically elected' organisation. For example, a delegation from the European Parliament went to Gaza in November 2008 and issued an invitation to all elected Palestinian officials, including Hamas, to visit. The Greek Cypriot leader of the delegation, Kyriacos Triantaphyllides, said in justifying the decision: 'We don't ask if they are members of Hamas or members of Fatah ... the [Palestinian Legislative Council] was elected in 2006 and it was democratically elected.'[20]

Opponents of Israel and their fellow travellers consistently pleaded on behalf of Hamas along such lines during the Israeli offensive in Gaza in December 2008 and January 2009. In so doing, all they accomplished was a demonstration of their own inability to understand *either* Hamas *or* democracy. For political modernity has been through these arguments before. Hitler's Nazis were also 'democratically elected'. The core idea inside the modern, Western political tradition is not democracy but *liberal democracy*. If 51 per cent of a population were to vote for the extermination of the remaining 49 per cent, the decision would not be considered legitimate because it was 'democratic'. Legitimacy derives both from the ballot box *and* from a commitment to a panoply of basic human rights, laws, customs and practices. The fact that an organisation as vicious as Hamas is popular is not a reason for praising it; it is a reason for reflecting on the shameful character of a Palestinian political culture which offers it so much support. If France's far-Right nationalist leader Jean-Marie Le Pen, who looks like a dripping wet liberal compared with Hamas, had won the French presidential elections in 2002 (he came second by a wide margin) this would not have been an occasion to celebrate his democratic credentials; it would have been an occasion to slate the French for electing him. The same is true of Hamas and the Palestinians.

The fact that so many in Europe are unable to see the point at issue is reflective of deep-seated weaknesses in Europe's own political culture which are particularly evident when it comes to discussions about Islamism. But it is not just basic mistakes about liberal democracy and legitimacy that are exposing such weaknesses.

Major media organisations wielding enormous influence across Europe and around the world have sometimes gone to astonishing lengths to avoid calling the people who prosecute Islamist ideological agendas through mass violence by their proper name. After 9/11 the British-based international news agency Reuters – along with the Associated Press one of the world's most influential news agencies – broke new ground (in the field of logic as much as in journalism) by issuing an edict banning its reporters and editors from describing the 9/11 bombers as 'terrorists' but allowing them to describe the atrocities they perpetrated as 'terror attacks'.[21] The BBC has also been very careful to avoid using the word 'terrorist' in relation to anti-Israeli groups in particular.

In the face of Islamist violence at home, the response has sometimes looked weak to say the least. In Spain in March 2004, Islamist terrorists left more than 190 people dead in coordinated bomb attacks aboard commuter trains in Madrid. The attacks came just three days before a parliamentary election and appeared to have had an important effect on public opinion. The centre-right government of José Marie Aznar, a staunch backer of President George W. Bush in the war on terror and in Iraq, saw its poll lead reverse. It lost power to a left-leaning government which promptly announced it was pulling Spanish forces out of Iraq. There are too many complexities surrounding the affair to state baldly that Spain simply surrendered in the face of terrorism. But it hardly helped dispel the suspicion that significant sections of the European population will bend to the Islamists' will if sufficient pressure is applied.

All too often, though, actual violence is unnecessary. The mere expectation of it from Islamists is enough to encourage retreat. The much maligned Bush doctrine was called *antici-*

patory defence – hit the terrorists before they've had a chance to plan an attack. The bien pensant European version could be termed *anticipatory surrender* – concede to Islamist instructions before they've even been issued. The practice is starting to look routine in Europe. In 2006, the Deutsche Oper in Berlin initially cancelled a production of Mozart's *Idomeneo* which features a scene with the severed heads of Christ, Poseidon, Buddha *and* the Prophet Mohammed for fear of offending Muslims. In the same year the Whitechapel Art Gallery in London balked at presenting photographic works by the surrealist artist Hans Bellmer for fear of offending local Muslims. In 2007, London's Royal Court Theatre backed away from a production based on *Lysistrata* by Aristophanes which featured a Muslim heaven. The responses across Europe to the Danish cartoon controversy (see next chapter) were in many cases craven, and that is putting it mildly.

This behaviour is being aped in some circles in the United States as well. In 2008, Ballantine Books, an imprint owned by American publisher Random House, pulled out from publishing Sherry Jones's *The Jewel of Medina*, a novel featuring Aisha, a wife of the Prophet Mohammed. Random House explained its decision in a press release on the following lines: 'After sending out advance editions of the novel THE JEWEL OF MEDINA, we received in response, from credible and unrelated sources, cautionary advice not only that the publication of this book might be offensive to some in the Muslim community, but also that it could incite acts of violence by a small, radical segment.'[22]

Such reasoning was rejected by a small British publisher called Gibson Square, which decided to take the book on. The publisher's London premises, also his house, was subsequently firebombed by Islamists. The columnist Mick Hume, formerly the editor of *Living Marxism* magazine, has explained the underlying problem clearly:

The threat to freedom here does not come from a few Islamic radicals, but from the invertebrate liberals of the cultural establishment who have so lost faith in themselves that they will surrender their freedoms before anybody starts a fight. The mere suggestion of causing offence to some mob of imagined stereotypes is enough to have them scurrying for a bomb shelter, their creative imaginations blowing up small protests into the threat of a big culture war. Of course, such pre-emptive grovelling only encourages any zealot with a blog to demand even more censorship. Who needs book burners if 'offensive' books are not allowed to be published in the first place? Why bother to protest against provocative plays if the theatres will turn the lights off for you beforehand?[23]

In the interests of promoting 'diversity', the cultural establishment is frequently keen to stress that the 'so-called' enemies of the West are 'misunderstood'. Thus it was that on 25 December 2008 Britain's Channel 4 TV gave Iranian President Mahmoud Ahmadinejad a seven-minute slot to make an uninterrupted speech on a day when the Queen's traditional Christmas message was broadcast as usual on other channels. Justifying its decision, the station said: 'As the leader of one of the most powerful states in the Middle East, President Ahmadinejad's views are enormously influential. As we approach a critical time in international relations, we are offering our viewers an insight into an alternative world view.'[24] On the contrary, Ahmadinejad was given the opportunity to deliberately mislead viewers with carefully worded propaganda. He was allowed to conceal, not reveal, his true world view. As leader of a nation whose despotic, anti-Semitic rulers promote, fund and arm terrorism, and who call for the destruction of Israel while seeking to acquire nuclear weapons, he was thus given the opportunity to present himself in the following terms: 'If Christ were on Earth today,' he said, 'undoubtedly He would hoist the banner of justice and love for humanity to oppose warmongers, occupiers, terrorists and bullies the world over. If Christ were on Earth today, undoubtedly He would fight against the tyrannical policies of prevailing global economic and political systems, as He did in His lifetime.'[25] What a decent and reasonable man, one might conclude.

It is important to locate all of the problems referred to in this section not simply inside the specific challenge mounted by militant Islam but also in the wider context of what some analysts now refer to as a 'self-hating' narrative about Europe's past, and the ideological edifice known as 'multiculturalism'.

Multicultural Europe

Multiculturalism should not be confused with a recognition that since the end of World War II many European countries have become much more ethnically and culturally diverse. Nor should it be confused with laudable attempts by individuals and groups across the political spectrum to combat racism by arguing that ethnic minorities should be treated fairly and their cultural traditions accorded respect.

Though advocates of multiculturalism have often attempted to hide behind these arguments, the central tenet of multiculturalist ideology is very different. As one well-informed observer has put it: 'Multi-culturalism is a response to the perceived dreadful shortcomings of our own culture ... Many exalt non-Western cultures on the understanding that they are more peaceful "spiritual" or "closer to nature" than Western man, and untainted by his arrogance, brutality and greed.'[26]

This also ties in to a sense of post-colonial guilt which pervades large swathes of Europe's opinion-forming classes. Multiculturalism, which, despite some recent reversals has been a guiding paradigm, in formal and informal incarnations, for social and educational policy across much of western Europe for decades, is thus primarily concerned with stamping out notions of the primacy of Western cultural norms in Western countries themselves. It is intimately tied up with the self-hating narrative alluded to above. Cardinal Ratzinger, in the same article quoted earlier in this chapter, described the general problem poignantly. '... The West,' he said, 'is laudably trying to open itself, full of understanding, to external values, but it no longer loves itself; in its own history, it now sees only what is deplorable and destructive, while it is no longer able to perceive what is great and pure.'[27]

Multiculturalism has not simply confined itself to relegating the status of national customs and religion. The English language itself has come under assault, as the infamous events surrounding the firing of Ray Honeyford, the head teacher of a school in the northern English city of Bradford, demonstrated in the starkest terms.[28] In Honeyford's own words:

I was sacked for my alleged racism and was never allowed to work as a teacher again ... In 1985, I was the head of Drummond Middle School in Bradford, where over 90 per cent of the intake was from an Asian background. My determination was that my pupils should be fully equipped to participate in British society, and should therefore learn English and our national history. But this ran utterly counter to the multicultural ideology that prevailed in the city's education authority and among local politicians, which was based on the belief that every racial group should be encouraged to cling to its own separate cultural identity.

I was put under severe pressure for refusing to submit to the dominant official creed. After demonstrations at the school led by anti-racist Leftwingers interested in fomenting trouble and not in education, I was forced to resign. The irony was that I had the backing of the vast majority of Muslim parents at my school, who were not interested in racial or political point-scoring. Indeed, throughout my 25 years as a teacher in mainly inner-city schools, I never had one single Asian parent ask me to provide more multicultural teaching. It was only the ideologues, the zealots, the craven party activists and bureaucrats who sought to impose their divisive thinking on schools.[29]

There can be severe penalties for questioning the multiculturalist orthodoxy. And they can be much worse than being branded a racist and losing one's job. In the Netherlands in 2002, the Dutch politician Pim Fortuyn was assassinated by a pro-Muslim, Leftist animal rights activist. Fortuyn, an openly gay former Marxist, had railed against the dangers of multiculturalism and opposed further immigration, fearing it would undermine the kind of Western, liberal-political culture from which people such as himself had benefited.

Had he lived another seven years he would have witnessed several worrying indications that some of his concerns were far from fanciful. In January 2009, a Dutch court ordered the prosecution of Geert Wilders, the leader of the populist Freedom Party, for the alleged 'instigation of hatred' against Muslims.[30] Crucially, Wilders had not incited violence, but he had made extremely critical, generalised and insulting remarks about Islam, including references to the Koran and some of its more violent-sounding verses as 'fascist'. (It is worth noting that the Left in particular should be deeply concerned about the precedent this might set. If false application of the word 'fascist' is now held to be actionable hate speech, many on that part of the political spectrum could be in danger of falling foul of the law. Labelling political opponents as fascists has, of course, been a staple of Leftist discourse for decades.)

Nasr Joemann, the secretary general of the CMO, the Dutch Muslim umbrella organisation, told Agence France-Presse that it welcomed the decision to prosecute. 'We are positive that this will contribute to a more respectful tone to the public debate,' he said.[31] This may be true, if only in the sense that one of the most important political questions of our time will increasingly be discussed under the shadow of censorship, if at all. Two days later, Douglas Murray, a mainstream, centre-right analyst who has highlighted the dangers of Islamism and multiculturalism, was banned from chairing a debate at the London School of Economics entitled 'Islam or Liberalism: Which is the way forward?' The university said it felt his presence would be provocative at the end of a week of sit-ins and protests against Israel's operations against Hamas in Gaza.[32]

Across western Europe, multiculturalism and its ideological offshoots have wrought havoc with basic democratic values and there is every sign that the situation is getting worse, the final destination unclear. Despite Britain's shock-therapy-style awakening to its dangers following the 7/7 bombings in London – and some spectacular admissions of the policy's failings[33] – it clearly has deep roots. In an article in October 2007, Murray related the following account about a Muslim schoolboy's views and, more importantly, the head teacher's acceptance of the expression of those views, on what should happen to women who fail to observe Islamic dress codes: 'At a school in east London recently, a student perfectly calmly expressed his opinion to me – and in front of his principal – that girls who did not cover themselves in 7th-century desert-garb would be raped. It was salutary to speak with his head teacher afterwards as he boasted of the broad range of opinions at his school. Advocating the rape of fellow pupils strikes me as an unwelcome addition to the debate.'[34]

It should not be necessary to point out that reasoned criticism of the European past, as well of the European present, is an entirely healthy and legitimate practice. Indeed, it is central to the democratic tradition. Only those with weakened mental capacities, however, could fail to see the distinction between self-criticism and self-hatred. For the primary aim of many influential opinion formers in Europe is not, as they claim, to conduct an honest appraisal of the wrongs of the past. Their motivation is not better to understand our failings in order to make us stronger. On the contrary, it is to build up and sustain an ideological edifice which points solely to a past of which

Europe should be ashamed. It is thus to delegitimise what commitment remains in Europe to a robust defence of Western, liberal democratic values. It is to encourage shame, doubt and, ultimately, weakness.

European political culture and Israel

It should be clear from everything that has been touched upon in this chapter that important aspects of modern European political culture present us with a remarkably bad fit with Israeli realities. Europe, as represented by many leading opinion formers, makes a virtue of post-nationalism and secularism while the Israeli state is constituted in terms of national self-determination and the primacy of a national-religious culture. While Europe, for a whole host of reasons, dissembles about the true nature of Islamist terrorism and the ideology which sustains it, Israel comes face to face with it on a daily basis and has no choice but to confront it. While Europe is chary, even contemptuous, of using military power to achieve political aims, for Israel it is an existential necessity.

Europe's deep-seated sense of guilt for the past also plays a crucial role. In attempting to expunge that guilt (colonialism and Nazism featuring most prominently) support for the Palestinians and opposition to the Israelis have equal and opposite significance. Highlighting the suffering of the Palestinians functions as a form of compensation for imperial domination of the wider Arab world. Exaggerating the wrongdoings of the Israelis functions as a way of at least partially exculpating Europe for Nazism and the attendant mass collaboration with it through an implicit (and, as we have seen, sometimes explicit) equivalence between Nazi crimes and 'Zionist crimes' (see pp. 55–9). The former are levelled down in significance as the latter are ratcheted up.

Post-colonial guilt in particular may also have mutated into what Manfred Gerstenfeld terms 'humanitarian racism'.

Gerstenfeld has elaborated on this theme with specific reference to anti-Israeli elites in the Nordic countries. But its perverse consequences can be seen across Europe. As Gerstenfeld defines the concept: 'Humanitarian racists consider – usually without saying so explicitly – that only white people can be fully responsible for their actions; non-whites, such as the Palestinians, cannot (or can but only to a limited extent). Therefore, most misdeeds by non-whites – who by definition are 'victims' – are not their fault but those of whites, who can be held accountable.'[35]

Israel is held to a higher standard than Arab and other Muslim countries whose actions are explained, and thus excused, by 'grievances'. Against this sort of criterion of judgement, Israel can never be justified in using military force to secure its aims, however vital. It will always lose in the battle for hearts and minds.

Taken together, these interrelated themes go some way to explaining one of the great paradoxes in the Euro-Israeli relationship: that hostility to Israel tends to sharpen at times when Israel itself is under attack such as during the waves of mass suicide bombings of the second intifada, the Hezbollah-inspired conflict with Lebanon in 2006, and the Gaza conflict of December 2008 and January 2009 which was precipitated by thousands of rockets fired over several years at Israeli civilians.

In such circumstances, the default assumption that grievances against Western democracies are legitimate when aired by non-white minorities translates into a belief that terrorism must be a product of desperation. In a sense, therefore, it might be justified.

With the ideological roots of terrorism having been air-brushed from the picture, Israeli military responses are seen as futile at best. At worst, 'senseless' Israeli retaliation merely contributes to a 'cycle of violence'. Israelis have no one to blame but themselves. When will they ever learn?

The broader civilisational pathologies may also have a role to play in this. Many Europeans are naturally drawn to think that Israeli military attacks will 'radicalise' Palestinians because, often, they themselves do not hold passionate beliefs about anything bigger than their own circle of loved ones. They cannot conceive of being motivated to kill or to die for something unless their passions have been aroused by the killing of someone close to them. Thus, they lack the emotional and mental capacity to recognise that ideology could really be a root cause of Palestinian or wider Islamist violence. Modern Europe may be fated not merely to misunderstand Israel but the Palestinians as well.

With all the above in mind, it should be no real surprise, therefore, if the relationship between Israel and many in Europe so often seems to be conducted in the form of two monologues drifting past each other rather than as a single dialogue founded on common assumptions. In important respects such common assumptions do not exist.

On a final note, there is an additional reason why the Holocaust should be such a double-edged sword in this relationship. For it seems highly likely that different lessons have been drawn from it. Quite apart from the pathologies in Europe about Zionism and Jews discussed elsewhere in this book, modern European attitudes to confronting manifest injustice in general and totalitarianism in particular do not inspire much confidence that one of the most important lessons about the Holocaust has been learned at all in Europe. While the mantra 'This must never happen again' has been repeated times without number in recent decades it seems reasonably to suggest that an essentially pacifistic, hyper-legalistic, hollowed-out European political culture would not really be able to summon up the energy to prevent such an event happening again should the circumstances arise. And this is not mere conjecture as events surrounding the Balkan wars of the 1990s, and particularly the Srebrenica massacre of more than 7,500 Bosnian Muslims in 1995, amply demonstrated.

Indeed, if the principles, standards and values applied by bien pensant Europe to Israel today were retrospectively applied to Europe itself in the 1930s and 1940s it is, in all seriousness, difficult to escape the following conclusions: the editorial pages of liberal newspapers across the continent would portray the Nazi Party as a 'grievance'-based organisation 'radicalised' by Western injustice; Nazi Germany's 'alleged' anti-Semitism would be dismissed by BBC journalists as the rhetoric of the oppressed and would be censored out of the reporting; Amnesty International would denounce the Royal Air Force's bombing campaigns as 'disproportionate' since German civilian deaths outnumbered British civilian deaths by 25 to 1; the European Parliament would condemn the targeted assassination of Reinhard Heydrich in Czechoslovakia as an 'extra-judicial execution'; and Winston Churchill would be indicted for a long list of 'war crimes' by the International Criminal Court in The Hague. Again, this is meant in all seriousness. Contemporary European values negate the possibility of contemporary European realities. Today's Europe could not have been built on the basis of the value system now being argued for by large numbers of the continent's own opinion formers. The Allies would have lost World War II.

As it relates to Israel and as it relates to itself, Europe has a credibility problem. Its civilisational integrity is open to a whole set of questions which have no easy answers.

But there is a specific item inside this general theme which needs more discussion. It has been touched upon in this chapter already. How is Europe managing its relationship with a new and growing constituency which brings with it a virulent hostility to Israel and whose political and religious values do not even derive from European traditions? What price the Islamist challenge?

CHAPTER 5

Muslims in Europe

According to a study conducted by *The Times* in 2007, Muhammad is now the second most popular name for baby boys in Britain after Jack.[1] In Belgium's capital, Brussels, it is the first most popular boy's name. The prevalence of the name is in large part due to the propensity of Muslim parents to honour the Prophet by naming their sons after him. Numbers matter greatly, but that is not the salient point. What matters more is the sense in which these examples indicate the degree to which European Muslims remain wedded to their own cultural (and often, by extension, their political) traditions rather than the traditions of their host communities. This illustrates something about the changing face of modern Europe.

Tellingly, there are no precise figures on the numbers of Muslims in Europe because most governments do not take the trouble to research them properly. But according to the best estimates, the Muslim population of western Europe currently stands at between fifteen and twenty million.[2] In Europe as a whole, including Russia and countries with very large Muslim populations such as Albania (70 per cent) and Bosnia-Herzegovina (40 per cent), that figure rises to between forty and fifty million. The number of Muslims as a proportion of the overall population remains small in most countries, ranging from 1 to 2 per cent in Norway and Italy, through 3–5 per cent in countries such as Britain, Spain, Germany and Denmark, to 7–10 per cent in the Netherlands and France.

Demographic trends (see below) suggest that these percentages will rise sharply in coming years mainly due to significantly higher Muslim birth rates. Mere citation of the numbers can, however, be deceptive. There is intense nervousness among Europe's governmental establishments about how to handle their Muslim minorities and a concomitant culture of denial about problems within them. Muslim minorities, therefore, may already punch far above their weight in terms of their influence on policy making.

Although wider questions about the influence of Muslims on the political culture of Europe are important, the key question for the purposes of this book is this: do Europe's rapidly growing Muslim populations pose a problem regarding Israel? The answer is that they do, that it is serious and that it may become far more problematic as time goes by. The evidence to back up that assertion is stark.

Consider the results of an extensive survey conducted by the Pew Research Center in 2006 which looked at specific attitudes to the Israel–Palestine conflict and related issues comparing the attitudes of Muslims with the general population.[3] The survey was conducted in Britain, France, Germany and Spain. Sympathy with Israel among Muslims in the four countries surveyed averaged at just 6 per cent, compared with 27 per cent among the population as a whole, Muslim and non-Muslim. Sympathy for the Palestinians, by contrast, averaged at 70 per cent among British, French, German and Spanish Muslims, compared to 29 per cent in the general population.

A similar pattern is in evidence when we look at Muslim and general popular attitudes to the election victory in January 2006 of the virulently anti-Semitic terror group Hamas. On average, 24 per cent of Muslim and non-Muslim respondents in the four European countries thought the Hamas victory was a good thing for the Palestinians.[4] This in itself is worrying since it suggests that around a quarter of the European population either has a favourable opinion of Hamas or has no real idea what the group stands for. For Muslim respondents taken in isolation from the overall sample the situation was far worse, with 47 per cent expressing a positive view of Hamas's election.

Putting these two sets of data together we get a truly alarming picture of the kind of attitudes to the Israel–Palestine conflict held by very large numbers of European Muslims. Not only do they have an overwhelming sympathy for the Palestinians, they are also strongly supportive of extremely violent and bigoted strands of opinion within Palestinian society.

When the polling turned to major international issues of relevance to Israel, there was also very convincing evidence that Europe's Muslims operate from within an entirely different world view as compared to the general populations. In every case, views of the United States and the war on terror are more negative among Muslims than the general population. One particularly striking set of findings concerned the desirability, or otherwise, of Iran acquiring nuclear weapons. In the general population in Britain, a mere 5 per cent thought a nuclear-armed Iran would be a good thing. For British Muslims that figure rose eightfold to 40 per cent. In France, the number rose more than fourfold from 7 to 29 per cent.

If opinion survey data is worrying, the way in which influential Muslims talk about Israel is nothing less than frightening, though we should not imagine that it is necessarily worse than the kind of discourse in Europe adopted by some non-Muslims. One hardly needs to cherry-pick to find examples.

During the Gaza campaign in January 2009, Yasmin Alibhai-Brown, a widely respected British Muslim commentator, wrote about the Israeli offensive in terms which are as extreme as they are typical. Writing about the people of Gaza she said: 'First systematically starved, the population was denied escape and more than 1,200 were slaughtered like animals in an abattoir.' Warming to her task she continued: 'On the letters pages Zionists say the violence – including phosphorus burns on children – are "regrettable" but necessary. A nation that asks the world not to forget what was done to its people by Hitler, has advocates who believe brutal ethnic cleansing is "regrettable". How many

Palestinian Anne Franks did the Israelis murder, maim or turn mad?'[5]

What is said by the commentariat is perpetuated by 'moderate' Muslim leadership organisations. The language and imagery is often brutal and inflammatory.

In 2004, Sir Iqbal Sacranie, then Secretary-General of the Muslim Council of Britain (Britain's leading Muslim umbrella group, with more than four hundred affiliates), issued forth in a manner which now barely raises eyebrows: 'We have time and again warned that Israel's murderous leadership would exploit the US presence in Iraq to escalate its ethnic cleansing of Palestine. Now the evidence is incontrovertible. What we are seeing is a creeping genocide of the Palestinian people. It is palpably clear that the Israeli campaign is calculated and deliberate. Most of the Palestinian children killed in recent days bore the marks of sniper bullets to their heads.'[6]

In 2006, Sacranie's successor at the helm of the Muslim Council of Britain, Dr Muhammad Abdul Bari, issued a demand for the recall of Parliament over the war in Lebanon of 2006. His language indicated growing confidence about Muslim influence in the UK: 'With the situation in the Middle East deteriorating daily, the vast majority of people in Britain and many British Muslims find it *unacceptable* that our elected representatives are not meeting as a matter of urgency to debate how the Government should be contributing to stopping the bloodshed and carnage. The ramifications of current events in the Middle East are global and can have potential fall-out in terms of community relations in Britain.' (My italics.)[7]

The line between a threat and a warning is sometimes thin. When the leading figure in the British Muslim community implies that British policy must be changed to avoid the possibility of public discord involving British Muslims that line becomes thin indeed. Either way, its power to affect policy lies precisely in its vagueness: there is not enough in such statements to constitute a direct threat, but there is just enough to get an aggressive and uncompromising message across to the authorities. It will not have been missed.

The MCB does, as it must, issue calls for Muslims to show restraint. But even as it does so it incites extreme sentiment against the Jewish state. In another tirade over Lebanon in 2006, an MCB press statement peppered with incendiary vocabulary – 'massacre', 'atrocities', 'slaughter', 'rape of Lebanon' – also included the kind of warning about British (and American) culpability for failing to slap Israel down that has now become routine: 'The continuing refusal of the United States and the United Kingdom to insist on an immediate ceasefire has diminished us in the court of world public opinion and has made us complicit in these atrocities in the eyes of hundreds of millions of Muslims around the world.'[8]

The message is clear: if you don't want hundreds of millions of Muslims on your case, conform to our agenda. In the same statement, the way in which the MCB covers itself against accusations of incitement is illuminating and worth deconstructing. It said: 'We well understand the immense anger among British Muslims at the actions of the outlaw Israeli regime, however, we urge all British Muslims to act in a dignified manner at all times and not to allow themselves to be provoked.'[9]

The call for restraint is thus accompanied by a nod of approval to an 'immense anger' which it legitimises as being understandable. Having raised the emotional temperature against Israel in a vicious and relentless tirade, the calls for Muslims 'to act in a dignified manner' and 'not to allow themselves to be provoked' sound confused and contradictory. You cannot incite hatred and expect your simultaneous calls for restraint to be regarded as serious by all among your audience. Once again, in its cumulative effect the tone is troubling and aggressive. This in itself is significant. People do not usually assert themselves in such a manner unless they feel that they are in a position of strength or at least that they are seen as potentially difficult customers to deal with.

In an open letter to Prime Minister Gordon Brown over Gaza at the end of 2008, the MCB once again set forth its demands of the British government. 'The illegal and inhumane bombardment of the Gaza Strip by Israeli forces has shocked us all. The images beamed around the globe show the horror of death and destruction unleashed against an Occupied People, contrary to all humanitarian standards. The mass outrage expressed on the streets of Britain is yet to be reflected in the actions of our government, *and this is unacceptable.*'[10] (My italics.)

In making such calls, they know what they are doing. Notwithstanding exceptional items such as France's decision to ban the Muslim veil in schools, European governments and the wider establishment are frightened of their Muslim populations. Muslim leaders sense it and play on it.

The Danish cartoons

No episode in recent years demonstrates the validity of that assertion with greater clarity than the sorry tale of the Danish cartoon controversy of 2005 and 2006. It ultimately led to the deaths of more than fifty people in several Muslim countries in the Middle East and beyond as well as the torching of Danish and other European embassies. The saga had its genesis in a series of cartoons published in the Danish newspaper *Jyllands-Posten* in September 2005. The twelve drawings mainly featured the Prophet Mohammed, one with a bomb in his turban with a lighted fuse. They were designed to raise in pictorial form the issue of Islamist intolerance and the violence associated with it. For many Muslims inside and outside Europe, however, the mere fact of portraying the image of the Prophet let alone of associating him with violence and extremism was considered blasphemous. As the controversy grew and more and more newspapers in Europe and around the world republished the cartoons a major crisis developed.

The way European political establishments handled it was highly illustrative. The strategy adopted almost everywhere across the continent was dual track (with the emphasis on the second track): first, condemn the violence and offer a (usually half-hearted) defence of the right to free speech; second, issue statements recognising the offence that the cartoons had caused to Muslim sensitivities and call on newspaper editors to act 'responsibly' (i.e. exercise self-censorship). The European Union's then Trade Commissioner Peter Mandelson thus denounced the reprinting of the cartoons in the following manner: 'The actions by other European newspapers now, in publishing these cartoons, is throwing petrol onto the original issue, the original offence that was taken.'[11] British Foreign Secretary Jack Straw said: 'I believe the republication of these cartoons has been unnecessary, it has been insensitive, it has been disrespectful and it has been wrong.'[12] After France's satirical newspaper *Charlie Hebdo* reprinted the cartoons in February 2006, French President Jacques Chirac described the move as a 'provocation'.[13] Germany's Chancellor Angela Merkel said: 'We need to learn to show mutual respect for each others' views and feelings as well as to develop our shared values.'[14] The editor of *Jyllands-Posten* eventually issued a grovelling apology for having 'offended many Muslims'.[15] Danish Muslim leaders were still not satisfied.[16] The editor of *France Soir*, Jacques Le Franc, was fired by the magazine's Egyptian owners for reprinting the cartoons.[17]

Daniel Schwammenthal of the *Wall Street Journal Europe* drew the big picture in stark terms.

The murder in 2004 of Dutch filmmaker Theo van Gogh by a Muslim fundamentalist in Amsterdam demonstrated the kind of risks critics of Islam are exposed to these days – even in Europe. Fundamentalists can find good cover – and followers – among the millions of Muslim immigrants on the Continent. *Jyllands-Posten* decided to publish the cartoons after complaints from an author that he could not find an illustrator who dared to draw images of Muhammad for his book. It was this atmosphere of fear and intimidation that the newspaper wanted to highlight. The Muslim reaction to these pictures only confirmed how relevant the topic is.

Using their combined economic muscle, death threats and street protests, a combination of state and nonstate actors are slowly exporting to Europe the Middle East's repressive system. What *Jyllands-Posten*'s editors are enduring is not unlike what dissidents under communism had to go through. The Islamists can't send the journalists to a gulag but they can silence them by threatening to kill them. Bomb threats twice forced the journalists to flee their offices this week.[18]

As the responses from senior politicians quoted above show, it is not just the journalists who are now afraid of offending Muslims in Europe. What is abundantly clear from almost every statement issued at the time from Europe's political classes was the pervasive sense of nervousness that the situation might get out of control as it had in predominantly Muslim countries around the world. Muslim leaders themselves set up a balancing act of their own: condemning violence and urging restraint against 'provocation' while joining with their co-religionists in denouncing the cartoons in the strongest possible terms as well as, in some cases, calling for legislative changes to outlaw such 'blasphemy'.

The Muslim Council of Britain spoke for many Muslim groups across Europe in calling for restraint among Muslims but in laying out the consequences in no uncertain terms for European governments if they failed to toe the line.

'The MCB acknowledges the fundamental right of peoples of all faiths to freedom of speech and expression. *This does not mean however that they should be free to create social unrest and instability*. Neither should that freedom be abused to undermine national interests at home and abroad."[19] (My italics.)

It should not be necessary by this stage in the discussion to explain the meaning of the warning contained in that statement, nor indeed the blatant contradiction between the first sentence and the following two.

In looking back at the whole episode, two points emerge as being fundamental. First, note the glaring difference between the way Muslims in Europe (and around the world) erupted in indignation at the *pictorial* association of Islam and violence and their relative silence about *real-world* suicide bombings by *real-world* Islamists in places such as Israel and Iraq. Where are the mass protests from Muslims in Europe at terror attacks in Tel Aviv and Baghdad conducted by Muslims who themselves explicitly assert a direct relationship between the teachings of the Prophet and their murderous actions? This in itself illustrates something profoundly significant about Muslim leaders' political and ethical priorities.

Second, it needs to be recognised that European governments and officials were in a certain sense acting rationally in the way they responded to the situation. They have a duty to their peoples to ensure social and civic peace. The fault was not so much in the way they reacted at the time as in the way European leaders over years and decades have allowed the problem to fester. Warning was first served on Europe about the threat from Islamism to basic Western values as far back as 1989 with the fatwa death sentence issued on the British-Indian writer Salman Rushdie by Iran's Ayatollah Khomeini. Rushdie's alleged crime was to have been disrespectful to the Prophet Mohammed in his book *The Satanic Verses*. In spite of the spectacle of Muslims burning his book on the streets of Europe combined with violent mobs calling for his death, the lessons were simply not learned.

As a result, when the problem exploded into the open again

sixteen years later, European governments found themselves pushed against the wall, their options limited. When fundamental Western values came under attack from Islamism, they ended up negotiating a desperately difficult dilemma: stand tall in defence of liberty and risk unrest on the streets of Europe, or slink back into a messy set of compromises in the fluffy middle ground between democracy and intolerance. They chose the latter.

In the general sense as well as in the particular case of Israel, it is important to underline that it is the senior figures in the Muslim community itself which lie at the heart of the problem and not ordinary Muslims. In Britain this has extended to the Muslim Council of Britain's grotesque policy of snubbing Holocaust Memorial Day, a policy which was only reversed for the 2008 event in the most grudging terms and apparently due to concerns about the public relations impact of their boycott.[20] Then, the grouping snubbed the event again in 2009 following Israel's Operation Cast Lead in Gaza. Four years earlier, Iqbal Sacranie, as Secretary-General of the MCB, had explained his aim of abolishing a memorial day dedicated to the Holocaust in the following manner: 'The message of the Holocaust was "never again", and for that message to have practical effect on the world community it has to be inclusive. We can never have double standards in terms of human life. Muslims feel hurt and excluded that their lives are not equally valuable to those lives lost in the Holocaust time.'[21]

In 2003, the MCB had issued a press release saying that, 'regrettably the memorial ceremony in its present form excludes and ignores other ongoing genocide and human rights abuses around the world, notably in the Occupied Palestinian Territories'.[22]

To compare Israel's treatment of the Palestinians with the Holocaust and to call it genocide is abhorrent. It could also be construed as diminishing the Holocaust by equating it with anti-terror measures. Such statements are deeply insulting to the Jewish people and are an affront to civilised values. Overall, the mentality we are dealing with is clear. Or, rather, it is clear to those who are not in a state of denial about Muslim political culture in Europe. In 2005, Iqbal Sacranie was knighted by the Queen on the recommendation of the British government.[23]

The employment of extreme language against Israel from Muslim leaders is now 'normal' in most west European countries. The Union of Islamic Organisations of France (UOIF), a leading French umbrella organisation accused of having ties with the Muslim Brotherhood, which it denies, also regularly issues statements condemning Israel in the strongest possible terms. Speaking of the events in Gaza at the beginning of 2008, it said: 'The UOIF condemns the escalation of violence which has pitted the Israeli occupied forces against the Palestinian population ... By starving an entire population and depriving them of essential humanitarian needs, the Israeli occupation has confirmed to the world the brutal character of its expansionist policy, where the suffering of the Palestinian population takes place on a daily basis.'[24]

Along with the incendiary and false accusation of 'starving an entire population', note the use of the words 'expansionist policy' to describe actions in Gaza, from which all Israeli soldiers and settlers were withdrawn in 2005. As in Britain, the Muslim leadership in France does not care whether what it says about Israel is true or false as long as the overriding need to demonise is satisfied.

With potentially 10 per cent of the population behind it, France's UOIF, like its British counterpart, also regularly flexes its muscles in front of the French government. In March 2008, it issued a statement, again over Gaza, in which it referred to the 'bloodbath' caused by the Israeli 'occupation' and demanded that the French government and the European Union condemn Israel in no uncertain terms.[25]

In January 2009, the Gaza conflict provoked yet another

round of extreme rhetoric against Israel in France (as it did from leading Muslim groups across western Europe). References to 'massacres of the civilian population' were ubiquitous.[26]

The statements of Muslim organisations in Germany are described by close observers as somewhat less virulent than elsewhere in Europe though there are indications that this may be changing, especially since the Muslim Brotherhood now has a powerful presence in the country (see below). Dr Juliane Wetzel, chair of the Center for the Study of Anti-Semitism at the Technical University of Berlin, commenting on the situation in 2006, flagged up other potential dangers which may apply more widely: 'Since the Muslim community in Germany is largely of Turkish origin,' she said, 'there is a lot less hatred toward Israelis and Jews than in comparable communities in Europe ... But in recent years, the youth here have apparently been influenced by Islamic Internet sites and satellite channels, and absorbed certain anti-Semitic stereotypes that they did not have in the past.'[27]

Whatever is happening on that front, the opinion polls show that ordinary Muslims in Germany remain far more hostile to Israel than the general population. In Germany, as elsewhere, mosques and other Islamic institutions provide ample opportunity to inculcate hatred of Israel without Muslim leaders necessarily being so bold when speaking to the mainstream media.

Across Europe, deep hostility to Israel is a unifying factor among Muslim groups from diverse backgrounds. The pan-European Federation of Islamic Organizations in Europe, which brings together groups from twenty-eight countries and which has an increasingly powerful presence in Brussels, professes to be a moderate institution. With links to the Muslim Brotherhood, its motto calls for 'a well established and effective Islamic presence in Europe'. However, in 2005, its then leader Ahmed al-Rawi voiced support for militant violence in Iraq and Israel indicating that 'moderation' may be a relative term in this case and might not apply where Israel and the United States are concerned.[28]

The general expansion of activities by the Muslim Brotherhood, whose adherents despise the Jewish state, across Europe has been noted by those who follow the issue closely. According to the Islamism analyst Lorenzo Vidino, a strategy has been in place for several decades: 'Since the early 1960s, Muslim Brotherhood members and sympathizers have moved to Europe and slowly but steadily established a wide and well-organized network of mosques, charities, and Islamic organizations. Unlike the larger Islamic community, the Muslim Brotherhood's ultimate goal may not be simply "to help Muslims be the best citizens they can be," but rather to extend Islamic law throughout Europe and the United States.'[29]

Until recently, such assertions might have been dismissed as scaremongering, or even as a pandering to 'Islamophobia' – a serious concept but one which in some quarters has now become little more than an anti-intellectual buzzword designed to shut down debate. However, comments from Britain's Chief Justice, Lord Phillips, in July 2008 and the Archbishop of Canterbury, Rowan Williams, in February of the same year, suggest that the incorporation of aspects of sharia law in Britain is now very much on the cards. Indeed, it is already happening (and not just in Britain). Archbishop Williams described the increasing use of sharia as 'unavoidable'.[30] Lord Phillips argued: 'There is no reason why Sharia principles, or any other religious code, should not be the basis for mediation or other forms of alternative dispute resolution . . .'[31]

Both men have defended their arguments saying there would be no question of sharia taking precedence over English law if the two ever collided and that they were merely referring to procedures that in many respects already take place in matters such as marriage, arbitration and family disputes. What is worrying is that, given the mentality we are dealing with, neither appears to have any sense that, as sharia becomes more and more a part of everyday life over such seemingly mundane matters, emboldened Muslim leaders may then start to press for more. If they do, it remains an open question whether Britain and other European countries will have sufficient confidence and belief in their own civilisational values to resist. As Vidino sees it, the Muslim Brotherhood, at least, will be no pushover: 'While the Muslim Brotherhood and their Saudi financiers have worked to cement Islamist influence over Germany's Muslim community, they have not limited their infiltration to Germany. Thanks to generous foreign funding, meticulous organization, and the naïveté of European elites, Muslim Brotherhood-linked organizations have gained prominent positions throughout Europe.'[32]

A full discussion of this subject is beyond the scope of this book. What matters here is what it shows about the assertiveness of Europe's Muslim groups and the timidity of governments and senior Establishment figures in dealing with them. European Muslim leaders are clearly not content to sit in the shadows. As the Muslim populations grow in size, it is inevitable that their leaders will press their demands, including on Israel, with ever greater forcefulness. This brings us directly to the question of how large and politically influential the Muslim populations of Europe will become.

Future shock?

There is now much controversy over the question of how large Europe's Muslim populations will become in the decades ahead. In 2004, the historian Bernard Lewis famously predicted in an article in the German newspaper *Die Welt* that Europe could become majority Muslim by the end of this century. In an article in the *Washington Quarterly* in the same year State Department analyst Timothy M. Savage suggested that even conservative predictions envisaged that 20 per cent of Europe's population would be Muslim by mid-century, with some estimates seeing the French Muslim population at 25 per cent of the total by 2025.[33] For its part, the US National Intelligence Council has estimated that Muslim populations in Europe will approximately double by 2025.

This increase will take place against a background of non-Muslim birth rates which in many parts of Europe fall well below what demographers refer to as the 'replacement rate' – the number of births per woman required to sustain a given population at current levels.[34]

For the very long term, demography is an inexact science and has produced some spectacular failures, from Thomas Malthus, whose 1798 *Essay on the Principle of Population* predicted mass starvation due to what we would now see as the laughable assumption that population growth would always exceed the available food supply, to Paul R. Ehrlich, whose 1968 book *The Population Bomb* predicted catastrophic falls in population due to famines involving hundreds of millions of people in the 1970s and 1980s and something close to the extinction of much of the human race not long thereafter.[35]

The problem with estimating the future size of Muslim populations in contemporary Europe is that the two key variables – immigration and relative birth rates – are subject to change. If the gates are opened to mass immigration from predominantly Muslim countries, and if Muslim birth rates remain at two to three times the levels of the general population, the kind of estimate put out by Bernard Lewis for a majority Muslim Europe may not be as far-fetched as it at first sight appears. On the other hand, if, as seems more likely, immigration policy becomes highly restrictive and Muslim birth rates converge with birth rates in the general population the outlook may be far less dramatic.[36] (The question of whether Turkey does or does not join the European Union will also be important.)

Whatever the scale of the increase, the relative birth rates we see before us today mean that Muslim populations will certainly get bigger. A doubling, at least, of the size of the Muslim presence in western Europe in the next two decades, from the current 5 per cent, seems inevitable. Does it matter?

Apart from anything else, it will matter because increased Muslim populations will become much more electorally significant. In countries which have electoral systems based on proportional representation, we may in some cases see the emergence of Muslim political parties popular enough to get into Parliament. Since proportional representation often produces governments which depend on junior coalition partners, such Muslim parties could emerge as kingmakers with all that that implies in terms of concessions and deals.

However, since Muslims do not vote as a homogenous bloc such a scenario is unlikely to come to pass until or unless Muslim populations become quite significantly larger than they are now or are even likely to become in most countries over the next couple of decades. A more plausible version of this scenario is that mainstream parties will much more actively seek to court Muslim voters by addressing causes that they and their community leaders hold dear. Many analysts have argued that Germany's Social Democrats squeezed in to power in elections in 2002 in part due to the party's active campaigning for Turkish-Muslim votes. In tight electoral races across Europe, this is likely to be the shape of things to come.

True, Muslim voters, like voters across society, appear to place greater emphasis on domestic issues such as employment and economic wellbeing than on foreign policy.[37] Even where foreign policy is a priority a European Muslim population of diverse ancestry will not necessarily place the Israel–Palestine conflict at the top of the list. British Muslims of Pakistani or Bangladeshi parentage appear more energised by events in Kashmir. French Muslims of Algerian extraction and German Muslims of Turkish descent may be more interested by developments in Algeria and Turkey respectively.

Nevertheless, the Israel–Palestine conflict is clearly an

emotive issue in Muslim communities across Europe. Their increasing strength will certainly act as an enhanced transmission mechanism for extremist views of Israel into European politics. At the very least, if mainstream parties are looking to attract new voters from these growing communities there will inevitably be a temptation of sorts to play to the gallery by emphasising both hostility to Israel and support for the Palestinians. During the Lebanon crisis in 2006, there were strong indications that British Prime Minister Tony Blair was well aware of the price he would pay in terms of Muslim votes for his courageously pro-Israeli position. One of his cabinet ministers was quoted by the *Observer* as saying: 'It was clear that Tony knows the situation, and didn't have to be told about the outrage felt by so many over the disproportionate suffering. He also completely understands the effect on the Muslim community – *both in terms of losing Muslim voters hand over fist and the wider issue of community cohesion.*'[38] (My italics.)

As suggested earlier in this chapter, it also needs to be emphasised that Muslim leaders have learned to play on governments' fears of discontent in their communities even at present levels. They may get bolder as their communities increase in size. But Muslim populations do not need to be especially large to extract concessions from governments which fear them. For governments, playing to extreme prejudices against Israel inside the Muslim communities of Europe will be an ever-present temptation, especially in periods of tension and conflict involving the Israeli military. Should politically radicalised Muslims spill on to the streets in large numbers in protest against some future flashpoint, it would be naïve, given current realities, to expect European governments not to take this into account, with some seeking to restore domestic peace and tranquillity with words of appeasement.

The final point to understand is that much will depend on whether European governments and the experts they rely on for advice can be persuaded to break out of the current cycle of denial about the deep-seated pathologies inhering in contemporary Muslim political culture. Despite the shocks of the Madrid train bombing in 2004, the July 2005 bombings on the London underground system and the killing of Theo van Gogh in 2004, there are worrying signs that the denial runs very deep.

Sifting through the contemporary academic literature makes for depressing reading. One of many such examples that could be quoted came with a book published in 2007 called *Islam in Europe: Diversity, Identity and Influence.*[39] I refer to it not because it is the most egregious instance but, on the contrary, because it is entirely representative of some of the best mainstream academic discourse on the subject. It is, therefore, a useful and illustrative case study. It brings together writers from eminent institutions in Paris, Athens, Budapest, Geneva, London, Birmingham (England) and Frankfurt: in other words, from across Europe.

The purpose of the collection, as set out in an introduction by one of the co-editors, is to promote a 'more nuanced approach' to the question of Muslims in Europe than is usual which takes account of the diversity of Muslim populations and which challenges the assumption that the religion of Islam alone can itself be taken as the sole or necessarily the primary locus of identity of a given individual – an assumption shared by populists in Europe and Islamic fundamentalists alike, they argue. From such a starting point the book embarks upon an interesting set of discussions of the kind one would expect from knowledgeable analysts.

It is vital, of course, that in trying to understand Muslims in Europe we do not descend into unreasonable generalisations which will take us further away from rather than closer towards a true understanding of what is going on. Still less that we fall into a lazy discourse which can cause pain and unhappiness to people who face discrimination and abuse from some of the nastiest political forces on the continent.

But it is at this point in the discussion precisely that this collection and the European discourse generally ceases to be part of the solution and starts to become part of the problem. The book is thus replete with references of the kind which warn of 'right-wing anti-immigration rhetoric',[40] of the dangers of 'people rushing to explain terrorist violence in the light of what they perceive to be distinctive about Islam',[41] of 'the two-dimensional worldviews encouraged particularly from Washington',[42] after 9/11, of 'the current climate of Islamophobia in Europe',[43] of Muslims' hopelessness when they encounter opposition to their 'right to wear Islamic clothing to school or at work ... [or] the desire that their limits of modesty be respected in swimming and gym classes',[44] and of a 'xenophobia' which is 'shared and expressed in different tonalities, with deliberate alarmism, overtly malignant as well as seemingly benign, as in the case of nativist political parties, certain sections of the press ... or notorious publicists such as Oriana Fallaci'.[45]

Leaving aside the dubious assumptions implicit in many of these remarks, the question that cries out from the pages is this: what about the rest of the debate? The discussion, in large part, is shot through with a narrative of denial in which pertinent evidence about deeply problematic commonalities inside Muslim Europe have been expunged or sidelined.

Why is it, for example, that as late as 2006, 56 per cent of British Muslims, 46 per cent of French Muslims, 44 per cent of German Muslims and 35 per cent of Spanish Muslims believed that Arabs did *not* carry out the mass terror attacks on the United States on September 11, 2001?[46] Why is there such a significant difference from non-Muslims in Europe in attitudes to Iran getting nuclear weapons, to American-led attempts to root out terrorism, to Israel and to Hamas? Why do European Muslim populations diverge so sharply from the rest? What does this say about the political values which their community leaders are encouraging? Why is it that almost all the terrorist attacks which either did take place in Europe in recent years or which were prevented by the security services were perpetrated by Muslims in the name of Islam and not by Jews in the name of Judaism, Hindus in the name of Hinduism or Christians in the name of Christianity? We are entitled to ask such questions. Indeed, intellectual honesty and a concern for the future of Europe *demand* that we ask such questions. Why, then, are such evidence-based arguments being swept under the carpet and ignored in discussion forums against Europe?

It is no defence to say that since the bombings in London and Madrid European governments have woken up to the threat of terrorism. Of course they have. What they have failed to do is to recognise that ideological extremism lies not at the fringes but in the mainstream. This does not mean that most imams tell their audiences at Friday prayers to plant bombs or glorify those who would do so, though there are instances in which this has certainly happened and continues to do so.[47] What it means is that the political culture surrounding a large proportion of Muslims in Europe is being pump-primed with prejudices about Western villainy and Muslim victimhood which at the fringes can then lead to violent outcomes.

With this in mind we must be emphatic in stressing that no Muslim leader or luminary can rightly be described as a 'moderate' while peddling hateful propaganda against the Jewish state.

During the Gaza crisis on the cusp of 2008 and 2009, the British political establishment received a loud and unmistakable wake-up call that its investments in cultivating 'moderate' Muslims may yield less than they had hoped. Ed Hussein, a reformed former member of the Islamist group Hizb ut-Tahrir who had been feted by the British authorities, released a blistering attack on Israel, and Britain's failure to condemn her actions. The tone and content of his remarks, issued via the foundation of which he is co-director, were all too familiar: 'The UK Government cannot seek to win hearts and minds across Muslim communities while failing to stop Israel from murdering Palestinians en masse,' he said. '[Prime Minister]

Gordon Brown and [Foreign Minister] David Miliband have reached out to Damascus and Darfur in recent weeks in an attempt to bring peace and stand for fairness. That is commendable. And in that spirit, where is the outright condemnation of Israeli atrocities and pressure on Israel to stop its inhumane operations?'[48] The following day, Hussein, who has been brave in condemning Islamism in other respects, wrote a commentary in the *Guardian*. He asked: 'How can the children of Holocaust survivors become such brutal killers?'[49]

At around the same time, another self-styled moderate, the Swiss-born Tariq Ramadan, also showed the extent of his moderation. In an article peppered with warnings not to give in to anti-Semitism ('antisemitism is anti-Islamic,' he said) or 'to turn the Israeli-Palestinian war into a religious conflict' he still could not resist the standard incendiary rhetoric. Israel's actions were referred to as 'massacres'. He argued that for Muslims 'a global movement of non-violent resistance to the violent and extremist policy of the state of Israel has become imperative'.[50]

It is and must be definitional of 'moderation' that reasoned discourse about democratic Israel is accepted and internalised. One can imagine the howls of protest that such a suggestion would bring. But, ironically, those who would protest are thereby unwittingly conceding that there is in fact something distinct and troublesome about Muslim political culture in Europe. For they are thus admitting that the expectation that Muslims should talk and act in a decent manner about the Jewish state is an expectation too far. But why is it an expectation too far? Only the tiniest percentage of Europe's Muslims are themselves of Palestinian extraction, in which case personal and family connections could explain, though not excuse, virulent hostility to Israel. The expectations of those who would balk at using Israel as the proverbial canary in the mine for Europe's Muslims thus reveal something that they are desperate to deny: Muslim political culture in Europe is hardwired into an extremist and globalised Islamist discourse in which the Jewish state is the subject of an unremitting demonology. If it is hardwired into that portion of Islamist discourse why should anyone believe that it is not hardwired into other parts of it too?

In a wide-ranging study published in March 2009 on the upsurge in anti-Semitism during and after Israel's Operation Cast Lead offensive in Gaza, the Institute for Global Jewish Affairs listed a range of cases in which Muslim groups had attempted, as the report put it, to 'conquer the public square' and not only in the battle against Jews and Israel.[51]

While 'many Muslims, through their mode of dress, increasingly emphasize their religion in the public domain', the report said, in Europe, Jews have become ever more wary over the years of overt expressions of their own identity. Jewish community leaders have warned against wearing kippahs on the street; 'On various occasions people wearing Stars of David were also advised to tuck them into their shirts.' As Jews have been forced to retreat from the 'public square', its would-be new owners have flexed their muscles against wider targets, as we have seen with great clarity in the various clashes between Muslim groups and press and artistic freedom over representations of the Prophet Mohammed, and critical discussion of the Islamic religion. The report also highlighted the infamous incident in Italy in January 2009 in which hundreds of Muslims used protests against Israeli actions in Gaza to take a literal stand in the public square but this time against Catholics, too:

'In Milan, a Muslim prayer session was held on the major square in front of the cathedral. This message can be interpreted in several ways. For instance: the Catholics pray inside, but the street, the public square, is for Muslim prayer. Or, the cathedral is empty, the street is full, and ultimately the cathedral will be a mosque. Many Italians understood the message; Interior Minister Roberto Maroni forbade future demonstrations in front of religious buildings. Later the Muslim organizers apologized to the cardinal of Milan.'

With all that is going on in this respect these days in Europe, one would have thought that there would be widespread acceptance of the need to debate the issues, however uncomfortable such discussion may be. But the denial is deeply embedded.

This can also be seen in the reaction to the few people who have had the temerity to raise the subject with the frequency that its seriousness deserves. Writers such as Mark Steyn and Melanie Phillips, to name two of the most controversial in the English-speaking media, have to varying degrees been ostracised by mainstream society, and especially by its bien pensant, cultural guardians.

Of course, both can be justly criticised. I know of no one who cannot be. But the distinction between a serious response to such writers and a response which smacks of timidity, intellectual shallowness even, is revealed in the extent to which it is understood that it is not so much the answers they give that matters as the questions that they raise. To say that Islamism, demographic change and civilisational confidence are not even worth talking about in modern Europe is surely to talk oneself out of some of the most important political conversations of our era. It is to relegate oneself to the status of a bit player. An understanding that these issues are of the profoundest importance is a prerequisite to a claim on seriousness. The trouble is that looking across Europe, especially western Europe, it is depressingly evident that the number of people who can now really make such a claim is few and far between. Steyn put his finger on the nature of the problem referring to a review in *The Economist* which dismissed his concerns about Islam in Europe as 'alarmist'.[52] As he put it: 'By "alarmist", *The Economist* and company really mean "raising the subject".'[53]It is hard to disagree. The subject does pop up in the European discourse from time to time, but in a desultory and superficial sense which indicates precisely the lack of seriousness just described.

And if the political-cultural establishment will not address the problem the risk is that extremists will, drawing greater and greater support from a public disillusioned about the way things are going and bewildered as to why mainstream actors seem to brush over it. The growth of Islamism may thus be met by a substantial improvement in the prospects for deeply undemocratic parties and individuals of the far right. There are signs that this is already happening across Europe.

What is overwhelmingly obvious in surveying the European political and opinion-forming scene is the existence of a meta-narrative which is clearly accusatory of many prevailing attitudes towards Muslims while lingering in a state of almost total denial about the depths of the problems inside Muslim communities themselves. It was this meta-narrative, to quote just one last example, which led the European Union in 2003 to try to suppress a report commissioned by the European Monitoring Centre for Racism and Xenophobia (EUMC) which concluded that rising anti-Semitism in Europe was mainly due to young Muslims. The cover story from the European Union was put out by none other than Javier Solana, the EU's foreign policy supremo. He claimed that the report did not meet 'quality standards'. The previously mentioned Juliane Wetzel, from the institution which conducted the research, explained the situation rather differently: 'The study put the EUMC in a difficult situation because it singled out the group [young Muslims], which they [the EUMC] seek to protect. They refused to publish it because it clashed with political correctness.'[54]

Attitudes to Israel inside Europe's growing Muslim populations are deeply problematic. They are also representative of a wider problem about integration in Western society and acceptance of Western values, the surface of which has only been scratched by political and cultural elites afraid of what they might find if they go deeper.

Of course, when it comes to Israel in particular it should not be forgotten that integration is a two-way process. Europe's Muslims, like all immigrant groups, will inevitably respond to the signals that emerge from the opinion formers of the host societies. In the case of Israel, the signals in Europe hardly point in the direction of enlightenment, as much of this book has been at pains to show.

But the Muslim question is not simply a matter which introduces itself domestically. Muslim countries, with combined populations exceeding a billion, need to be dealt with on the international stage. In the business of international diplomacy there are deals to be done and relationships to foster. As we do those deals, and tend to those relationships, we come face to face with political cultures marked by extreme hostility to Israel, and to the Jews. When they cough, do we catch cold?

CHAPTER 6

The diplomats' dilemma

Try these for a couple of generalisations: the closer you get in government to foreign ministries the more hostile the attitude to Israel; the closer you get to defence ministries the more friendly the attitude to Israel. The point is hard to prove with reference to reliable surveys, but it accords with my personal experience, and I submit that it makes sense. Diplomats engaged in the practice of building bridges and forming friendships on the international stage are not going to do themselves favours by stressing their affection for Israel. Walking into a meeting of the Arab League or OPEC humming Hatikvah would not be a great strategy for achieving objectives.

The incentives for defence ministries – naturally more hawkish and likely to be respectful of Israeli military prowess and sophistication – take them in the opposite direction. These are generalisations indeed. But even in the United States, the one part of the apparatus of government which sometimes comes in for criticism from pro-Israel groups is the State Department. Interests count in the world of international diplomacy and for a whole host of reasons that stacks the deck against Israel.

This book has not been designed to trace the history or contemporary realities of state-level relations between Israel and Europe. The focus has been and remains on the opinion formers. But ultimately it is not possible to compartmentalise everything to the extent that the world of the opinion formers as I have defined them can be made to stand in isolation from the business of international statecraft.

When top-level politicians use their high-profile public positions to hold forth on international affairs they themselves function as opinion formers. In office or retired, they and their senior diplomats also mix in influential circles, often having good contacts with foreign correspondents, editors, columnists, academics and people who work in think-tanks. They make regular appearances on radio and television. In many cases, they bring with them into the debate about Israel a particular way of interacting with the world, a more or less 'realist' perspective which gives primacy to the exercise of power rather than to questions of justice, fairness or even truthfulness.

As a starting point for approaching international relations such patriotic considerations are reasonable, if not spectacularly principled. From such beginnings there arises a much more generalised, usually less intense, sometimes quite casual hostility to Israel which proceeds from a sense that the Jewish state represents an unnecessary danger to Western wellbeing, an obstacle to stability in a strategically vital part of the world and an impediment to good relations with countries crucial to energy security. When Daniel Bernard, the former French ambassador to London asked 'Why should the world be in danger of World War III because of these people?', he was reflecting a state of mind which sees Israel as the awkward squad in international relations. It was a statement which is rarely made with such brutal frankness. But, in one form or another, it is commonplace.

As another example, consider an open letter published in several British newspapers in 2004 addressed to then Prime Minister Tony Blair from no fewer than fifty-two of Britain's most senior retired diplomats.[1] The letter focused on the Israel–Palestine conflict as well as Iraq. In sum it was a damning indictment of Blair's alleged subservience to President George W. Bush. It noted with horror President Bush's acceptance, and Tony Blair's endorsement, of policies pursued by then Israeli

Prime Minister Ariel Sharon which they described in terms of being 'one-sided and illegal and which will cost yet more Israeli and Palestinian blood'. They went on to argue that: 'This abandonment of principle comes at a time when, rightly or wrongly, we are portrayed throughout the Arab and Muslim world as partners in an illegal and brutal occupation in Iraq.' Leaving aside the suggestion that it is Bush and Blair who were engaged in an abandonment of 'principle' in backing Israel, it is the rest of that sentence which betrays the mindset we are discussing. It is how things will look in the Arab world, how we are 'portrayed', that concerns them. The weasel words 'rightly or wrongly' can do nothing to alter the reality of what is at work here. Taken together with another revealing assertion that the Israel–Palestine conflict represents 'a problem which, more than any other, has for decades poisoned relations between the West and the Islamic and Arab worlds', the diplomatic mindset, at least as it is represented by the authors of the letter, reveals itself clearly.

I cannot be certain about what is going on in the mind of any one individual. I do not therefore accuse the above quoted group of retired diplomats of consciously manipulating their words in a manner that contradicts what they really think. I do not doubt their sincerity. (Indeed, my worry is that they might well be sincere.) What I am arguing is that there are powerful anti-Israeli dynamics bound up with the practice of international diplomacy and that key elements of their letter represent an appeal to submit to them.

But an appeal for the West to adopt policies towards Israel which will improve our image in the Arab and Islamic world sets us on a course towards some perverse conclusions. To improve our image it may well be necessary to adopt elements of their narratives. What if those narratives about Israel are characterised by hatred and deceit? What if the discourse in the Arab and Islamic world is shot through with some of the foulest anti-Semitism to have appeared in the world since the era of the Third Reich? What if they have no concern for the victims of suicide bombing in Israel? What if they are unable to come to terms with the fact that they opposed the very existence of Israel at its inception and several times launched wars of aggression to destroy it? What if their own countries are harbouring or funding or arming anti-Israeli terror groups? What if they are tyrannies or dictatorships?

Where precisely does it leave us when, to ingratiate ourselves, we aim for the middle ground between honesty and dishonesty, enlightenment and bigotry, democracy and tyranny? Do we simply conclude, in the sardonic words of Lord Janner, that 'Arab oil is thicker than Jewish blood'?[2]

It should be clear that Israel faces dynamics working against it on two levels. First, the diplomatic balancing act between Israel and its enemies risks encouraging concessions at one level or another to ferociously anti-Israeli narratives in the manner just described. Second, in order to justify such concessions there is an obvious incentive to sanitise Arab and Muslim political culture by downplaying or denying its true nature, especially as it relates to Israel. This reinforces the problem Israel faces in explaining to the world the context in which it operates and the character of the regimes and groups that it confronts.

The way in which the dynamics of diplomacy can influence the narratives that we ourselves ultimately adopt concerning Israel has also been well illustrated in relation to the diplomatic efforts in the quest for peace. In senior American diplomat Robert Malley's highly controversial account of the failure of the Camp David negotiations in 2000 (see p. 19) he challenged the widespread (and in my opinion convincing) view that most or all of the blame should have been laid at the door of then Palestinian leader Yasser Arafat. Writing with Hussein Agha in the *New York Review of Books*, he offered a wide-ranging set of arguments to support his case. But the question of whether their case is convincing can be left aside for a moment. The way that they constructed their arguments was illuminating in its own right. 'In short,' they said, 'the failure to reach a final agreement is attributed, without notable dissent, to Yasser Arafat. As orthodoxies go, this is a dangerous one. For it has larger ripple effects. Broader conclusions take hold. That there is no peace partner is one. That there is no possible end to the conflict with Arafat is another.'[3]

The point they are trying to make comes across loud and clear: the narrative of events which portrays Arafat as the root cause of the breakdown of negotiations is fraught with risks. Diplomatic initiatives to revivify the peace process are unlikely to be undertaken if this is the conclusion you come to. If you are interested in peace at all, accept that view at your peril.

Note how the appeal to reason here is thus merged with an appeal to be mindful of the political and diplomatic consequences of the place our powers of reason may take us. But objective and reasoned analysis cannot be conducted under such terms. The truth is the truth whether it is inconvenient or not and whether, in a sense, it is 'dangerous' or not. What we have in this one tiny example is a window into the diplomatic mindset I am referring to. What is said about the Israel–Palestine conflict is not only being said because it represents an honest and clear analysis of events. It is coloured by the need to consider the political ramifications as well.

I am convinced that the way in which many senior politicians and diplomats talk about Israel is affected by precisely these sorts of considerations. The painful underlying reality of Palestinian rejectionism and the brutal facts about Arab, Muslim and Palestinian political culture are simply considered too inflammatory to talk about and too depressing to internalise. What emerges, then, is a narrative which has been forced through a distorted prism. Painful and inconvenient truths are edited out of the story. The case for Israel suffers accordingly.

Europe's big three and Israel

The year 2008 provided some of the best case studies in recent years of European diplomatic balancing acts in relation to Israel. The leaders of all three of Europe's most powerful countries made widely publicised keynote addresses to the Israeli parliament, the Knesset. For German Chancellor Angela Merkel and British Prime Minister Gordon Brown the speeches were the first ever to the Knesset by a German or British head of government. Nicolas Sarkozy's speech was the first by a French president since François Mitterrand's address in 1982. As setpiece speeches at the heart of Israel's democracy, every single word was carefully crafted with painstaking attention to detail. Nothing was left to chance. We can therefore learn a lot both from what *was* said what was *not* said.

As one might expect, all three speeches were sprinkled with references to the Holocaust. Chancellor Merkel in particular devoted the lion's share of her address to it. 'The Shoah fills us Germans with shame,' she said. 'I bow my head before the victims. I bow before the survivors and before all those who helped them so they could survive.'[4] There is not the slightest reason to believe that Merkel (or Brown and Sarkozy, both of whom made similar remarks) was being anything other than genuine. Europe's leaders do not simply reiterate contrition and sympathy about the Holocaust as a matter of form. When they refer to the systematic murder of six million Jews in Europe they do so in recognition that this was indeed the iconic crime of the modern era. The three leaders also paid homage to Israel's extraordinary achievements in overcoming adversity to build a successful, modern democracy. Prime Minister Brown reminisced about the tales his father – a minister in the Church of Scotland – would tell about his trips to Israel: ' ... there was never a time as I was growing up that I did not hear about, read about or was not surrounded by stories of the struggles, sacrifices, tribulation and triumphs as the Israeli people built their new state,' he said.[5] 'And I am proud to say that for the whole of my life, I have counted myself a friend of Israel.'

President Sarkozy, who alluded to his upbringing by his Jewish grandfather, said: 'I would like to address all Israelis, Israelis whose ancestors hoped for centuries that one day that there would once again be a Jewish nation. A Jewish nation like all others, free, free at last to choose its fate, free at last to decide for itself. I want to address the people of Israel, the so brave people of Israel, who have chosen democracy and freedom, and owe these to no one but themselves, to their courage, energy and intelligence.'[6]

These words, and the many others in similar vein in all three speeches, should be remembered by anyone inclined to generalise about hostility to Israel in Europe. Much of what has been written in this book has concerned strands of thinking which are deeply hostile to the Jewish state. But that is exactly what they are: 'strands of thinking'. They do not represent Europe in its totality. To be sure, they represent a warning about what Europe could become. But no one motivated by an underlying hatred of Israel could talk about that country in the manner just described by Merkel, Brown and Sarkozy. No one who thinks about Israel as a pariah, no one who deals in the vile currency of analogies with Nazi Germany or apartheid South Africa or who calls for academic and trade boycotts would engage in discourse of this kind.

And yet, in both what was *also* said and what was *not* said, their speeches reflected precisely the kind of diplomatic compromises which can lead to a distorted picture.

The key problem concerns the way in which European leaders feel duty bound to offer pro forma concessions to Arab and Muslim sensitivities even as they heap upon Israel praise. Deep-seated problems in the political culture are almost always ignored. President Sarkozy, prefacing his criticisms with words to the effect that he had earned the right to state his views clearly because he had established his credentials as a friend of

Israel, said there could not 'be peace without a complete and immediate stop to all settlement activity'. There can't be peace, he said, 'if the Palestinians are prevented from moving around or living on their territory. There can't be peace without the resolution of the Palestinian refugees' problem with due regard for Israel's identity and destiny. There can't be peace, even though I know how painful this is, without recognition of Jerusalem as the capital of two States and guaranteed freedom of access to the Holy Places for all the religions. There can't be peace without a border negotiated on the basis of the 1967 agreement and exchanges of territory making it possible to build two viable States.'

The balancing act was palpable. In calling for such concessions from Israel he also referred to the need for the Palestinians to do more to combat terrorism. He acknowledged that the 'truth is that no one can hope to re-establish Palestinian people's rights by denying the Israeli people theirs and calling for Israel's destruction. The truth is that this endless conflict must end. The truth is that the violence must stop. The truth is that this hate, which sets peoples against other peoples, must be extinguished.'

In a desperate attempt to please all sides, President Sarkozy came within a whisker of moral clarity but then withdrew from it as he repeated the old mantras. He is entitled to his view in suggesting that settlement activity should stop, that the Palestinian refugee problem must be resolved and that a final peace agreement should be more or less founded on the 1967 borders. Politics is about compromise and when a deal can realistically be done Israel will have to make compromises too, as the Jewish state has done in the past. But in terms of the core reasons for the conflict, the existence of the refugees in the first place, the reasons for restrictions on Palestinian movement, and the hate which 'must be extinguished', he shirked the issue.

It is not Israeli schoolchildren who are programmed to believe that Palestinians, Arabs and Muslims are subhuman. It is not

Israeli religious leaders who day in day out, week in week out heap scorn and racist contempt on their counterparts in the region. It is not Israeli newspapers which print cartoons and articles portraying people as bloodsuckers, vampires, apes and pigs. It is not due to Israeli rejectionism that opportunities for a two-state solution were missed in 1947, 2000 and 2001. It is not due to Israeli aggression in 1947-8 that the refugee problem arose. It is not due to Israel that a war took place in 1967 which led to the occupation of the West Bank. It is not out of spite for the Palestinians that roadblocks and travel restrictions have been put in place. It is out of fears, fully justified by horrific experience, that free movement will be exploited by terrorists to slaughter Israeli civilians. President Sarkozy and the team that constructed his speech with him cannot possibly have been oblivious to all this. At the very least they must have known that a powerful argument about the situation can be constructed on precisely these lines and that a rounded appraisal of the conflict must at least refer to it. Why then, is it entirely absent? What is it that the French state is so frightened of? Whom is France trying to please? Whose interests is France deferring to? Whose narratives is it conceding to?

Gordon Brown continued where Sarkozy left off even as he called for 'the Palestinians' to act 'with persistence and perseverance against the terrorists who attack' Israel, as if the terrorists were somehow not Palestinians themselves, as if Palestinian television (Fatah-controlled as well as Hamas-controlled) had not sought to glorify suicide bombing, as if children in the West Bank were not taught daily to despise Israel and to read maps of the region in which Israel has been literally erased as if it did not or should not exist. In a flourish, he then appeared to dismiss the moral and political complexity of the settlement question with the brusque admonishment to Israel that it should be 'freezing and withdrawing from settlements'.

Again, there is no reason why a British prime minister should not call for change from Israel on the settlements. But why exactly was it presented in such clear-cut terms? By what kind of ethical *modus operandi* should the British prime minister be endorsing the principle that Jews cannot be allowed to live in a territory because the majority of the population has been taught to despise them? Why, for example, should the Jews of Hebron, which for three thousand years had a vibrant Jewish population until it was expelled en masse by Palestinians following a massacre of sixty-three Jewish civilians in 1929, simply hand over their homes under the principle of Judenrein? Under precisely what kind of moral imperative should we allow for the de facto signposting of the West Bank with the words: 'No Jews Allowed'?

And yet, close attention to the diplomatic wording of Brown's comments on the settlements suggests that this may not have been what the British prime minister was saying or implying at all. It is certainly an interpretation that could easily be drawn and it is one that the Arab and Muslim audience would certainly feel entitled to draw. But note what Gordon Brown actually said: Israel should be 'freezing and withdrawing from settlements'. Not '*the* settlements', or '*all of the* settlements'; just 'settlements'. With clear echoes of the 'definite article' saga surrounding UN Security Council Resolution 242 (see pp. 24–27) Brown was thus leaving Israel the option to retain some settlements while withdrawing from others: the question of which would be vacated and which would remain being a matter for negotiation as US policy in recent years has consistently implied.

It is a marvellously illustrative example of the multiple audiences often being addressed in diplomatic parlance. Nonetheless, it is unlikely that many would spot it if it was not pointed out to them.

What is necessary here is to put aside the personal and to see these leaders as incarnations of the political and diplomatic compromises that their states have decided to make in the

Middle East. Their ways of speaking reflect a perception of national interests, particularly the interests involved in sustaining the relationship with the oil-rich Arab world but also, to be fair, a desire to retain a robust relationship with Israel. In a speech to the Knesset, the diplomatic mindset knows what is at stake and knows what is required of it.

Not, of course, that the newspapers back home picked up on this. Given the condition of the opinion-forming classes in Britain it would have been nothing short of miraculous if they had. The mass circulation *Daily Mail*, usually a fierce opponent of Brown, opined: 'It takes guts for a visiting Prime Minister to stand up in the Jerusalem parliament and deliver some blunt home truths to Israeli MPs about their failures in the Middle East peace process. Gordon Brown displayed that courage yesterday.'[7] The paper, noting his condemnation of Iran, then went on to praise him for his 'even-handed statesmanship'. In a sense, of course, this is precisely the problem. To an anti-Israeli audience in Britain, Brown appeared to be doing nothing more or less than serving up diplomatic mantras designed to placate both sides while emphasising Israeli wrongdoing over settlement policy. The diplomatic balancing act and the pathologies of anti-Israeli discourse back home met in a sickly-sweet embrace.

And it is when the two do not meet that the politicians run into trouble. The reception in Germany of Angela Merkel's speech to the Knesset, in which she eschewed the balancing act of her British and French counterparts, was mixed to say the least. It may well be that Merkel had shown greater moral fortitude in refusing to bring forth the usual diplomatic mantras. It may be that as the first German leader to address the Knesset she merely felt it would have been inappropriate. This was a historic moment for Germany and it was no time to dissemble.

Important German media outlets had no such qualms. *Süddeutsche Zeitung* wailed at Chancellor Merkel saying: 'Germany must be careful not to make (US President

George W.) Bush's cardinal mistake and be biased in the peace process.'[8] The paper added: 'Merkel must maintain her independence and criticise Israel directly for its occupation and settlement policy. A genuine friend tells the truth.' Fritz Kuhn, parliamentary leader of the Green party, told Germany's SWR public radio: 'You have to make clear during this visit and every other visit that preliminary efforts in the peace process are expected of Israel.'[9]

True to form, Hamas, the ruling Palestinian group in Gaza, lambasted Merkel in its own inimitable terms saying she had 'closed her eyes to the holocaust that this entity [Israel] has perpetrated in the Gaza Strip, focusing only on the Holocaust committed by the Nazis against Jews in her country, the extent of which is a subject of doubts and exaggerations'.[10] Such is the price a European politician pays, and such is the language in which the bill is handed over, when they refuse to play the standard, diplomatic game.

It is acceptable, indeed it is necessary, for Western politicians to have economic and diplomatic relations with the Arab and Muslim world. Diplomacy is often a messy business, particularly when dealing with dictatorships. Over the centuries, however, we have learned that conflict between nations that do not share each others' values can in many cases be avoided by establishing relationships between governments and binding them together through trade. This may mean that we make some grubby deals. But most of us accept that that is a price worth paying if it lessens the likelihood of conflict. The incentive to maintain working relations with the Arab and Muslim world is redoubled because of our obvious over-dependence on its oil (and their dependence on our money to buy it).

But there is a dividing line between sensible diplomacy and mutually advantageous trade relations on the one hand and appeasement on the other. That line is crossed when we cease to be true to our values, when we fail to show robustness in their defence and when we start to buy into narratives which are abhorrent to everything of which our own societies are constituted. For professional diplomats and senior politicians engaged in international diplomacy it is an occupational hazard.

Britain's former Europe Minister Denis MacShane gave a sense of the pressures that can be brought to bear on principled politicians and diplomats in reflecting speculatively on how he would have handled what he correctly termed the 'anti-Semitic orgy' that was the UN anti-racism conference in Durban, South Africa, in 2001. In his book *Globalising Hatred: The New Anti-Semitism*, he pondered on the reaction that he would have had to face from his superiors in the British governmental establishment (collectively known as Whitehall) had he been there and done the right thing. He said:

'I hope, had I represented Britain at that event, I would have had the courage to pull out the UK delegation *and risk the wrath of superiors in Whitehall who were bending over backwards to placate Islamist ideologues* [my italics], including those who have supported the murder of innocent Jewish children and women. As I read with mounting concern the raging hate against the Jewish people expressed at the conference and its linked events the scales began to come off my eyes about the way the democratic governments of the world had underestimated the arrival of latter-day anti-Semitism as a new organising force in world politics.'[11]

This is the heart of the diplomats' dilemma. For less principled men and women than MacShane, the day-to-day business of dealing with unpalatable regimes operating within degraded political cultures can quickly leave one numb. Later it can leave one bereft of moral compass. Relationships with local politicians and societal figures quickly become personal. Friendships develop. Distinctions start to become blurred. Value judgements become unfashionable. Major failings in the political culture start to be edited out of the consciousness. A culture of denial can easily take hold. There is a job to be done.

It is unlikely that a single diplomat reading these words would deny that the temptations are there, though most would add that they have never succumbed to them themselves! The central point to recognise is not that diplomats are bad people. They are not. It is that there are powerful dynamics at play which are difficult for them to resist. There is only one Israel. There are fifty-seven members of the Organisation of the Islamic Conference. All fifty-seven of those members of the OIC are virulently hostile to Israel. In their international diplomacy, as in their promotion of political ideas back home, hatred of Israel is often turned into a fetish.

Additionally, there is in fact convincing circumstantial evidence that diplomatic relations between Europe and Israel have been very significantly influenced by a need to placate Arab and Muslim hatred of the Jewish state. Perhaps the most instructive case in point surrounds the European response to the Arab oil embargo of 1973 which caused oil prices to quadruple. One does not need to go as far as the Egyptian-born writer Bat Ye'or whose book *Eurabia: The Euro-Arab Axis* posits the 'transformation of Europe into "Eurabia", a cultural and political appendage of the Arab/Muslim world'.[12] But her account of the way in which Arab countries succeeded in blackmailing European governments, via the so-called 'Euro-Arab Dialogue', into adopting aspects of their anti-Israeli agenda is worryingly convincing.[13]

The price of the deal, as Bat Ye'or describes it, was that several European countries, led by France, would set the tone for Middle Eastern discourse by downplaying oppression in the Arab world and partially indulging in a dishonest little propaganda war against Israel. In return they would get stable oil supplies and access to Arab markets generally. Not that they would take the Arab and Muslim agenda in all its parts and all its forms. It would just be enough to curry favour in the right places without going too far in a continent still haunted by the memory of the Holocaust. Thinking and acting in this manner would soon become routine in foreign ministries across the continent. Little by little the true nature of Arab and Muslim political culture would be sanitised. Little by little the justice of the Israeli cause would be diminished.

One highly significant way in which this manifested itself was the incorporation into European diplomatic discourse at around this time of the specious Arab interpretation of United Nations Resolution 242. That interpretation – perhaps better expressed as a wilful *misinterpretation* – attempts to suggest that Israel is duty bound by international law to withdraw unilaterally from all the territories occupied following the 1967 war. In reality, the resolution, drafted by the British, quite deliberately and consciously *refused* to call on Israel to withdraw from all the territories in recognition that the pre-1967 borders were not defensible (see pp. 24–27). The extent to which indulgence of Arab prejudices against Israel was taken sometimes beggars belief. France, in deference to the opposition of the Arab League, even wobbled over supporting the Egyptian–Israeli peace agreement of 1979.

But the European document which really set the tone for relations with Israel was the European Union's Venice Declaration of 1980.[14] As Bat Ye'or sees it, the declaration 'endorsed ... all the Arab requests'.[15] Since the declaration specifically endorsed the 'right to existence and to security of all the states in the region, *including Israel*' (my italics), she may be accused of exaggeration.[16] Nonetheless, the extent of European diplomatic subservience to the Arab and Muslim case against Israel was obvious. The Venice Declaration for the first time offered the PLO a key role in the negotiation process. It should be remembered that the PLO at the time was formally committed to the complete and total destruction of Israel. Also, the drift of the document is blatantly biased. Israel is the only state named whose actions and policies are deemed an obstacle to peace. The word terrorism does not appear once. Amazingly given how recent they were at that time, there is not a word of direct condemnation of the Arab states which started the 1967 and

1973 wars. Neither is there a word of understanding for Israel's plight in the region. Expressions of sympathy and calls for justice are exclusively focused on the Palestinians.

As the Irish historian Rory Miller recounts, the Venice Declaration sent the Israeli government apoplectic with rage with the cabinet comparing it to Munich 1938 'and condemning the Community's endorsement of the "Arab SS known as the PLO"'.[17]

It was this very document that set the standard for European diplomatic discourse about Israel until the Oslo era at least and, arguably, led the Palestinians to believe that there would be no price to pay in Europe for terrorism. It came, of course, in the wake of the oil shock of 1973 and the one that followed it in 1979 after the Islamist takeover of Iran by Ayatollah Khomeini. Fears of upsetting the oil producers pervaded.

As suggested in this chapter and elsewhere, the negative forces emanating from international diplomacy do not have a free run. When I talk about Europe's leaders engaging in a balancing act that is exactly what I mean. Israel and Europe have a burgeoning trade and technology relationship. Formal relations with the European Union have been continuously upgraded. More generally, in surveying the international scene the fact that the United States is pro-Israeli must act as something of a counterweight to all of the negatives. What it cannot do is to wipe those negatives away. The anti-Israeli dynamics remain, even if they are to some extent held in check. From the highest levels this normalises and legitimises a way of talking about Israel which trickles down into society below.

Agenda slippage

Ultimately, none of the arguments in this chapter should be taken to mean that there is something unusual about politicians and diplomats seeking to strike a balance between competing interests. It would be to misunderstand the point of this chapter to conclude here that Israel is being singled out, or that the realities of the Middle East are being distorted due to malice.

The point is, rather, that due to the realities of Arab and Muslim bigotry against Israel, Western politicians and diplomats desirous of maintaining friendly relations with Arab and Muslim countries find themselves confronted by the obvious temptation to concede some ground to their agenda. This *agenda slippage* affects the way Israel is portrayed. A European propensity to yield to the imperatives of international diplomacy at the expense of a truthful and principled approach to the Middle East is the consequence.

On a concluding note, surely, one might protest, the same incentive–disincentive equation applies to the United States. If the dynamics inherent in international diplomacy are as powerful as I have suggested, why has America not yielded to them as Europe has? Occasionally, of course, the United States does yield to such pressures. It is not hard to find (rather obviously) pro forma diplomatic statements from the United States issued to placate Arab and Muslim sensitivities. But these form the exceptions rather than the rule. Mainly, I think, the answer to that question is that the United States is so much more powerful than Europe – collectively in the form of the EU or as its individual nations – in international diplomacy. It is far harder to push around. It is also less dependent on Middle Eastern oil and gas. It will certainly feel the pressure, but it is far better placed to withstand it.

Moreover, American political culture is much better disposed towards Israel in the first place. When European leaders and senior diplomats adopt a critical stance towards Israel it will be broadly welcomed back home rather than punished. American leaders and top diplomats know that there may be a price to pay for unfair criticism of Israel in the American media and in Congress. Unlike in Europe, it is not a cost-free option.

CHAPTER 7

Ideology against Israel

One of the most puzzling features of the polemic against Israel is the way in which it unites groups, individuals and institutions which in other respects despise each other. More precisely, it unites streams of ideological thinking which, on the face of it, appear completely incoherent. What kind of common denominator could bring together traditionalists on the old, conservative Right with self-declared progressives on the Left? To add to the confusion, why is it that people who look as though they should be friends – Democrats in the United States and Leftists in Europe – find themselves so divided when it comes to discussion of Israel?

It looks like a mess. And in such circumstances there is always a temptation to seek solace in simple explanations. Most prominent among them is that this is all very much easier to understand than it is sometimes made out to be: unlike America, Europe is inherently anti-Semitic. This anti-Semitism is spread more or less evenly across the political spectrum and, therefore, it translates into widespread hostility to Israel. Europeans hate the Jews. Consequently, they hate the Jewish state.

There are good reasons for believing that this analysis is profoundly mistaken. For one thing, there is no real evidence to support the contention that traditional anti-Semitism is the driving force behind hatred of Israel. In fact, some of the best available evidence directly contradicts it, as the discussion below will show. Moreover, I believe there is a far more convincing explanation of the roots of anti-Israeli sentiment which resolves the apparent contradictions noted above very effectively. It does so through a recognition that the main ideological platforms on which the anti-Israeli narrative is constructed are actually united by something quite significant, though what unites them is a negative. In their different ways they have both lost out in the modern world. The Israel–Palestine conflict concentrates anger and resentment at this sense of loss in a manner that promotes remarkable unity between them and in a place which has no precise equivalent. To be sure, anti-Semitism is picked up along the way. But it does not explain how the bandwagon started rolling in the first place.

However, this presupposes the discussion which follows. First, it is necessary to set a few matters straight.

Which Left? Which Right?

Political people have a tendency to identity with the parties they support just as football fans identify with their team. Terms such as 'Left' and 'Right', particularly the former, engage our emotions as well as our intellects. It can all get very tribal, and sometimes a little childish. People do not like hearing criticism of traditions with which they associate. For those who view politics in such terms this will be a painful discussion. To deconstruct political ideologies in order to locate the root causes of anti-Israeli demonology is to delve into some dark and unpleasant places. Since the bulk of the campaign against Israel is being mounted by forces within the Left it is inevitable that much of what follows reveals aspects of the Left-wing tradition which are far from positive, and that is putting it mildly. There is nothing much that can be done to soften the blow. One is either interested in serious discussion or one is not.

All I can say is that the points that I raise do not impinge upon the entirely honourable and decent aspects of the Left-wing tradition which have focused on the struggle for social justice at home and an internationalist solidarity abroad that sees the deprivation and suffering of anyone as a call to action for us all. Those aspects of the Leftist tradition have a solidity and a permanence about them. They represent a central theme in the Western democratic tradition and anyone who supports that tradition, whether they agree with its conclusions or not, should be proud that it is there.

Terms such as Left and Right can be slippery and imprecise. On some important issues, some parts of the Left are closer to some parts of the Right than they are to other parts of the Left. The same applies to the Right, as it must, in reverse. Political parties are coalitions formed from a variety of different interest groups and a variety of ideological starting points.[1] The conflicts within them can be as sharp as the conflicts between them.

If 'Left' and 'Right' are slippery terms, what about 'Socialist', 'Liberal' or 'Conservative'? For many who have called themselves socialists all they are trying to do is to stress the centrality of the social dimension of human life to their public policy priorities. They emphasise concern for the socially deprived without necessarily committing themselves to a particular way of achieving their aims. Most self-designated socialists certainly incline towards a greater rather than a lesser role for the state, but does that mean they envisage the nationalisation of the means of the production? Does it mean they accept that economies need to be privately owned but then regulated and reinforced by welfare systems? Or is it something in between? And what about the political dimension? Are they democratic socialists? Are they populist socialists? Are they totalitarians?

And Liberals? Are we talking about classical liberals emphasising individualism, human rights and free markets? In this case, most observers would place them on the right of the political spectrum. Or are we talking about social liberals – the sense in which the term is commonly used in the United States? In this incarnation liberals tend to stress social and lifestyle priorities and human rights as well as a broad acceptance of market economics tempered by a belief in the reformative power of the state in tackling social deprivation and gross inequality.

Most of us would place people adhering to such views on the centre-left.

Finally, what is a Conservative? Is it someone who stresses tradition and the status quo over the possibilities and prospects for a brighter future through radical reform? If so, were Margaret Thatcher and Ronald Reagan really conservatives? Are we talking about social conservatives and religious conservatives? Or are we using the term as shorthand to designate anyone on the right, from free-marketeers to landowning aristocrats?

The political outlook of very few people can be explained in terms of a single ideological stream in any case. Most of us are influenced by a variety of political ideologies, whether we recognise it or not. To borrow from the terminology of global-warming theorists, what matters here is what might be called the 'ideological forcing effect': all other things being equal, what will be the effect on the climate of opinion through the introduction of one ideological stream or another?

A central theme of this chapter is that, regardless of whether one is nominally on the Left or nominally on the Right, the further away from, the more suspicious one is of, liberal democratic capitalist values the less likely one is to be supportive of Israel. The more closely one is associated with an ideological standpoint supportive of the liberal-democratic, capitalist order the more supportive one is likely to be of Israel (and, not incidentally, the United States).

On the European Left, there are two broad camps of anti-Israeli thinking. One is the far Left, composed of adherents to Marxism and its attendant offshoots and endless mutations. Henceforth this group is referred to as the *radical Left* since it exhibits a fundamental opposition to, or at least a deeply held lack of sympathy for, liberal-democratic capitalism.

I am well aware of the infinitely fissiparous nature of the Left and I am equally well aware that attempts to reinvent the Left at various times have led to it adopting labels such as 'New

Left'. It is amazing how many New Lefts there have been. But I am not convinced that (for this discussion) this really matters. There is no observable, real-world difference in the degree or intensity of the hostility to Israel between any of the factions and fractions of the radical Left.

For my purposes, the radical Left refers to all far Left ideological platforms which are more or less totalitarian in character or which exhibit a thoroughgoing hostility to liberal-democratic capitalism. This includes Leninists, Trotskyites and Stalinists as well as adherents to the Frankfurt School and its associated splinters, supporters of Che Guevara and Fidel Castro, the hotch-potch of much of the above which inaugurated a shift in far Left thinking in the late 1960s, and fellow travellers and flirters with such traditions today in far Left parties and movements. I am casting a wide net. But all of these platforms are in important respects related and, in my opinion, form part of the same overarching political tradition.

Hostility to Israel inside this camp is often extremely intense. Occasionally one finds exceptions. These are usually Jews (but sometimes non-Jews, too) who retain a sense of nostalgia for the Israel of the kibbutzim. Sometimes they are not really members of the radical Left at all. They may be unconscious of other ideological currents which would better define them. Then again, they may be genuine adherents, but only in the sense of holding a philosophical attachment to the more interesting, analytical elements of Leftist ideology such as the Marxism of the Paris Manuscripts.[2] Whatever the reason for the absence of hostility to Israel in their thinking, I submit that they are exceptions which prove the rule.

The other important camp on the Left is the modernised, liberal or social democratic Left. This camp, far larger these days than the radical Left, is itself divided. There is a significant minority within it which, like most American Democrats, is supportive of Israel. Former British Prime Minister Tony Blair is an obvious representative of this strand of thinking. While it is certainly arguable that Blair would be better described as a political centrist, there is no question that the Liberal Left does contain vocal supporters of Israel. 'Friends of Israel' groupings in labour and social democratic parties across Europe cannot be dismissed as mere tokenism. The majority of people on the Liberal Left, however, are hostile to Israel, as anyone who follows the debate in Europe must be aware. It is this strand of thinking which dominates large sections of the European media. I refer to it as the Liberal Left since its attitudes to policy making, especially in the domestic arena, are much closer to an activist kind of liberalism than to communism or to any other radical Leftist platform.

The Right in Europe, taken as a whole, is generally far more supportive of Israel though there are distinct camps on this side of the political spectrum as well. Clearly, the far Right exhibits a hostility to Israel which is driven by traditional anti-Semitism. But groups and people of this kind are extremely marginal. The political significance of far Right parties such as Jean-Marie Le Pen's *Front National* in France or similarly obnoxious groupings elsewhere in Europe is not in question. The point is, rather, that they do not have a presence inside the mainstream opinion-forming community. They are not pumping opinions into the European discussion about Israel in the leading newspapers or in artistic and cultural circles.

The most important section of the mainstream Right which is hostile to Israel encompasses traditionalists or *ancien régime* conservatives. Henceforth they are referred to as the Old Right since the predominant feature of their thinking is nostalgia. They have a strong, though minority, presence in most right-wing parties in Europe and are well represented inside parts of the state bureaucracy, especially foreign ministries.

The dominant factions in most right-wing parties in Europe are now guided by aspects of neo-liberalism or a modernised, centre-right conservatism. For want of a better term, I refer to this group as the Liberal Right since it has largely internalised the progressive attitudes to women and minorities, for example, which were once championed primarily by the Left while simultaneously embracing an attitude towards economic and social matters which veers towards the thinking of the great, classical liberal economists. Inside this group are to be found Israel's strongest supporters in Europe. In a general sense, most American Democrats could fit just as easily inside the embrace of Europe's Liberal Right as inside the Liberal Left though in terms of their thinking about Israel they would find more friends on the Liberal Right.

These, of course, are rough and ready guidelines. They will not satisfy the pedants and the purists. But generalisations are necessary. And, as generalisations go, I believe that they capture the realities of the political debate in Europe as fairly as possible given the scope of the discussion at hand. How does it all break down in terms of hostility to the Jewish state?

The radical Left and Israel

In a discussion constructed on several levels, replete with complexities and demanding of an appreciation of subtlety, there is at least one claim about the radical Left's stance on Israel that can be dispensed with more or less effortlessly.[3] That claim is that hostility to the Jewish state is driven by a natural, ideologically determined predisposition to side with the oppressed against the oppressor. Hostility to Israel, it is alleged, is a particular instance of a general concern for human rights, and justice for the underdog. In many versions, this line of thinking ties itself into the shift against Israel on the Left following the 1967 war when Israel took control of the West Bank and Gaza. As Israel became an 'occupier' and an 'oppressor', how could any self-respecting radical do anything other than rail against it?

It doesn't take much knowledge of twentieth-century history to see the gaping hole in the argument. Doyens of the radical

Left may like to style themselves as champions of the oppressed but no objective observer could possibly agree. With the sole exception of Nazism, the ideology responsible for the greatest instances of tyranny and oppression in the modern era was of, course, global communism. From the Soviet Union and China, through Ethiopia under Colonel Mengistu, Cambodia under the Khmer Rouge and a host of others, the death toll runs into the high tens of millions.[4] That was how radicals behaved where they got into power. Where they did not, a very high proportion of them in the West either openly championed such tyranny or sought to downplay it, deny its existence or to excuse it by dissembling.[5] By a very wide margin, the most oppressive regime on the planet today is communist North Korea. The regime in Pyong Yang is hardly under a barrage of criticism from a radical Left outraged at North Korean human rights abuses.

All this cannot be excused as a minor inconsistency, the kind of innocent hypocrisy or oversight that all of us, from time to time, are capable of. The stand-off between totalitarianism and democracy provided one of the greatest tests of moral and political character since the modern era began in the wake of the French and American revolutions. The part of the Left referred to in this section either sided with totalitarianism or refused to take sides under the ruse that there was nothing to choose between one side or the other. This, then, is clearly a systemic pathology. It speaks of a complete and thoroughgoing dismissal of freedom and human rights from the central features of the ideological world view. Of course, human rights arguments may be used for tactical and presentational reasons, but this does not mean that the rest of us should take them seriously. From any fair and reasonable analysis, the idea that radicals, communists and their fellow travellers derive their hostility to Israel from a general concern for human rights is manifestly ludicrous.

So where does their hostility come from? If it is not human rights what is it? One argument that sometimes drops into this discussion is that virulent hostility to Israel on the radical Left can at least partly be understood as a legacy of Soviet propaganda. It is true that the Soviet Union, especially in its later years, made great efforts to discredit the Jewish state. One of its most prominent instruments was the Anti-Zionist Committee of Soviet Public Opinion, formed in 1983. It was established primarily to blacken the name of Israel in order to counter the aspirations of many Soviet Jews to emigrate, but also to curry favour with anti-Western movements worldwide as well as with client and prospective client states in the Middle East.

I have some small personal experience of how they operated. As a student of Russian on a five-month study trip to Moscow I met and interviewed the First Vice-Chairman of the Committee, Samuel Zivs, in January 1989. Expounding on the similarities between Nazism and Zionism, Zivs handed me a booklet entitled *The Criminal Alliance of Zionism and Nazism*.[6] My notes from the meeting recorded that 'he specifically alleged that the only significant difference between Israeli policy towards the Palestinians on the West Bank, in Gaza and in south Lebanon, and Nazi extermination policy against the Jews was the slower rate at which Palestinians were being killed'. It is a trope that far Left circles have been propagating for years.

But as a general explanation for radical Left hostility to Israel, and even as an aid to understanding the genealogy of some of its most unpleasant modes of expression, the Soviet legacy is unconvincing. In the first place, by the 1970s and 1980s most communist, Marxist and far Left movements in western Europe were not in fact slavishly loyal to the dictates of Moscow. Indeed, many drew inspiration from Trotsky who could not even be mentioned in the Soviet Union until the end of the Gorbachev era. They would back Moscow over Washington, but the idea that, in the vast majority of cases, far Left Europeans were mere receptacles for the pronouncements of the Soviet propaganda machine is simply not true. Also, Soviet propaganda died with the Soviet Union and its empire. It stretches credulity to argue that two decades after the fall of the Berlin Wall the radical Left is still heavily influenced by a propaganda machine that has long since disappeared.

A more convincing explanation is to be found inside the key precepts of radical thinking and the way in which they have developed and mutated over time. This, rather than 'reds under the bed', is the key to understanding what is really going on.

Last stand of the totalitarians

It would be perfectly reasonable to write a history of the ideological Left framed in terms of a constant stream of retreats from positions once held with a passion akin to religious fanaticism. Quite apart from the moral and humanitarian catastrophe of global communism, the core ideological tenets of radical Left thinking have simply been refuted by experience. Nonetheless, it is still with us. The old, radical Left decorates the political landscape of Europe like a forest of dead trees. It is dried out, intellectually brittle, but unmistakably there. How can this be possible?

The most important point to understand is that while the positive side of the programme is gone – few but the most deluded believe there is the slightest chance of a revolutionary socialist agenda being taken up by any government anywhere in the West, and little chance of it having much success elsewhere either – the negative side of the programme still has traction. In other words, while it is difficult to subscribe to radical Left ideology in terms of what it has always *supported*, it remains quite possible to subscribe to it in terms of what it has always *opposed*. And what it has always, consistently, opposed is the liberal-democratic, capitalist system.

But merely to oppose capitalism in the form of airy, ideological gestures has never been enough. Opposition to capitalism has always gone hand in hand with a vehicle for change:

a force which can translate theory into practice. In Marx's famous words: 'The philosophers have merely sought to interpret the world; the point is to change it.'

In its classical incarnation the Western proletariat was designated as this vehicle for change. In its Leninist incarnation the proletariat was to be led by a vanguard party. By the 1960s, however, it was quite clear to many radicals that the Western proletariat was not going to be a force for change whether led by a vanguard party or not. The workers were happy, contented and clearly getting richer rather than poorer. Western capitalism was the patient that obstinately refused to die. From where could salvation be found?

A crisis inevitably ensued and it inaugurated a major shift in thinking. This shift would refocus attention on the revolutionary potential of Third World liberation movements as well as on discontented minorities back home in the manner most powerfully described by the German 'critical theorist' Herbert Marcuse, whose 1964 publication *One-Dimensional Man* became one of the most widely read books in its genre.[7] Anticolonialist writers such as Frantz Fanon, the French (Martinique-born) author of the much celebrated *The Wretched of the Earth* (1961), also become hugely influential.[8] If the Western proletariat could no longer be expected to upset the capitalist system perhaps others could. Enter groups like the PLO.

To repeat, the argument that the radical Left moved against Israel after 1967 because of concerns about human rights and occupation is not credible. The real reason for the move against Israel was because a general realignment at around the time of the 1967 war necessitated a reconfiguration of the ideology. Israel had become an enemy not because of anything it had done: anyone could see that the occupation of the West Bank had followed a war caused by Israel's enemies. Israel had become an enemy in the mind of the radical Left because it was now on the wrong side of the barricades.

In the famous 'Seven Points' of the main PLO faction Fatah in January 1969, point 7 showed an acute awareness of precisely what was going on and how to play on it. It said: 'The struggle of the Palestinian People, like that of the Vietnamese people and other peoples of Asia, Africa, and Latin America, is part of the historic process of the liberation of the oppressed peoples from colonialism and imperialism.'[9] The attempt to tie in the Palestinian cause with other anti-capitalist and anti-Western causes was thus quite explicit, and it was readily taken on board.

Tracing the post-war history of Leftist attitudes to Israel, Ben Cohen, a writer and analyst with the American Jewish Committee, has added some interesting insights. The Suez crisis of 1956, he has argued, 'was perhaps the last occasion where it was possible to oppose great power ambitions in the Middle East without denouncing Zionism at the same time'.[10] Insinuations that the West had fallen under the spell of Zionism, that Zionism was a facet of Western imperialism and that anti-Zionism represented an important platform in the struggle against imperialism still lacked resonance. As Cohen sees it: 'Israel had not yet been categorised, in the moral hierarchies of the Left, as an "oppressor" state,'[11] and, as importantly, the Palestinians had not yet established themselves as a coherent anti-colonialist force. Until the PLO was formed in 1964, the Palestinian cause had not yet entered the world of political 'praxis'. Once that moment had come, the shift in thinking could begin to take place.

Although the broad ideological shift represented something new on the Left in the sense in which it captured the spirit of the times, it did not in fact mark a complete departure from the orthodoxy. In an essay entitled 'The Magyar Struggle' on the national uprisings which shook parts of Europe in 1848, Friedrich Engels had written freely about how some nations and peoples should be seen as representing progress and others reaction, some representing 'the revolution', others 'the counter-revolution'. The nod of approval to genocide and the violence of the language in the cause of a pitiless Manicheism which extends beyond class to notions of race and nation are central. In the words of Engels:

... at the first victorious uprising of the French proletariat, which Louis Napoleon is striving with all his might to conjure up, the Austrian Germans and Magyars will be set free and wreak a bloody revenge on the Slav barbarians. The general war which will then break out will smash this Slav Sonderbund [separate or special alliance] and wipe out all these petty hidebound nations, down to their very names. The next world war will result in the disappearance from the face of the earth not only of *reactionary classes* and dynasties, but also of entire *reactionary peoples*. And that, too, is a step forward.[12] (My italics.)

The Jews had once filled an important role for the Left. Their suffering had provided ammunition for discrediting 'bourgeois society'. In the immediate post-war era, the Holocaust, seen through the lens of radical ideology as an extreme variation of the exploitative and oppressive potential latent in developed capitalism, had made Jewish causes, including the State of Israel, popular. To put it with brutal frankness, Jews, especially dead Jews, had been useful. They served the cause of 'progress'. Simultaneously, from 1945, the future founders of the State of Israel found themselves in conflict with the British Empire. They were an anti-colonial force to be reckoned with. By the end of the 1960s priorities had changed. Embodied in the State of Israel, the Jews had, to use the lexicon of Engels, become a 'reactionary people'.

If the reconfiguration of the ideology in the 1960s could be said to have represented phase one of the shift against Israel, a second phase, this one even more decisive for the radical Left, can be identified in response to the trauma associated with the West's victory in the Cold War two decades later. With communism gone, the Western proletariat having long been written off as a lost cause and most of the Third World liberation movements either defeated or now in government and them-selves embracing capitalism (even the ANC, for goodness sake) it seemed for a while that history, for the radical Left at least, had indeed come to an end. Underpinned by the United States, and in economic terms now even supported by China, cap-italism had gone global. The question posed in Lenin's famous 1902 pamphlet, 'What is to be done?' had no obvious answer. One could scour the globe in search of revolutionary potential and do so in vain.

To cut a long (and almost unbearably tedious) story short, a candidate was, of course, located in the form of militant Islam. As former Italian President Francesco Cossiga put it in a scath-ing attack on the country's ex-communist Foreign Minister Massimo D'Alema in 2006: '... most former communists like him believe that now that the myth of the Soviet Revolution is over the new myth may be represented by the Islamic revolu-tion.'[13] In 1979, the radical French philosopher Michel Foucault wrote glowingly about the return of Ayatollah Khomeini to Iran in an article in Italy's *Corriere della Sera* entitled 'A powder keg named Islam'.[14]

This 'Unholy Alliance', as David Horowitz has called it, between the radical Left and Islamism has struck many obser-vers as curious, to say the least.[15] How can people who have spent their lives campaigning in the West for the rights of women, homosexuals and ethnic minorities, let alone for secu-larism and pacifism, make common cause with some of the most violent religious bigots on the planet?

But there is no mystery at all here so long as one is prepared to see the radical Left for what it is rather than for what it has claimed to be. If Islamism's potential was not exactly revolu-tionary in the sense that there was anything in its positive agenda that resonated with radical Left thinking in the West, they were at least aligned in terms of what they opposed. There were obvious precedents. Communists and Nazis had joined forces under the Nazi–Soviet pact of 1939. Both opposed

Western capitalism. United by what they opposed, they found a way to cooperate.

Grotesquely and perversely, Islamism has provided plenty to get excited about. It was big enough and certainly ruthless enough to have a serious chance of making its presence felt, as the attacks on New York and Washington on September 11, 2001 showed for all to see. The prime target, the World Trade Center, was not merely a building packed with thousands of innocent people, though it was certainly that. It was a symbol of the West and of global capitalism. The attacks caused ripple effects around the world. Currency markets and equity markets crashed. The entire global banking system was temporarily plunged into crisis. The international transportation system briefly came to a near standstill with ramifications for both passengers and merchandise. The strategic thinking of the most powerful nation on earth was turned upside down. Since the end of the Cold War nothing and no one had come close to this. Many on the radical Left looked on it as a major defeat for America, and one that had been richly deserved.

The central point to understand is that in the absence of a positive platform, the radical Left's 'alliance' with Islamism is entirely logical. What matters is what is being opposed. As for Israel, the Jewish state not only stands right on the front line of the battle but it is also symbolic for Islamism of everything that it feels insulted by. Israel is capitalist. It is democratic. It is Western. And, it is in their face. To make common cause with the most effective possible opponents of Western capitalism and not to make common cause with virulent hostility to Israel would make no sense. For the radical Left, virulent hostility to Israel is now a political imperative.[16]

It should also now be clearer why there is such a large overlap here between opposition to Israel and anti-Americanism, an overlap which has been remarked upon widely. It exists on several levels. First, as has been suggested, Israel is on the front line of a global, anti-Western struggle with enormous ramifications for the radical Left. But Israel is not simply a microcosm of the United States, a representation in miniature of the US-led capitalist system. That also applies to Switzerland. Few on the radical Left are truly fired up with a burning hatred of the Swiss. Israel is more than a symbol. Like America, it is fighting the fight and fighting it across the most sensitive fault line in the modern world. Flowing from this, there is a second, unforgivable attribute of the Jewish state which also applies to America. It is a liberal-democratic capitalist country which has the audacity to defend itself.

But in the thinking of the radical Left, states which are illegitimate in the first place have no such right. They exist on sufferance against the day when, ultimately, they will be destroyed. The grievances of their opponents are always legitimate. This is why a section of the European and American population, driven by the radical Left, opposes *all* military campaigns pursued by Western democracies. From Bosnia and Kosovo to Afghanistan and Iraq, as well as a host of other cases, the use of force is always denounced. It makes no difference whether the cause could be described as just or unjust.[17] To the radical Left the nuances and fine distinctions involved in discussions along such lines are irrelevant. Western powers with their 'grubby imperial pasts', with their 'wealth built on slavery and exploitation', can never be right to go to war. There can be no just outcomes from unjust beginnings. Israel, denounced also as a colonialist enterprise reminiscent of the imperialism of the European past and the American present, can never be right in the manner of its self-defence. Islamism, the new, great ally in the struggle against the West, has declared that it has no right to exist. The Left has followed suit.

If Israel mounts air strikes against militants firing rockets it is, therefore, denounced. If Israeli soldiers go door to door to root out bomb makers, as in Jenin in 2002, it is denounced. If it targets terrorist leaders, it is denounced. If it builds a barrier to prevent suicide bombers crossing into Israel from the Palestinian territories using the most non-violent means possible, it is denounced. All attempts are denounced. Israel has no right to self-defence. It must simply sit back, and take whatever is coming. The Jewish state must go quietly into the night.

Radical chic

Aside from the content of radical Left hostility to Israel its most remarkable attribute is its style. That style is marked by a deep intensity, a searing contempt and a use of language which reflects a need to delegitimise the opponent completely. This, I believe, has led many observers to conclude that only anti-Semitism could really explain what lies beneath. But they are missing the point.

It is vital to recognise that this manner of talking about Israel is entirely in keeping with radical Left ideological traditions and is applied widely. The *totalitarian* mind requires a *total* delegitimisation of the opponent. In debate, there can be no room for an opponent with saving graces, whoever it is. The radical Left, the primary energising platform in the West for vehement hostility to Israel, does not do reasoned, nuanced criticism. It does hatred and demonisation. This is why radical Left politics has always been so intensely personal (and, one might add, so violent).[18] It is impossible to have gone to a west European university at more or less any time since the 1960s without seeing radical Left demonisation in action. One of its most familiar tactics involved the widespread employment of the word 'fascist'. Opponents could not be accepted as well-meaning people who simply had a different point of view. They had to be tarnished and thus rendered objects of hate by association with a form of politics which all decent people regard as abhorrent. Margaret Thatcher was, therefore, a 'fascist'. Ronald Reagan was a 'fascist'. George W. Bush was certainly a 'fascist'. The police were 'fascists'. Business leaders were 'fascists'. NATO was 'fascist'. Israel was 'fascist'. Every opponent was 'fascist'. It was a form of discourse participated in by millions.

In a book on the political journey from far Left radicalism of former German Foreign Minister Joschka Fischer, political analyst Paul Hockenos has described the way in which the radical Left of the 1960s and 1970s would work itself into a frenzy. Note in this brief extract, describing a gathering in 1972, the cult-like atmosphere, the regimented silence for the leader figure and, of course, the lexicon employed:

Hundreds of people crammed into the Frankfurt university's fabled lecture hall IV (the former location of Adorno's standing-room-only lectures) for a teach-in sponsored by the [Red Army Faction] support group, Red Aid. The crowd went silent when a reel-to-reel tape recorder was switched on. The high-pitched singsong voice of Ulrike Meinhof cast an eerie spell over the hall. She called upon all 'left wing comrades' to jettison their 'fear and hopelessness' and 'to stop hiding behind the masses.' She implored them to abandon their futile pacifism and to arm themselves in an international struggle against imperialism.[19]

And, Hockenos explained: 'The armed factions reduced the student movement's concerns to their crassest possible expression ... Indeed they claimed to be at war with the "fascist state".'[20]

This was totalitarian politics in action. Groups like the Red Army Faction clearly represented an extreme on the extremes. But their way of talking about the world was entirely typical of a radical Left discourse which captured the hearts and minds of a whole section of the European population.

As I have said before, many people looking at the European response to the Israel–Palestine conflict too often get bogged down in attempts to analyse seriously the accusations that Israel is an 'apartheid' state, an outpost of 'imperialism' or that it is 'fascist' or 'Nazi'. But once one understands the mindset from where these accusations in the West mainly originate there is really no mystery about what is going on. Once the radical Left has sunk its claws into an opponent, this is how it always talks about them. No Leftist called Margaret Thatcher a fascist because they seriously thought that Britain in the 1980s was going the way of Benito Mussolini's Italy. Nor did they expect anyone hearing the accusation to believe that. When Nobel Laureate José Saramago (see page 60), who is a communist, compares Israel to Nazi Germany he is not for one moment expecting anyone to think that Ehud Olmert, Ariel Sharon, Benjamin Netanyahu or any other Israeli leader is in any way comparable to Adolf Hitler. The same is true of accusations of Israeli 'apartheid'. To the radical Left, the accuracy of the content of these charges is irrelevant. What matters is the effectiveness of the terminology in leveraging disdain and contempt. The totalitarian mind is energised by the need to hate. The discourse, therefore, is hateful.

There are, as there always have been, sections of the Left which have been anti-Semitic because of allegations that Jews are associated with capitalist exploitation. But these have tended to be a small minority and have been outnumbered by others who have often been at the forefront of the campaign against anti-Semitism at least in its old incarnations. Nowadays, Jews *as individuals* are basically irrelevant to the radical Left unless they are anti-Zionist, in which case, as I have suggested, they perform an important propaganda function. Generally though, there is no leverage to be had from Jews in terms of the struggle against 'bourgeois society'. Jews have tended to do well in postwar Europe. They hardly represent a pool of seething discontent from which to draw recruits.[21]

In radical Left thinking these days there is also a marked tendency, conscious or unconscious, to downplay the centrality of Jewish suffering in the Holocaust, possibly due to the fact that Israel and its supporters are now routinely accused of exploiting it. While individual Jews are irrelevant, key episodes in Jewish history are an embarrassment. They get in the way of the business of the day. In August 2008, Britain's *Jewish Chronicle* ran a story about a petition circulated by the Socialist Workers Party, one of Europe's most influential remaining radical Leftist parties, against the far Right British National Party (BNP). According to the report, the petition said: 'The BNP deny the holocaust [sic] where thousands of LGBT [lesbian, gay, bisexual and transgender] people, trade unionists and disabled people were slaughtered.'[22] In the roll-call of the dead, one rather important group of Holocaust victims has been – how shall we put it? – forgotten.

The Liberal Left and Israel

This is all very well, it might be argued, but why, in a book which is concerned with thinking about Israel in the mainstream and which consciously avoids the easy targets on the fringes, has so much space been devoted to a radical Left which has now been pushed to the margins? Who in the twenty-first century really cares what a small band of neo-totalitarians thinks about Israel or, indeed, anything else? Part of the answer is that the radical Left may have been largely swept out of mainstream political parties but it still retains influential strongholds in academia, in charities, in trade unions, in left-wing newspapers, in mutated form in the anti-globalisation movement and in some sections of the environmentalist movement. Also, some of Europe's (and indeed America's) cultural and political icons are still energised by radical Left prejudices. For every Noam Chomsky in the United States there are a dozen equivalents in Europe. People listen to what they say.

But the more important response to such a question is that it is impossible to understand the Liberal Left, especially in its attitudes to Israel, unless one understands the radical Left ideological world view with which many among its number once associated or, in one form or another, flirted.

Half a transition

Many (possibly the majority) on the Liberal Left in Europe are political refugees from a radical Left homeland that has been left largely in ruins by the victorious armies of the Right. This truth is a brutal one for many on the Left. It may still take a generation or two before it has been fully internalised and events such as the 2008 financial crisis have served to rekindle hopes that all may not, after all, have been lost. It is also a truth which has occasioned much soul-searching and not a few attempts at self-justification for the sins of the past. Numerous books have been written on the subject, particularly about (and by) the so-called 'sixty-eighters' who embraced radicalism in the 1960s and 1970s but who subsequently wound their way towards the political centre. Paul Berman's sympathetic account, *Power and the Idealists*, is a celebrated example.[23]

The Liberal Left in Europe has indeed undertaken a radical shift in outlook, especially as far as its domestic agenda is concerned. But how complete has the transition really been? There are good reasons for thinking that many on the Liberal Left have emerged into the modern world contaminated with aspects of the radical Left agenda which have a profound impact on attitudes (and modes of expression) towards Israel. In a general sense, it is extraordinary how some of the old ways of thinking and talking have persisted. Consider an example from the most reformed Leftist party in western Europe, the British Labour Party which, since the days of Tony Blair, has tellingly billed itself as *New Labour*.

In February 2008, sixty-five Labour Members of Parliament signed a parliamentary motion praising the 'achievements' of former Cuban dictator Fidel Castro. The wording is pure radical Left. The motion argued:

That this House commends the achievements of Fidel Castro in securing first-class free healthcare and education provision for the people of Cuba despite the 44 year illegal US embargo of the Cuban economy; notes the great strides Cuba has taken during this period in many fields such as biotechnology and sport in both of which Cuba is a world leader; acknowledges the esteem in which Castro is held by the people and leaders of Africa, Asia and Latin America for leading the calls for emancipation of the world's poorest people from slavery, hunger and the denial of human rights such as the right to life, the right to shelter, the right to healthcare and basic medicines and the right to education; welcomes the EU statement that constructive engagement with Cuba at this time is the most responsible course of action; and calls upon the Government to respect Cuba's right to self-determination and resist the aggressive forces within the US Administration who are openly planning their own illegal transition in Cuba.

No mention of the thousands of people shot or otherwise done to death, the tens of thousands incarcerated and the millions who fled from his tyranny into exile. This cannot be dismissed as a rearguard action by a rump of radical Left renegades. In the same month no less a figure than the deputy leader of the Labour Party, Harriet Harman, spoke for many in describing Castro as a 'hero of the Left', while issuing the obligatory pro forma acknowledgement that it was time for Cuba 'to move on'.[24]

In moving on, people like Harriet Harman and millions of like-minded people across Europe on the Liberal Left carry with them a sense, if not quite of comradeship then at least of camaraderie with their radical Left predecessors. They do not usually allow themselves to believe that important parts of the past constitute something to be ashamed of. As the historian Martin Malia, looking across Europe, has put it:

The status of ex-Communist carries with it no stigma, even when unaccompanied by any expression of regret; past contact with Nazism, however, no matter how marginal or remote, confers an indelible stain. Thus Martin Heidegger and Paul de Man have been enduringly compromised and the substance of their thought tainted. By contrast, Louis Aragon, for years under Stalin the editor of the French Communist Party's literary magazine, in 1996 was published among the classics of the Pleiade; the press was lyrical in praise of his art, while virtually mute about his politics ... Likewise, the Stalinist poet and Nobel Laureate, Pablo Neruda, in the same year was sentimentalised, together with his cause, by an acclaimed film *Il Postino* – even though in 1939 as a Chilean diplomat in Spain he acted as a de facto agent of the Comintern, and in 1953 mourned Stalin with a fulsome ode. And this list of unparallel lives could be extended indefinitely.[25]

The previously mentioned Red Army Faction (also known as the Baader–Meinhof Gang), which murdered thirty-four people and wounded dozens of others from the early 1970s until 1993, is looked on by far too many Liberal Leftists in Germany with a certain fondness. The terror group is glamourised with T-shirts and badges. It is talked about by many on the German Liberal Left in terms of a group of mischievous and misguided idealists: they were wrong but their hearts were in the right place.

Even when people on the Liberal Left do not go so far as to express their admiration for communist dictatorships and terrorist groups, they sometimes cannot help themselves from slipping back into the old ways. They are susceptible to what could be called 'the totalitarian spasm'. This can be activated by anything from outrage at American foreign policy to the perceived excesses of financial markets.

In 2005, the chairman of Germany's Social Democratic Party Franz Müntefering famously railed against private equity firms and hedge funds as 'swarms of locusts'[26] in an outburst which would not have looked out of place in the far Left cells of 1970s German radicalism, or indeed in Stalin's Russia. It was the totalitarian rhetoric of dehumanisation. Müntefering's comments attracted widespread applause on the German and wider European Left. Modes of discourse and styles of looking at the world which some may have participated in for decades do not suddenly vanish without trace. Changing one's entire world view is not like a trip to the tailor's to replace an old suit with a new one.

There is no reason to suggest that the Liberal Left is some kind of wolf in sheep's clothing. But there is every reason to suggest that many among its number still retain a residual, emotional connection with the darker aspects of radical Left thinking.

There should be nothing so surprising in this. When one enters the political fray on one side or another one enters a political tradition. Even people on the Liberal Left who are too young to have had a radical Left past, who never had one in the first place, or who consider themselves fully modernised still may have a sense, often a profound one, that they are part of a Leftist tradition in which many different kinds of people have also shared. In France and Italy communists governed or joined in opposition with Liberal Left parties for decades after the end of World War II. Prior to that, 'popular front' groupings united broad spectrums of Left-leaning parties in alliances against the 'Right'. The sense in which they had all been 'in it together' is often very real, as is the nostalgia.

Crucially, it seems that the transition to a modernised, reformed Liberal Left among many opinion formers in Europe has focused on domestic items in the Leftist tradition over and above international agendas. Voters, whom opinion formers are trying to influence, are, in the main, notoriously unengaged in international affairs. The focus of attention for the vast majority of citizens in a given country is almost always domestic. The political transformation which saw the Liberal Left triumph over its radical Left rival was based primarily on an under-standing that Left-leaning political parties would find it increasingly hard to get into government by advocating eco-nomic policies that voters know will harm them.

No serious Left-leaning party is advocating nationalisation

of the means of production or five-year plans. Most are now aware of the dangers of rising unemployment inherent in over-regulated labour markets, though their populist instincts may sometimes get the better of them. The general drift everywhere has been towards liberalisation, deregulation and privatisation (the 2008 financial crisis notwithstanding). The opinion formers have largely followed in tandem.

However, it would be a great mistake to believe that this transformation has extended from the domestic into the inter-national arena where retention, perhaps in more muted form, of the old, traditional Leftist attitudes has been a relatively cost-free option. Hence the persistence of anti-Americanism which is heavily concentrated in Left-leaning parties, even as their domestic priorities are carried through in thrall to the basic precepts of the US-led capitalist system. Philosophically this is self-contradictory. But the contradiction can be borne because it is either not seen or not cared about by the vast bulk of the domestic audience. For ordinary voters, as long as Leftist parties are providing the goods in terms of reasonably strong econ-omies, the scribblings of anti-American opinion formers in the high-end newspapers or the casual anti-Americanism of socially privileged, Leftist elites in Paris, Brussels and London is neither here nor there. This remains, in other words, as a free pass for modern-day Liberal Leftists to locate themselves firmly inside Leftist traditions without alienating key supporters.

It is also vital to recognise that, despite the radical Left's defeat in important parts of the economic and even social domain, it can still draw on important elements of its tradition with justifiable pride. For there is no question that the primary driver in European post-war society for a more enlightened attitude to minorities, and in favour of an end to imperial domination, came from the Left. Anti-colonialism and anti-racism were quintessentially Leftist and Liberal causes. Often the battles were fought in the teeth of Conservative opposition and prejudice.

George Orwell, perhaps the most formidable and certainly the most celebrated writer in the democratic Leftist tradition, illustrated the point eloquently in his essay of 1936, 'Shooting an Elephant'. As a reluctant British police officer in imperial Lower Burma, Orwell recounts how he had been called to deal with a rampaging elephant that had already stamped a local – a 'coolie', in the racist lexicon of the time – to death. At the end of his essay, he recalls the discussions and the controversy that his shooting of the elephant had aroused:

'Among the Europeans opinion was divided,' he wrote. 'The older men said I was right, the younger men said it was a damn shame to shoot an elephant for killing a coolie, because an elephant was worth more than any damn Coringhee coolie.'[27]

There were plenty of racists on the Left and plenty of non-racists on the Right. But for much of the twentieth century there is no doubt about which political forces stood in favour of progress in this sphere and which opposed them.

Taking all this together, it is necessary to recognise that the Liberal Left, however modernised in its approach to domestic politics, is extremely susceptible to an alignment with radical Left thinking on an issue such as Israel which is billed as combining anti-racist, anti-colonialist, anti-apartheid, anti-capitalist and anti-American elements. It provides an affirmation that the left-wing tradition is real. It is a place they can go for a validation that not everything from the past was in vain. It helps them feel alive again, relocating them in a world free from the painful concessions and excruciating compromises that have characterised the modernisation of the Left since the end of the Cold War. It is related to anti-Americanism, but it is constructed out of a far more potent cocktail of ideas, prejudices and pathologies.

It is a cause which is also far more likely to yield results. There is, after all, little hope that the struggle against America can be won. Liberal Left anti-Americanism is more like a self-indulgent whine than a serious political platform. In terms of translating hostility into political outcomes, the case has little mileage. America is not going away. The same cannot necessarily be said for Israel whose predicament is far more precarious. There is a genuine real world struggle to attach oneself to. No one will accept boycotts of American universities or boycotts of the American economy. To boycott Israel is a different matter.

The Leftist anti-globalisation activist Naomi Klein has made the point explicitly. Calling for an anti-apartheid-style boycott of Israel in January 2009 she said: 'Why single out Israel when the US, Britain and other western countries do the same things in Iraq and Afghanistan? Boycott is not a dogma; it is a tactic. The reason the strategy should be tried is practical: in a country so small and trade-dependent, it could actually work.'[28]

Of all the shibboleths of the Left, hostility to Israel is proving the most tenacious. It is the last great refuge for a tradition in its death throes. To repackage the famous dictum of German sociologist August Bebel writing about anti-Semitism in the nineteenth century, it is 'the socialism of fools'. But for Liberal Leftists still clinging on to radical Left traditions – as opposed to their more enlightened colleagues who have ditched them – foolishness may be all that they have left. It is possible, indeed it is to be hoped, that much of this Liberal Left hostility to Israel is generational and that it will eventually peter out. If that happens, younger adherents, untainted by the past, could come through and make of the European Left what it always should have been – a socially active equivalent of the American Democratic Party. It remains to be seen.

As a codicil to this section, it is worth considering one final thought about Liberal Left ideological hostility to Israel. For there is something deep inside *secularist* 'progressive' thinking, in particular in Europe, which may go some way to explaining the kind of visceral disdain with which many on the Liberal Left relate to Israel and indeed Jews anywhere whose identity is wrapped around an affinity with the Jewish state. Writing in the *Church Times* in February 2009, Canon Giles Fraser argued: 'Like it or not, the very identity and existence of the State of Israel is bound up with Judaism. Israel makes no sense without the Hebrew scriptures. But, because a large part of the Left has so wedded itself to the belief that progress comes with secularisation, it cannot accept a religious explanation for anything; so it immediately thinks of it as a form of prejudice.'[29]

Perhaps the point needs to be made more tentatively since Leftists in Europe do not in fact adopt a contemptuous stance against all religious endeavours. Self-declared progressives are practically silent on the Islamic foundations of a whole host of countries around the world. They frequently support the introduction of sharia in European countries as an instance of 'multicultural diversity'.

Nonetheless, there appear to be different standards for 'non-white' religions as opposed to 'white religions'. Religion may be excused or overlooked if it forms part of the identity of an 'oppressed people' – particularly if, like Islam, it is seen to be mounting a challenge in one form or another to the West. The anti-religious dimension of Liberal Left progressive thinking is only unleashed as a tool for leveraging hostility to people, nations and projects who have already been designated as part of the 'reactionary' camp.

Hence the propensity to lampoon churchgoing (and white) former American President George W. Bush for his religious beliefs while remaining silent about churchgoing (and black) current American President Barack Obama and his religious beliefs. Hence the tendency to brush over the religious foundations of Islamist groups such as Hamas and Hezbollah while devoting vastly disproportionate attention to 'religious zealots' among the Israeli settlers, especially if they speak with an American accent. And hence the mocking tones in which Jews and Israelis are characterised when they offer biblical justification for the recreation of the Jewish state in Palestine. The lurid obsession of many on the Left with scriptural references to the Jews as the 'chosen people' is part and parcel of the same agenda.

It is possible that it is here precisely that anti-Semitism and anti-Zionism become conceptually indistinguishable for some incarnations of the secular progressive mindset. The deepest roots of Jewish identity are inextricably bound up with the Jewish religion even, via the cultural inheritance, for Jews who regard themselves as secular. When a political project such as Zionism – designated a 'reactionary' endeavour for other reasons as well – derives its ultimate justification from religious foundations, hostility towards it is redoubled. Secularist indignation adds a new and bitter twist to an already poisoned well.

The Old Right

The Left is not alone in the campaign against Israel. No serious observer of anti-Israeli sentiment in Europe and the wider West can be oblivious to the reality that Leftist hostility to the Jewish state is in important respects buttressed by sections of the Right. The inventory of anti-Israeli discourse provided in the first part of Chapter 1 offers examples from across the political spectrum.

As I suggested earlier in this chapter, traditionalist conservatives have largely been superseded in parties of the Right in Europe by a fully modernised form of right-wing thinking heavily influenced by liberalism and, to some degree, by neo-conservativism from the United States. The revolution in politics inaugurated by Margaret Thatcher in Britain in the 1980s captured this shift better than in any other country in western Europe. But in less flamboyant fashion new- or liberal-Right thinking has made deep inroads into political parties across the continent and, indeed, across the world. The liberal Right supports Israel for the equal but opposite reasons that the anti-Israeli Left opposes it. Israel is on the right side of their barricades just as it is on the wrong side of the Left's.

But why would traditionalist, *ancien régime* conservatives – well represented in establishment institutions such as foreign ministries, some parts of the media, academia and high culture – depart from their nominal bedfellows on the liberal Right over Israel? What is it in their ideological world view that matters here?

Latent old-style anti-Semitism may be part of it. France's Old Right, nationalist President Charles de Gaulle, for instance, famously described the Jews as an 'arrogant and domineering people'. The patrician former British Conservative Prime Minister Harold Macmillan once quipped that the number of Jews in Margaret Thatcher's cabinet made it appear 'more Old Estonian than old Etonian' – Eton being the exclusive private school at which so many in the old British Establishment had been educated; Estonia serving as a signpost for the east European ancestry of many British Jews.

This sense that the Jews represent a tendency to upset the natural order of things may, for some on the Old Right, morph into a belief that the Jewish state performs the same function globally. When the Old Right is asked to contemplate or engage with the Middle East its underlying assumptions fit far more comfortably with Arab realities than Israeli ones. The quasi-feudalistic features of many Arab states and the pre-modern cultures which are a facet (though not a totality) of all of them represent a remarkably good fit with Old Right nostalgia for a world long gone. Those who hanker for the days when rank and position in society were determined by family associations, when society was disciplined by deference, when political power was exercised for the people but not by the people, find in this region a congenial place of rest. The 'Arab tent' may not be as cosy as the country houses of Britain's Home Counties or the chateaux of the Loire Valley but inside its flannel walls its hosts offer more in the way of common values than could ever be hoped for from the 'arrivistes' of Tel Aviv. Sharing so much in common with the 'uncivilised' Americans,

and seen as an 'imposter' in a region governed by other traditions, the Jewish state has upset old world certainties. Arab
traditions satisfy Old Right nostalgia in a way that Israeli realities do not.

It is hard to make the point in anything other than impressionistic terms. But as I suggested in introducing this chapter,
there is a hint that both Old Right and Old Left hostility to
Israel is somehow related to a sense of loss. This, at least, they
have in common. In their different ways, the certainties that
they once clung to have been superseded. As with the radical
Left, the Old Right has much to feel resentful about. The
'natural order' has been upset, irrevocably destroyed even, by
upstart ideologies and the upstart nation *par excellence*, the
United States of America. The Pax Americana, though not
much of a 'pax', they grumble, has attempted to inaugurate a
new world order in which they are left shouting from the
sidelines even as the ground gives way beneath their feet. For
the Old Right, as for the Old Left, the certainties of the past
are gone. The spirit of deference has been replaced by the spirit
of enterprise and meritocracy and by elites which (or at least
claim to) embody such values.

But there is another important factor at play here which
complements this and gives it traction. The Old Right has
always been strongly motivated by a kind of realpolitik in its
understanding of international relations. This, perhaps, is why
it is still so well represented in foreign ministries where the
management and enhancement of power is usually the daily
reality. Unlike the radical Left, it is not idealistic in the sense
of having a grand ideological programme. Realpolitik is often
dressed up in the language of something more idealistic. European empires did have a sense of mission in terms of 'civilising'
what in the patronising terminology of the day were considered
'lesser' or 'barbarian' cultures. The 'civilising mission' was under-
scored in most cases by a sense that legitimacy derived from the
old certainties, from the old social and ethical mores, the old

structures and the traditions which gave them meaning. Nonetheless, it was also about power.

Realpolitik understood in its most basic incarnation will inevitably work against Israel because of the sheer number of countries opposed to the Jewish state on the international stage. It is not just numbers. Many of Israel's most vociferous opponents are rich in oil and gas (see Chapter 6). If the guiding paradigm is the exercise of power, it is obvious that a slant against Israel will make the management of diplomacy that much easier. The realpolitik tendencies inherent in (though not, of course, exclusive to) the Old Right work against Israel in themselves. When combined with its nostalgic tendencies, this creates a powerful dynamic pushing Europe's Old Right firmly in opposition to the Jewish state of Israel.

East European exceptionalism

This brief odyssey through the political mind of Europe would not be complete without a visit to the one part of the continent which exhibits very little in the way of hostility to Israel – formerly communist, central and eastern Europe. Having spent more than a decade living and working in the region, the fact that it represents a significant exception in terms of attitudes to Israel is something to which I can personally testify. Universities are not decorated with posters comparing Israel to apartheid South Africa. Trade unions do not occupy themselves with motions calling for boycotts. The anti-Israeli invective so common in western Europe is largely absent from the media. It is not that the Israel–Palestine conflict is ignored. It is rather that it is reported more or less as it should be: an objective reporting of the facts untainted by an ideological slant hostile to the Jewish state.

Why is the contrast with western Europe so stark? Again, an understanding of the main ideological currents goes a good way to providing an answer.

The most fundamental difference between the political cultures of central and eastern Europe and the political culture of western Europe is, as one might suspect, related to the direct experience of communist totalitarianism. The experience of communism has inevitably put the leading intellectuals and opinion formers on guard against fanatically authoritarian ideologies. Liberal democracy is viewed as a prize that has had to be fought for and one whose existence cannot be taken for granted. All the leading opinion formers are of an age when the revolutions against Soviet-imposed totalitarian rule were the most important and politically formative experience of their lives. The fact that Israel is a vibrant liberal democracy fighting against ideologies and regimes which are all, in their different ways, anti-democratic is something that is easy to relate to.

However, there is a more important consideration to bear in mind. If the direct experience of authoritarianism was enough to explain sympathy for (or at least an absence of hostility to) Israel, then we would expect to see a similar pattern in west European countries such as Spain and Greece which did not become democracies until the mid-1970s. (Spain was subject to a coup attempt as late as 1981.) In Spain and Greece the leading opinion formers are also mainly drawn from a generation for which the emergence of democracy was a formative, political experience. But on the question of Israel, we see no similarities in these countries with central and eastern Europe at all. On the contrary, the opinion-forming classes in both countries are among the most hostile to the Jewish state in all Europe.

It seems that what is much more important than the general experience of non-democratic rule *per se*, is the particular experience of *socialist* totalitarianism. For the most significant difference between the way in which political culture is configured in central and eastern Europe, from the way it is configured in the west of the continent, is that in the east radical Leftist ideology has been completely and thoroughly discredited. To be sure, there are opinion formers (and politicians) who are motivated

by Left-populism. There are also many social democrats. But
few carry with them any trace of the totalitarian thinking of the
past. Indeed, many social democrats in the region go to great
lengths to dismiss any association with communism at all. In
an ideological sense, and in the sense in which ideology affects
the opinion-forming classes, the Left in central and eastern
Europe is far more thoroughly de-Sovietised, far more completely disassociated from anti-capitalist sentiment, than its
counterpart in western Europe.[30] The ideological juice – primarily drawn from the radical Left but suffused in the Liberal
Left, too – which feeds anti-Israeli sentiment in western Europe
has dried up, evaporated. Most Leftists in central and eastern
Europe are simply committed to domestic causes such as
improving conditions for the low paid, raising pensions,
improving healthcare and education, and working for greater
social equality generally. Since these causes imply nothing whatever in terms of attitudes to the Israel–Palestine conflict, the
central and east European Left is far more reasoned in its
approach to it. Active or residual anti-capitalist sentiment is
absent or marginalised, a fact which explains why anti-Americanism is such a minority pursuit in the region as well.

When one looks at the condition of the Right in central and
eastern Europe there are also marked differences with the other
side of the continent. The complexities in this question are vast
and in generalising about an entire region there are obvious
dangers. However, it still seems that there are some generalisations which will hold up to scrutiny and which are relevant to this discussion. The first is that opinion formers leaning
to the Right (and this is the majority in central and eastern
Europe) came into the post-communist world with a disposition fully receptive to modernised right-wing thinking.
Neo-liberalism was the obvious strand of right-wing thinking
to adopt and it has a powerful presence in most right-wing
parties across the region, as well as among large sections of
academia and the media. The baggage of the Old Right had

been mostly lost during a communist period which lasted two generations.

True, after the fall of communism, there was a revival in some quarters of a Catholic-led Right (in Poland and Slovakia, for instance) which has often, though not always, been accompanied by populist-nationalism (as in Hungary, for example). But even this strand of thinking (which sometimes carries with it strains of anti-Semitism) has little in common with the Old Right in western Europe and it does not translate into any significant degree of hostility to Israel anyway. It is nostalgic to be sure. But its nostalgia is for a world far more distant (yet far more localised geographically) than the nineteenth- and early twentieth-century heyday of the Old Right in western Europe. It harks back to the settled village life of centuries past: a life dominated by family and church; a rustic ideal far removed from the modern-day 'evils' of promiscuity, abortion and rampant consumerism. Its nostalgia is not only different by time, it is also different by place. The Middle East has no real presence on its mental map. Indeed, the outside world plays little role in its thinking at all except in so far as it concerns threats from outsiders or, in some cases, emigration to America. The Jews in the Diaspora have certainly played a role in their past. But the State of Israel is remote from their thinking, as are the Arabs. In so far as anti-Semitism of the old east European Right could be said to play a role in attitudes to Israel, perversely it may be a positive one: far better that the Jews are there than here, they might think: 'there' is where they belong, as the Bible itself teaches us.

The differences on either side of the continent in terms of attitudes to Israel can sometimes lead to some astonishing intra-European misunderstandings, particularly on the part of indignant west Europeans convinced, as ever, that they are in a position to do the judging on this issue. During the Gaza conflict in January 2009, the Brussels correspondent of the Inter Press Service news service – which has correspondents and bureaus across Europe – penned a commentary lambasting support for Israel from the Czech Republic which, at the time, held the EU's rotating presidency. In a piece which descended into unintentional self-parody, the writer, David Cronin, scorned what he called 'Prague's patent bias towards Israel', adding: 'The Czechs' steadfast support for Israel sits uncomfortably with their apparently stout defence of human rights elsewhere.'[31] On the contrary, the Czechs' steadfast support for Israel is entirely in keeping with their stout defence of human rights elsewhere. History has taught the Czechs, and other central and east Europeans, important lessons about human rights and democracy. Appeasement and a failure to confront totalitarian movements can lead to a human rights catastrophe of the kind that Hamas and groups like it would certainly inaugurate if Israel gave them half a chance.

Czech support for Israel is testament to a broader truth about the formerly communist countries of central and eastern Europe as compared to their counterparts on the west of the continent: communism left them materially behind but, in important respects, their emergence from it left them conceptually ahead. The leading opinion formers emerged from communism far better intellectually and morally equipped to understand important civilisational issues than many who would seek to judge them in the West.

The final point to note about the ideological landscape of central and eastern Europe is that it provides an extraordinarily powerful refutation of the main counter-argument to much that has been said in this chapter, namely that the real ideological driver of hostility to Israel is a revived form of traditional anti-Semitism. If that argument held up, if anti-Semitic starting points led to anti-Israeli outcomes, we would expect to find a more pronounced anti-Israeli sentiment in the most traditionally anti-Semitic part of Europe. But as the case of central and eastern Europe shows, the relationship does not hold up. Opinion polls suggest a widespread persistence of anti-

Semitism in the region but do not suggest widespread hostility to Israel. A survey by Pew in spring 2008 found that 36 per cent of Poles had unfavourable views of Jews compared with just 9 per cent of Britons.[32] Yet Poland exhibits some of the most pro-Israeli sentiment in Europe while Britain exhibits the opposite.

If the related argument that hostility to Israel is in part driven by a need to exculpate collaboration with the Nazis in the Holocaust – by vastly exaggerating Israeli wrongdoing – holds up, we would similarly expect to find particularly strong evidence of anti-Israeli hostility in the parts of Europe where the Holocaust actually took place. While there is some evidence that this may be at play in German public opinion (see pp. 91–92), there is little evidence supporting it in central and eastern Europe.

In a final effort to save the argument about a direct relationship between traditional anti-Semitism and hatred of Israel, many proponents resort to intimations that it does exist but at some deep psychological level which cannot be precisely located. Perhaps there is a kind of Jungian archetype which, when one strips out all real-world phenomena, reveals itself as the core explanatory wellspring of hostility to meritocratic and 'rootless' modernity. Perhaps this then translates in some way into a hostility to the Jews and Israel (as well as to the United States). Perhaps. It seems an interesting line of enquiry. But in the absence of evidence it must be considered less convincing than the arguments from political ideology outlined above.

American cousins

At the very beginning of this chapter a curiosity was alluded to in that the American Left and the west European Left have radically different attitudes to Israel. Of course, there is deep hostility to Israel in the Chomskyite far Left in the United States and the reasons for its hostility are the same as with the far Left in Europe. But the far Left in the United States has always been much more marginalised than it has in Europe. The concept of communist parties in government in the United States is more the stuff of fiction and sardonic humour than of political realities. The far Left has a presence in some of the universities and it has an important tradition in some of the major cities.

But the mainstream political Left associated with the Democratic Party is very different. Broadly speaking, the reasons for the absence of hostility to Israel on the mainstream American Left are similar to the reasons for the absence of such hostility on the mainstream Left in central and eastern Europe. Neither is located in a tradition which is *essentially* anti-capitalist. American Democrats (at least those who make it to Congress) carry little if any baggage from previous generations of far Left thinking. Democrats have, in the main, occupied a place just to the Left of a centre-ground which itself has always been well to the right of the centre-ground in Europe. Unlike most Leftist parties in Europe there is practically no significant political ancestry in the socialist tradition. Instead of socialism, American Democrats have tended to draw ideological inspiration from an activist liberalism which seeks to use the power of the state in a slightly more welfarist direction than its great Republican rival while remaining committed to the classical liberal traditions embodied in the American Constitution.

Democrats are not, of course, anti-American and see no problem in their country's near hegemonic international role. On the contrary, though they would express it differently from Republicans, they are usually committed to a sense of America's destiny as a force for good in the world. Their attitudes to the use of military power, though muted temporarily by the experience of Iraq, are different from the attitudes of the European Left. American Democrats are not fired up by a virulent hostility to Israel because their vision is simply not clouded by ideological pathologies which run riot in western Europe. It is a healthy, principled and reasoned stance reflective of broad-based support for Israel across the American mainstream.

That, of course, is the situation we have become used to describing. But some recent developments have raised questions about its durability. It is to a discussion of that question that we now turn.

CHAPTER 8

Contagion: Is America next?

The election of Barack Obama in November 2008 and his
subsequent inauguration in January 2009 inevitably raised questions about America's commitment to the State of Israel. This
was more than the usual trepidation among Israel's supporters
that political change at the helm of the Jewish state's closest
ally might mark a step into the unknown. Obama had run on a
platform of 'change' – the leitmotif of his campaign. He looked
different; he sounded different; he promised to *be* different. His
every word and personal association was preyed upon for clues
as to what that might mean.[1]

Sober observers suspected from the outset that beneath the
bluster from supporters and opponents alike, there would probably be far more continuity to the Obama presidency than some
had hoped for and others had feared, especially in foreign
policy. It did not take long for signs of such continuity to show
themselves in the case of Israel. His first top-level nomination –
Rahm Emanuel, for White House Chief of Staff – was the son
of a Jerusalem-born former member of the Irgun, the Zionist
group which had fought for a Jewish state under the British
Mandate. Emanuel had even served as a civilian volunteer
supporting the Israeli military during the first Gulf War. It was
not just Rahm Emanuel. The anti-Israeli constituency had long
fretted about Obama's running mate for the vice-presidency,
Joe Biden, a non-Jew who had gone on record as describing
himself as a 'Zionist'.[2] Hillary Clinton, for Secretary of State,
had a track record of strong support for Israel and of implacable
opposition to Iran, Israel's greatest foe.[3]

Obama's team aside, between election and inauguration the Israeli conflict with Hamas erupted in the Gaza Strip, spewing molten lava across the world. The silence from Obama was deafening: a clear, though tacit, indication that the new American president would have no truck with the frenzied denunciations of the Jewish state emanating from Europe or anywhere else. It was an unlikely prospect in any case. A presidency might change overnight; a political culture does not. Even in Europe, as I have been at pains to show, hostility to Israel is nowhere near as striking at the peaks of the political landscape as in the subterranean caverns below.

But at some point, the tectonic movements of cultural change must inevitably push peaks, caverns and everything else together, rolling them forward in a tumbling mass which forges anew the look and feel of political life. This is why the opinion formers are so important and why the way they are drifting needs to be closely watched. Ultimately, they will make their presence felt. Hence the subject of this book. And hence the key questions animating the chapter at hand: could it happen in America? Is there a route map by which the virus of anti-Israeli prejudice might spread from important sections of the mainstream opinion-forming classes in Europe into the fringes of the discourse in the United States, and then up and out to the American mainstream?

At first sight, the fundamentals would suggest that it is unlikely. American political culture is made out of different stuff from its European counterpart. It is more profoundly democratic. It is possessed of a sense of destiny in which it is America's mission to protect fellow democracies in precisely Israel's predicament. It is unencumbered by the kind of post-imperial guilt which has made it so difficult for Europeans to take sides with a prosperous Western society in conflict with Third World despotisms. It respects, rather than disdains, the use of military force in defence of values which it holds dear.

America's ideological foundations make it much less susceptible to anti-Israeli influences and pathologies.

Its Muslim population is much smaller; its Jewish population somewhat larger; its Christian adherence immensely more significant. The American character, like Israel's, is national rather than post-national. Its historical beginnings and mythologies therein as a settler nation of persecuted refugees fleeing tyranny for freedom do not represent a precise fit with the Israeli experience, but there are sufficient similarities to promote a sense of kinship. These are the foundation stones of America's truly 'special relationship' with Israel and they will not be easily dislodged.

Unfortunately for Israel's supporters, however, there is more to say here. For one thing, the description above is replete with generalisations – reasonable generalisations, but generalisations nonetheless. For another, this is not the whole picture. America and Europe share much in common. America, lest anyone forget, was a creation of Europeans. It was formed in opposition to Europe but simultaneously, from ideas, legal traditions, peoples and a language which are European in origin. America and Europe cannot look at each other with equanimity. Each contains within itself, at least to some extent, the potential of the other. There are aspects of America in Europe and there are aspects of Europe in America.

Of course, too much has happened since the foundation of the American republic to talk seriously about anything more significant than partially overlapping identities. Europe will never become America and America will never become Europe, whatever anti-Americans in Europe and anti-Europeans in America may rave about. Still, the export and import of ideas and political agendas across the Atlantic remains a constant possibility.

For American attitudes to Israel, the greatest risk, perhaps, comes out of a widespread desire in post-Bush America to rebuild bridges around the world, to make America popular again. There is much to be admired in such a disposition. But there is also a risk of playing to a rogues' gallery in a world where hostility to Israel is worryingly widespread. As the second great pillar on which Western civilisation is constructed, Europe is well placed to exert renewed influence on America. A willingness to listen more closely to the discourse in Europe could easily translate into the absorption of some unedifying prejudices about Israel. Having defined American support for the Jewish state as one of the 'problem areas' in the transatlantic relationship, there may be a temptation for some to modify traditionally supportive positions.

Americans thinking along these lines will bring themselves into contact with the kinds of prevailing narratives discussed in this book. The risk is that they will start conceding ground to them in the search for a congenial middle way. The temptation to buy a little European goodwill by selling a little decency about Israel may be difficult to resist. It has certainly been difficult to resist for a Europe looking to shore up good relations with the Arabs.

If Israel can be portrayed as a liability to the United States this will impinge upon the nature of the relationship. It is not hard to find examples of influential American commentators who are talking and thinking broadly along such lines.[4]

As far as the risk of contagion is concerned, it is important to bear in mind that political culture these days is a less insulated affair than it once was. The extraordinary expansion in the last decade of the internet in general, and the move to online platforms in the mainstream media in particular, has meant that ordinary as well as elite level Americans are now much more prone to influences outside the United States than they were in the past. Since Europe is more or less comparable to the United States in terms of its economic and democratic development, its internet penetration levels, its educational levels and in terms of the way in which its media collates and then disseminates information it is in a particularly strong position to influence the American mind.[5] Britain, for obvious linguistic reasons as well as because of its deep traditions of top-class journalism, is already making inroads.

During certain periods in the Iraq War there was evidence that American readers turned to British sources in large numbers. According to one report on the subject in May 2007 the internet edition of the BBC was getting five million unique users in the United States per month at the time the data was collated.[6] The *Guardian* got 4.5 million and *The Times* 3.3 million. These numbers compare extraordinarily well to several leading American publications. The *Washington Post* was getting 5.5 million users, Fox News 5.8 million, *USA Today* 7.5 million, ABC News Digital 8 million and the *New York Times* 10 million. Other figures paint a less spectacular picture of British successes in the US market.[7] But the prospect that British and other European media may be starting to have an impact is real. Since two of the three British media organisations referred to – the BBC and the *Guardian* – are notorious for their anti-Israeli bias the notion that there is a risk of contagion by the method described cannot be dismissed as fanciful.

On a number of occasions I have stressed that there is nothing new about fiercely anti-Israeli polemicists plying their wares in the United States. The likes of Noam Chomsky, Norman Finkelstein, the late Edward Said and now his nephew, UCLA professor Saree Makdisi, have been doing a very efficient job of demonising the Jewish state in America all on their own. They have not needed help from Europe. In their writings and the writings of like-minded Americans all the same kinds of mantras that we see in Europe are present: a downgrading or denial of the core historical realities such as the fact of Jewish acceptance and Palestinian/Arab rejection of peace agreements all the way back to the beginning of the conflict;[8] a similar refusal to come to terms with the violence and bigotry inherent in Palestinian and Arab political culture as it relates to Israel and the Jews; ahistorical and anti-intellectual comparisons with apartheid South Africa; careless or malicious equations of Zionism with racism and colonialism; distortion and denial about Palestinian terrorism; and so on and so forth.

I have the suspicion that Israel's fiercest detractors in America are somewhat more enamoured than their European counterparts with the idea of destroying the Jewish state via the so-called 'one-state solution' – the suggestion that a bi-national state of Palestinians and Jews along the lines of Lebanon or Yugoslavia (extraordinary as it may sound[9]) would be a better idea than a Jewish state and a Palestinian state living side by side. European hostility towards Israel tends to be more nihilistic – it tends to denigrate and demonise without offering up the pretence of a 'solution'. The 'one-state' idea seems to crop up with alarming regularity in the United States. Or so, at least, it seems to me. Nonetheless, the broad aims and the central elements of the discourse are the same and they often proceed from similar ideological starting points.

As I have also said before, though, what has really tended to distinguish the United States from Europe is that the likes of Chomsky, Said et al. have never quite been able to make serious inroads in mainstream society. Certainly they have acquired a following. Certainly they have had their commentaries published in top newspapers. Certainly their writings are on display (and sell well) in major bookstores. They have captured territory inside the Left-leaning humanities departments of several leading American universities where one Palestinian moderate has wryly observed that there sometimes appears to be more support for Hamas than in the Palestinian territories.[10] But despite all this, their thinking has remained marginal in the sphere of high politics and in wider civil society. Democrats and Republicans in Congress, in the overwhelming majority of cases, have not been swayed by them. Religious leaders, mostly, and trade unions have found little mileage in currying support via Israel bashing. Public opinion remains consistently supportive of the Jewish state with polls, more or less regardless of the precise nature of the question posed, showing much stronger support among ordinary Americans for Israel than for the Palestinians and the wider Arab community. Even though the anti-Israeli polemicists have broken through in the top media outlets from time to time, in comparison with the situation in Europe their relative influence is tiny.

That, at least, is how things have always seemed. In more recent times there has been a great deal of concern expressed by American supporters of a reasoned and honourable approach to Israel and the Middle East that the mainstream may now be under threat.

One study from the (admittedly pro-Israeli) Committee for the Accuracy of Middle East Reporting in America (CAMERA) surveying op-eds in three of America's leading newspapers – the *New York Times*, the *Washington Post* and the *Los Angeles Times* – suggested that anti-Israeli voices were now outweighing pro-Israeli voices, at least in terms of guest columnists.[11] The survey, conducted over a nineteen-month period from January 2006 to July 2007, found that in articles dealing directly with the Israel–Palestine conflict 55 per cent either pushed a pro-Arab or anti-Israeli perspective. By comparison, 27 per cent were deemed supportive of Israel or critical of the Arabs, with 19 per cent deemed neutral. Since the survey looked only at guest writers and not staff columnists this does not mean that the three newspapers can be accused of holding an anti-Israeli bias. One of the purposes of having guest columnists is to provide readers with perspectives that are not shared by regular columnists. If the staff writers are, in the main, pro-Israeli, the survey may in fact show that the top American newspapers are being scrupulously fair, upholding the entirely honourable journalistic tradition of presenting their readers with a balanced range of opinions and allowing them to make up their own minds. However one reads the data, one thing is for sure: the notion put about by Chomsky and Co. that America is a land in which consent in support of Israel has been manufactured by a supine media is demonstrably false.

The main concerns in recent years have largely centred on the writings of former US President Jimmy Carter, and professors John J. Mearsheimer, of the University of Chicago, and Stephen M. Walt, of the John F. Kennedy School of Government at Harvard. The concerns have been raised precisely because these are not marginal figures. They are respected participants in mainstream political society.

President Carter's book, *Palestine: Peace not Apartheid*, as well as *The Israel Lobby and U.S. Foreign Policy*, the book jointly written by Mearsheimer and Walt, have not fared well at the hands of the critics, and that is an understatement. The demolition job on Mearsheimer and Walt conducted by Walter Russell Mead in an article in *Foreign Affairs* in 2007 is so devastating as to have rendered their book's essential content null and void as a would-be contribution to serious debate.[12] Abraham H. Foxman, director of the Anti-Defamation League, has also, to quote another example, written a blistering critique – *The Deadliest Lies* – focusing on both books.[13]

I do not intend to re-publicise the arguments of Carter or Mearsheimer and Walt in any detail. But I will allow just one instance from each as illustrations of the mindset we are dealing with, and to show how such mainstream players exhibit in their writings the same kind of subterfuge as their European equivalents.

First, Jimmy Carter. In attempting to justify the use of the word 'apartheid' in the title of his book, Carter gave the following explanation in an interview with the online bookseller Amazon.com in January 2007: 'Forced segregation in the West Bank and terrible oppression of the Palestinians create a situation accurately described by the word,' he said. 'I made it plain in the text that this abuse is not based on racism, but on the desire of a minority of Israelis to confiscate and colonize Palestinian land.'[14]

I submit that anyone writing about international politics who can argue that the word 'apartheid' – which describes a system of racial segregation specifically created by white supremacists to subdue dark-skinned races viewed as inferior – can be appropriately used to describe a situation which that very same person, in the very same paragraph, admits 'is not based on racism' has thus discarded any claim to intellectual credibility. Carter must know what he is doing in using such an emotive word as 'apartheid'. And in using it he clearly places the emotional effect of the word above its true, analytically verifiable, content. It is demonisation pure and simple. Sadly, this is entirely indicative of the state of mind of the author and the lamentable quality of his thinking.

The one instance I will offer from Mearsheimer and Walt (an instance also quoted, though with slightly different emphasis, by Foxman) is equally unforgivable and equally indicative. Mearsheimer and Walt's primary aim is to show that an extraordinarily powerful Jewish lobby has effectively hijacked US foreign policy in order to support Israel at the expense of American interests. So as to make the case convincing, the authors need to show that the moral arguments (never mind the strategic arguments) for supporting Israel are worthless. As one among many 'proofs' of long-term Israeli mendacity towards the Palestinians, the authors draw on a quotation from Golda Meir, prime minister of Israel from 1969 to 1974, that has long been used and abused by the worst anti-Israeli propagandists. They write in their book: 'In the six decades since Israel was created, its leaders have repeatedly sought to deny the Palestinians' national ambitions. Prime Minister Golda Meir, for example, famously remarked that "there was no such thing as a Palestinian."'[15]

This is an astounding distortion of Meir's meaning made even worse by the fact that the distortion is revealed for what it is by more extensive elements from the same quotation that the authors decide to bury in the footnote: 'Meir also said,' Mearsheimer and Walt add in footnote 82 to chapter 3, 'it was not as though there was a Palestinian people in Palestine considering itself as a Palestinian people and we came and threw them out and took their country away from them. They did not exist."[16]

The point Meir is making, it emerges from the footnote, is perfectly respectable. She is simply referring to a fact that no serious historian could dispute: the Arabs who inhabited Palestine prior to the establishment of Israel did not have a completed sense of themselves as a distinctive national group separated from other Arabs in the region, imbued with a clear sense of *Palestinian national identity* and seeking statehood on that basis. The leaders of Arab states at the time would have been in complete agreement. And no one could dispute her associated remark that no Palestinian state had ever existed. There is a general point here about national consciousness which could be applied to about a half dozen European national groups inside the Habsburg Empire in the nineteenth and early twentieth centuries. Indeed, it could be applied to Zionism itself. National consciousness is not something one buys out of a catalogue. It is something which matures, something which is nurtured and fought for, something which develops in response to events. Palestinian nationalism grew in such a manner. It did not exist in completed form at the time that the Jews were pushing for the establishment of Israel. Indeed, many respected historians have argued that it took some time after that before it did.

But to see just how misleading Mearsheimer and Walt are in their writing, let us return to the body of the text. It begins with an outright falsehood which is then 'proved' by an outright distortion. The falsehood is that Israel has denied Palestinian national ambitions for six decades. This, of course, is factually incorrect. Jewish leaders accepted the United Nations proposal in 1947 and the proposals brokered by Bill Clinton. The Palestinians flatly rejected these offers. And this is to name but two clear instances where Israel showed itself willing to accept a Palestinian state.[17] (It also stands in complete contrast to the reality that it is Palestinian and Arab rejectionism of Israel's right to exist as a Jewish state that has formed the core of the conflict since it began.) The partial quotation from Golda Meir, ripped out of context in order to 'prove' the false assertion that precedes it, then appears as a statement of Israel's deep-seated perfidy: no point talking about Palestinian human rights, they want to imply, the dastardly Israelis haven't even been ready to recognise the Palestinians as a people!

The mind boggles at how academics holding decent positions at top universities can bring themselves to behave in such a manner. It is not as though it could possibly have been a simple mistake. Their own footnote proves the case against their own argument.

As Benny Morris, whose writings they quote (much to his disgust), put it in response to the wider content of their book: 'Their work is riddled with shoddiness. Were "The Israel Lobby and U.S. Foreign Policy" an actual person, I would have to say that he did not have a single honest bone in his body.'[18]

What is more important for the purposes of this argument is that these books provide evidence that the same sort of utterly degraded writing about Israel as is now so commonplace in Europe has made inroads of a kind in the American mainstream.

Of course, this is not the same thing as saying that the likes of Mearsheimer and Walt or Jimmy Carter have written in the way that they have because of what they have read from Europe. As I wrote in the introduction, it may not be a coincidence that the essential content of Mearsheimer and Walt's book first appeared as an essay in the *London Review of Books*. But the writers will still have been influenced by a multiplicity of different factors and there is no evidence that the state of affairs in Europe is first among them.

There is, though, one case in recent years which does in fact provide clear evidence that the notion of a contagion effect from

Europe is more than speculative, and it shows precisely how it can work in practice. In Chapter 6, I referred to a letter from fifty-two retired senior British diplomats lambasting Tony Blair for endorsing the pro-Israeli policies of George W. Bush. Blair ignored the letter which simply repeated a set of easily refuted anti-Israeli clichés. However, a whole slew of respected senior American diplomats – several of them former ambassadors to Arab countries – had obviously been following events in Britain closely. They penned a letter of their own, to President Bush.[19] The sixty signatories made it quite clear that they had drawn their inspiration from the open letter written to Blair:

'We former U.S. diplomats applaud our 52 British counterparts who recently sent a letter to Prime Minister Tony Blair criticizing his Middle East policy ...', they said in their first sentence. If anything, their tone was even more hostile to Israel, showing once again that, when given an appropriate opportunity, Americans can compete with the worst of them in demonising Israel. At one point the letter referred to 'Israel's Berlin Wall-like barrier', an allusion to the highly effective security barrier which was put up in response to hundreds of Palestinian suicide bombings against Israeli civilians emanating from the West Bank.

It is a forlorn and wrenching statement on the anti-Israeli mind made all the worse by the sheer casualness and carelessness of its inhumanity. These are men and women of high rank and education whose craft is centrally concerned with precision in the use of words. They refer to the Berlin Wall, a wall that was erected to stop the oppressed citizens of a totalitarian state from fleeing to freedom in the West. They say that a security barrier put up by Israel to stop suicide bombing and slaughter is analogous to that. Are they saying that communist East Germany put up a wall in order to prevent people from strapping themselves up with Semtex, loading themselves up with ball bearings and nails, and walking into cafés and bars in order to blow part innocent men, women and children apart? Are they saying that

that was why the Berlin Wall was put up? Or if it is not that, are they suggesting that Israel is like a communist, totalitarian state so hated by its own people that it has found it necessary to build a barrier to stop its citizens from fleeing to freedom and prosperity in Nablus and Ramallah? Is that why they believe Israel's security barrier was put up?

In writing a letter to their president not a single one of them, out of sixty, could see the grossness of the error they were making. Any stick will do, it seems. This is a sickness, and, *no*, America is not immune.

CONCLUSION

Something has clearly gone wrong when it has become increasingly difficult to tell the difference between some of the language, tone and content of mainstream commentary on Israel in Europe from the daily polemic against the Jewish state in the Arab and Muslim world.[1]

Who does the anti-Israeli constituency really think is benefiting from all this? Even if one takes a generous view of their motivations (and I think there are good reasons for not doing so in most cases) what could possess anyone to believe that the hysterical tones in which the case against Israel is now being made could offer the slightest benefit to the Palestinians? I don't just mean that there is something deeply perverse about middle-class Westerners feeding and validating the very culture of denial, demonisation and victimhood in the Palestinian and Arab world which has always been the Palestinians' core problem. I mean, even when Israel deserves censure, even when there are good grounds for protesting at Israeli behaviour, isn't it blindingly obvious that the use of ridiculous and defamatory analogies with Nazism or apartheid, the repetition of entirely distorted renditions of the historical context, and the making of casual and reflexive denunciations of criminality gives Israel a free pass to ignore *all* criticisms, including the reasonable ones? Which school of political campaigning did these people go to?

But as I have suggested on a number of occasions, an appeal to reason may miss the point. Whatever it touches, the anti-Israeli agenda always brings out the worst. It brings out the worst in journalists who cast aside their principles of balance and objectivity. It brings out the worst in seasoned commentators who substitute hysteria and foot stamping for calm analysis and enlightened discussion. It brings out the worst in trade unions which put a hateful agenda above the interests of their members. It brings out the worst in diplomats who debase themselves by pandering to tyrannies against a democracy. It brings out the worst in artists and writers who submerge their commitment to beauty and truth in ugliness and lies. It brings out the worst in the great traditions of Left and Right which default back to their shabbiest instincts and their darkest prejudices.

The sickness here is civilisational. It reflects and draws upon the worst and the weakest in Western political culture: its lack of self-belief, its ideological pathologies, its historical traumas, its relativism, its tendency to appease. It has rekindled an old problem which has sometimes appeared in traditional garb but more usually in a fully modernised, neo-anti-Semitic form in denigrating the most important Jewish project of our time. America, as I have said, is not immune.

There is nothing remotely challenging in establishing that the overwhelming majority of the charges made against the Jewish state are either outright falsehoods or are decontextualised to such an extent that they are manifestly made in bad faith. No one of any degree of seriousness could claim that liberal-democratic Israel's human rights record is worse than North Korea's, China's or Sudan's and that it therefore deserves the level of censure it attracts. There is not even the slightest shred of intellectual justification for charges that Israel is like Nazi Germany or apartheid South Africa. There is no reasonable case that Israel's foundational legitimacy is any less secure than that of a whole host of other countries around the world. No one who has read the history of the conflict could seriously make of Israel the prime culprit, let alone the only culprit. Nor yet, given the nature of the threats it faces and the political cultures which produce those threats, that Israel demonstrates a uniquely unreasonable stance in the manner of its self-defence.

As I have stressed on several occasions throughout this book, I do not believe there is convincing evidence that the root cause of the hostility to Israel is old-style anti-Semitism. Most of the people participating in hateful discourse against Israel did not start out in a frantic search for an outlet for their hatred of Jews only to find a place of rest on an anti-Israeli platform. In a sense, if the underlying problem really was a chauvinistic form of anti-Semitism it would be easier to deal with. Much to their credit, mainstream Western opinion formers will have no truck with brute racism these days. Presented with credible evidence that that was in fact what they were indulging in, most would quickly back down and take the lesson.

But this problem will not be resolved by such simple, didactic means. It is not just about taking and learning lessons. The anti-Israeli agenda has not taken such deep root in Europe due to a misunderstanding here or a gap in the knowledge there which could easily be rectified if only its practitioners knew a bit more history or were a little better informed about the contemporary context. That would help, but it would not solve the underlying problem.

The more one enters the world of the Israel-haters, the more obvious it becomes that it is a pathological condition, itself reflective of multi-layered pathologies inside it and constitutive of it. This touches on the character of modern Europe and its ability to deal with what the Israel–Palestine conflict throws up.

That is really what this book has been about. Too many Europeans labour under the illusion that they are doing the judging on this issue. They have got it the wrong way around. The Israel–Palestine conflict is judging Europe. It is testing its strengths and weaknesses. It is teasing it and scratching at its rawest wounds. It is cross-examining Europe before the court of history in a trial where witnesses to the character of the defendant are not at the moment presenting an uplifting picture.

I repeat that not everything about Europe's relationship with Israel is bad. In the sphere of high politics there is much to be applauded. It is when we turn to the opinion formers – the self-appointed guardians of Europe's conscience, the architects of its metaphors, the workmen of its guiding narratives – it is here that we run into problems. It is here that we enter an altogether darker world, haunted and tormented by the ghosts of Europe's past. The people who inhabit this world enfeeble Europe and cast doubt on its future.

For these are not just problems *of* Europe, they are problems *for* Europe. The pathologies inside Europe's character that have produced such a miserable response to Israel's predicament in the Middle East are precisely the same pathologies that undermine Europe's ability to perpetuate and reinvigorate its own civilisation back home. There is a pragmatic as well as a moral dimension to this. The meta-narrative, of which the anti-Israeli narrative is merely a part, is formed from creeping structural weaknesses in the political architecture. We saw that meta-narrative poking its way through in Europe's terrible mis-handling of the Yugoslav crisis of the 1990s. We have seen it in Europe's patchy responses to the war in Afghanistan. We have seen it in its dealings with a neo-authoritarian Russia. We have seen it in Europe's timorous manner of approaching extremism in its Muslim populations. In all of these cases most of the same underlying pathologies as we see in the response to Israel are at play. Often, the self-same people are involved.

The moral dimension is closely related. The prevalence and persistence of the anti-Israeli agenda in Europe is a stain on its integrity. It impinges upon Europe's ability to be taken seriously. Cocooned in their own self-righteousness, large numbers of influential Europeans simply have no idea of the damage that is being done to Europe's reputation. Contempt in Europe for Israel will be repaid by contempt among the civilised for Europe. There are a hundred reasons for Europe to clean up its act on

Israel. Self-preservation and self-respect are just two of them.

Ultimately then, it is not Israel that is the state beyond the pale. Europe is putting *itself* beyond the pale as the forces of reason and decency cede ever more ground to an edifice of hatred and lies. It is not over yet. There is still much to play for. As Dore Gold, Israel's former ambassador to the United Nations, once put it: ' ... the struggle for Europe's soul is still an open one.'[2] And so it is. But it won't remain open forever.

Jerusalem and London, 2008 and 2009

NOTES

Introduction

1. The reference is to the title of Andrei S. Markovits's book, *Uncouth Nation: Why Europe Dislikes America*, Princeton University Press, Princeton, 2007.
2. *David Ben-Gurion – a Brief Biography & Quotes*, posted 23 October 2001. http://www.palestineremembered.com/Acre/ Famous-Zionist-Quotes/Story638.html
3. Ibid.
4. Quoted in Sarah Honig, 'Fiendish hypocrisy II – the man from Klopstock St.', *Jerusalem Post*, 6 April 2001. Also quoted in Alan Dershowitz, *The Case for Israel*, John Wiley & Sons, Hoboken, 2003, p. 55.
5. For an account of Robert Malley's views on the negotiations see his essay written jointly with Hussein Agha: 'Camp David: The Tragedy of Errors', in the *New York Review of Books*, vol. 48, no. 13, 9 August 2001.
6. 'Camp David: An Exchange'. Letter by Dennis Ross to the editor of the *New York Review of Books*, vol. 48, no. 14, 20 September 2001.
7. Quoted by Daniel Pipes in 'Accept Israel as the Jewish state?' *Jerusalem Post*, 29 November 2007.
8. Ibid.
9. Ibid.
10. Ibid.
11. There are many examples of this. For one, see Wafa Amr, Ahmed Qurie in 'INTERVIEW – Palestinian PM says two-

state solution in danger', Reuters, 8 January 2004.

12. Khartoum Resolution, 1 September 1967, paragraph 3.

13. Eugene V. Rostow, 'The Illegality of the Arab Attack on Israel of October 6, 1973', *American Journal of International Law*, vol. 69, 1975, pp. 283–4.

14. Lord Caradon, interviewed on Kol Israel in February 1973, http://www.icaj.nl/nieuws/vn242.htm + http://www.camera.org/index.asp?x_context=2&x_outlet=118&x_article=1267

15. Yossi Klein Halevi, 'Fenced In', *The New Republic Online*, 30 October 2003.

16. See, for example, Ilan Pappé, *The Ethnic Cleansing of Palestine*, Oneworld Publications, Oxford, 2006.

17. UN General Assembly Resolution 194, paragraph 11.

18. Editorial: 'Israel's EU upgrade', *Jerusalem Post*, 19 June 2008.

19. See, for example, Aron Heller, 'Jewish leaders: Nazi imagery incites violence', Associated Press, 20 January 2009.

20. Ibid. The Dutch lawmaker in question was reported as saying that he himself did not join in that particular chant.

21. Some surveys show a decline in feelings of support for Israel from younger Jews. See http://www.ynetnews.com/articles/0,7340,L-3446492,00.html

22. Michael Oren, *Zohan and the Quest for Jewish Utopia*, *Azureonline*, Autumn 2008, no. 34.

23. There is evidence that some black slave owners bought their relatives to free them from bondage. That did not diminish their propaganda value to racists.

24. Bernard Lewis, 'The New Anti-Semitism', *The American Scholar*, vol. 75, no. 1, Winter 2006, pp. 25–36. Available online at http://www.zionism-israel.com/log/archives/00000008.html

25. Fascist or extreme single-issue movements may closely approximate to it but, unlike the radical Left, they are not welcome in mainstream circles.

26. Bernard Harrison, *The Resurgence of Anti-Semitism*, Rowman & Littlefield, Plymouth, 2006.

27. Alan Dershowitz, *The Case for Israel*, John Wiley & Sons, Hoboken, 2003.

28. Neill Lochery, *Why Blame Israel?*, Icon Books, Cambridge, 2005.

Chapter 1

1. Markovits, op. cit., pp. 152–7.

2. The way of talking about Israel in Germany, still heavily influenced by post-Holocaust guilt, is not *identical* to the way of talking about Israel in Britain, the post-imperial power whose Mandate under the League of Nations provided the backdrop for the creation of the Jewish state. But what is truly remarkable about the discourse on Israel in western Europe is how the same old tropes are repeated again and again more or less regardless of whether the country in question could be called 'Nordic', 'Anglo-Saxon', 'Latin', 'Francophone', 'Germanic' or whatever. There are good reasons for this which I attempt to explain in terms of west European political ideologies and the ways in which Europe sought to reinvent itself after the catastrophe of World War II.

3. In some cases, the sense in which the type of discourse described is problematic will, for most readers, be obvious. The first two or three subsections contain material which is frankly disturbing. Others are not so clear-cut. Still others may contain commentary that is in fact reasonable. There are also questions about tone and emphasis which cannot easily be answered when presented with words and phrases conveyed in written rather than verbal form.

4. Johann Hari, 'Israel is suppressing a secret it must face', *Independent*, 28 April 2008.

5. This was originally quoted by Barbara Amiel, Conrad Black's wife.

6. Deborah Orr, 'I'm fed up being called an anti-Semite', *Independent*, 21 December 2001.

7. 'Nobel peace laureate compares Israel to Nazi Germany', Associated Press, 19 December 2004.

8. 'German Bishops Rile Holocaust Memorial', Associated Press, 10 March 2007.

9. Ibid.

10. 'Finnish minister stands by criticism of Israel', Reuters, 31 August. In his subsequent words of clarification the minister was quoted in the article as saying: 'I have recognised that these are very, very sensitive issues, and obviously one should be more careful about wordings which either unintentionally, but sometimes even intentionally, are misrepresented and create a false impression. For that I am sorry.'

11. 'Norwegian envoy: Israel, Nazis the same', Etgar Lefkovits, *Jerusalem Post*, 21 January 2009.

12. 'British MP: Israel exploits guilt over Holocaust to murder Palestinians', *Jerusalem Post*, 15 January 2009. (The report was sourced to the Associated Press.)

13. Ibid.

14. Tom Gross, 'The media aims its missiles', *Jerusalem Post*, 3 August 2006.

15. Manfred Gerstenfeld, 'Calling Jews, Nazis', *Jerusalem Post*, 19 April 2004.

16. Tom Paulin poem, 'Killed in Crossfire, *Observer*, 18 February 2001. © Faber and Faber Ltd.

17. See the cartoon at the following link:
http://www.adl.org/Anti_semitism/arab/cartoon_072202.asp

18. 'Gaza resembles concentration camp', *Jerusalem Post*, 8 January 2009.

19. Ibid.

20. Jihad El-Khazen, 'The Pope should not visit a Nazi nation', *Dar Al Hayat*, 13 January 2009.

21. Quoted in 'Jewish group slams Irish politician's Goebbels jibe', Agence France-Presse, 19 January 2009.

22. 'Swedish city cancels Holocaust event', *Jerusalem Post*, 27 January 2009.

23. Philip French, 'When brothers in arms went on the warpath: Philip French says that a film about Jewish guerrillas sends out a very mixed message', *Observer*, 11 January 2009.

24. 'Author Saramago sets off storm by comparing blockaded Palestinian town to Nazi death camp', Associated Press, 26

March 2002. Saramago said: 'What is happening in Palestine is a crime which we can put on the same plane as what happened at Auschwitz, at Buchenwald. Even taking into account the differences in time and place, it is the same thing.'

25. Quoted by Paul Berman, 'Bigotry in Print. Crowds Chant Murder. Something's Changed', *Forward*, 24 May 2002. This is Berman's translation from the original which appeared in the Spanish newspaper *El País*.

26. 'Boycott Israel in Davis Cup': Social Democrat, The Local – Sweden's News in English, 13 January 2009, http://www.thelocal.se/16874/20090113/

27. 'European Parliament member condemns racist Israeli policies', 23 July 2007, *ArabicNews.com* http://www.arabicnews.com/ansub/Daily/Day/070723/2007072309.html

28. Eamonn McCann, 'Gaza Horror: How many Palestinians have to die before world says stop', *Belfast Telegraph*, 15 January 2009.

29. Jonny Paul, 'UK charity warned about anti-Israel campaign', *Jerusalem Post*, 1 May 2008.

30. War on Want press release: 'Wall of death'. Retrieved on the War on Want website on 17 January 2009 at:
http://www.waronwant.org/Wall%20of%20death%20+4375.twl

31. Chris McGreal, 'Worlds apart', *Guardian*, 6 February 2006.

32. See Wiesenthal Center to European Parliament President: 'Apartheid Israel exhibit disqualifies EU role as partner in quartet peace initiative', Simon Wiesenthal Center, press release, 28 May 2003.

33. 'BACKGROUNDER on Professor Ilan Pappé: When Ideology Trumps Scholarship', Committee for Accuracy in Middle East Reporting in America (CAMERA), http://www.camera.org/index.asp?x_context=8&x_nameinnews=122&x_article=994

34. Eric Rouleau, 'The "ethnic cleansing" of Palestine; Israel faces up to its past', *Le Monde Diplomatique*, 1 May 2008.

35. Seumas Milne, 'Expulsion and dispossession can't be cause for celebration: the demand to make Palestinian rights a reality

is no longer simply a matter of justice but also of self-interest', *Guardian*, 15 May 2008.

36. Assaf Uni, 'Norway up in arms after author asserts Israel has lost right to exist', Haaretz.com, 12 August 2006.

37. 'Swedish church leaders and writers call for Israeli boycott', Agence France-Presse, 18 January 2003.

38. 'D'Alema accuses Israel again: "It's just a punitive expedition"', *La Stampa*, 13 January 2009.

39. Patrick Wintour and Matthew Taylor, 'MP loses job over suicide bomb claim', *Guardian*, 24 January 2004.

40. Ibid.

41. Leading article: 'Call yourself a liberal, Mr Kennedy?', *Independent*, 24 January 2004.

42. Ken Dilanian, 'In Europe, old anti-Semitism in a new stripe', *Philadelphia Inquirer*, 30 November 2003.

43. 'MEP says she feels like strangling Israel's ambassador', *European Jewish Press*, 30 April 2007, available at: http://www.ejpress.org/article/news/western_europe/16358

44. Quoted in Anna Pelegri Puig, 'Israel fights off war crimes charges in Gaza', Agence France-Presse, 20 January 2009.

45. 'UNISON urges Miliband to condemn Gaza "war crimes"', *Morning Star*, 4 March 2008.

46. 'Danish lawmaker wants Israeli foreign minister detained for investigation into war crimes charges', Associated Press, 28 August 2006.

47. 'Lebanon: Deliberate destruction or "collateral damage"? Israeli attacks on civilian infrastructure', Amnesty International, 23 August 2006.

48. Editorial: 'Gaza's misery has to be stopped', *Financial Times* (FT.com), 24 January 2008.

49. 'Switzerland: Israel Violating Intl Law In Gaza Offensive', Dow Jones News Wires, 3 July 2006.

50. 'Switzerland lambasts Israel over UN and hospital attacks', Agence France-Presse, 16 January 2009.

51. 'Gaza: Aid agencies call for suspension of enhanced EU–Israel agreements', Brussels, 7 January 2009. See the statement

at http://www.oxfam.org/en/pressroom/pressrelease/2009–01–07/gaza-aid-agencies-call-suspension-enhanced-eu-israel-agreements

52. Oxfam, press release, 9 July 2004.

53. 'France, Germany criticise Israel for Hamas leader's assassination', Agence France-Presse, 18 April 2004.

54. Robert Wielaard, 'EU nations condemn Israel for attack', Associated Press, 22 March 2004.

55. 'Presidency conclusions', Copenhagen European Council, 12 and 13 December 2002.

56. 'German minister calls Israeli offensive in Lebanon unacceptable', Agence France-Presse, 15 July 2006.

57. Quoted in 'Israel defends Gaza op to UN chief', *Jerusalem Post*, 28 January 2008.

58. 'Bombing Gaza is not a solution', FT.com, 28 December 2008.

59. 'Parliament calls for international observers to be sent to Gaza and for an international peace conference to be held', Agence Europe, 17 November 2006.

60. 'Euromed lawmakers group urges "immediate ceasefire" in Middle East conflict', Agence France-Presse, 9 August 2006.

61. 'EU says Israeli attacks in Lebanon, Gaza excessive', Reuters, 18 April 2001.

62. 'EU Presidency Statement on further escalation of violence in Gaza and Southern Israel', 2 March 2008.

63. Opinion: 'Merkel's Mideast Stance Ignores German-Arab Ties', Deutsche Welle, 9 August 2006.

64. 'Britain's Labour MP interviewed by Al-Jazeera on Iraq, Blair, BBC Monitoring Middle East, July 11', from Al-Jazeera TV, 9 July.

65. See Trevor Asserson's BBC watch at www.bbcwatch.co.uk; Tom Gross's www.tomgrossmedia.com, www.honestreporting.com, www.justjournalism.com, www.camera.org

66. Paul Taylor, 'INTERVIEW – Senior Saudi prince offers Israel peace vision', Reuters, 20 January 2008.

67. Pew Research Center, *Pew Global Attitudes Project: Spring 2006*

Survey. The Pew Global Attitudes Project bears no responsibility for the analyses or interpretations of the data presented here.

68. 'International Poll: No consensus on who was behind 9/11', WorldPublicOpinion.org, 10 September 2008.

69. MEMRI, Special Dispatch series, no. 2014.

70. MEMRI, Special Dispatch series, no. 1453.

71. MEMRI, Special Dispatch series, no. 1217.

72. MEMRI, clip 1972, broadcast 31 December 2008.

73. MEMRI, Special Report, no. 11.

74. Kate Clark, BBC correspondent in Cairo, 'Interpreting Egypt's anti-Semitic cartoons', BBC, http://news.bbc.co.uk/1/hi/world/middle_east/3136059.stm

75. MEMRI, Special Dispatch series, no. 2278.

76. See archived reports of anti-Semitism in the Arab world from the Anti-Defamation League at www.adl.org

77. See Palestinian Media Watch reports at www.pmw.org.il

78. Brian Whitaker, 'Selective Memri', guardian.co.uk, 12 August 2002.

79. The Hamas charter is available in translation at a number places. For example: http://www.mideastweb.org/hamas.htm

80. 'We Do Not Wish to Throw Them Into the Sea', *Washington Post*, 26 February 2006.

81. 'Who are Hamas?' http://news.bbc.co.uk/1/hi/world/middle_east/1654510.stm, posted 25 January 2007, retrieved 23 November 2008.

82. 'Hamas blames US "Jewish lobby" for financial crisis', Agence France-Presse, 7 October 2008.

83. MEMRI, Special Dispatch series, no. 1964.

84. See Craig Whitlock, 'Al-Qaeda Leader Uses Slur Against Obama in Web Video; Zawahiri Says Next President Has Proved to Be "House Negro"', *Washington Post*, 20 November 2008.

85. 'French media authority seeks penalties against Hezbollah-linked network', Associated Press, 7 December 2004.

86. Ibid.

87. Smadar Haran Kaiser, 'The World Should Know What He Did to My Family', *Washington Post*, 18 May 2003.

88. Ibid.

89. *Transatlantic Trends* surveys and archives are available at: www.transatlantictrends.org in several languages including English. The data was averaged out by the author.

90. 'Attitudes Towards Israel and the Palestinian-Israeli Conflict in Twelve European Countries', Anti-Defamation League, May 2005. The poll, whose results were averaged out by the author, is available online at: http://www.adl.org/israel/Eur_Poll_Israel_May_2005.pdf

91. The Pew Research Center for the People and the Press, 'Americans and Europeans differ widely on foreign policy issues', 17 April 2002. The poll can be found at: http://people-press.org/reports/display.php3?PageID=453. The Pew Global Attitudes Project bears no responsibility for the analyses or interpretations of the data presented here.

92. 'Israel and Iran share most negative ratings in global poll', BBC World Service Poll, 6 March 2007. Available online at http://news.bbc.co.uk/1/shared/bsp/hi/pdfs/06_03_07_perceptions.pdf

93. Etgar Leftkovits, 'German poll equating Israeli, Nazi tactics "very worrisome"', *Jerusalem Post*, 9 December 2004.

Chapter 2

1. Christopher Hitchens, 'Stand up for Denmark! Why are we not defending our ally?', *Slate*, 21 February 2006. Article available at: http://www.slate.com/id/2136714/fr/rss/

2. The European Monitoring Centre on Racism and Xenophobia (EUMC), 'Working Definition of Anti-Semitism' 2004. http://eumc.europa.eu/eumc/material/pub/AS/AS-Working-Definition-draft.pdf

3. Ibid.

4. Colin Shindler, *What Do Zionists Believe?*, Granta Books, Cambridge, 2007, p. 62.

5. John Phillips, 'Italian cartoonist dropped after Israel furore', *Independent*, 13 January 2005.

6. Bernard Wasserstein, *Vanishing Diaspora: The Jews in Europe since 1945*, Hamish Hamilton, London, 1996. The questions of how to revivify Jewish identity in the Diaspora (and this also applies at some level to the United States) is not easy to answer and may in fact have no answer. As Wasserstein says (p. 289): 'In the last resort peoples decide their own fate. As Nahum Goldmann put it: "Peoples disappear in history by suicide, not by murder." If the Jews of Europe do, in the end, disappear, it will be because, as a collectivity, they lost the will to live.'

7. Barbara Amiel, 'Without Israel Judaism is pointless', *Jerusalem Post*, 23 February 2001.

8. For an eloquent and incisive analysis of the question of anti-Zionist Jews see Anthony Julius's two-part essay, 'Jewish Anti-Zionism Unravelled', on Z Word at www.z-word.com

9. The Black Hundreds was an anti-revolutionary movement operating in the last decades of Tsarist rule in Russia. It was reactionary through and through, exalting the autocracy and participating in anti-Semitic propaganda and pogroms.

10. For a discussion of this and other related matters see Manfred Gerstenfeld, 'Anti-Israelism and Anti-Semitism: Common Characteristics and Motifs', *Jewish Political Studies Review*, 19: 1–2 (Spring 2007).

11. Edward H. Kaplan and Charles A. Small, 'Anti-Israel Sentiment Predicts Anti-Semitism in Europe', *Journal of Conflict Resolution*, vol. 50, no. 4 (August 2006). The quotation is from the Abstract.

12. Robert Wistrich, 'Anti-Zionism and Anti-Semitism', *Jewish Political Studies Review*, 16: 3–4 (Fall 2004).

Chapter 3

1. See Johann Hari, 'The spiteful return of anti-Semitism', *Independent*, 17 August 2006.

2. Markovits, op. cit., p. 191.

3. Lewis, op. cit. Available online at http://www.zionism-israel.com/log/archives/00000008.html

4. Josef Federman, 'Olmert: Israel risks South Africa-like struggle without peace settlement', Associated Press, 29 November 2007.

5. Donald Macintyre, 'This is like apartheid', *Independent*, 11 July 2008.

6. Similar attempts at validating virulently anti-Israeli discourse came after an outburst from Israel Deputy Defence Minister Matan Vilna'i who, in March 2008, commented to Israeli Radio that Palestinians in Gaza risked bringing an even bigger disaster on themselves than they were trying to visit upon Israel through rocket fire. In so doing, he used the word 'shoah' which in Hebrew means 'disaster' but is most often used in reference to the Holocaust. In context, it is quite clear what Vilna'i meant. For the Israel haters it came as manna from heaven.

7. 'Deconstructing Apartheid Accusations Against Israel', Gideon Shimoni interviewed by Manfred Gerstenfeld, Middle East Strategic Information (MESI), 24 March 2008.

8. Baudouin Loos, 'An Interview of Ilan Pappé', *Le Soir*, 29 November 1999.

9. Benny Morris, 'Politics by other means', *New Republic*, 22 March 2004. The text of the review is available at: www.tnr.com/politics/story.html?id=942ccf90–97f0–4c32–a1f3–411bd908dcb0

10. Ilan Pappé, 'Benny Morris's lies about my book', George Mason University's *History News Network*, 4 May 2004. The text is available at: www.hnn.us/articles/4482.html

11. The Development Studies Programme – Birzeit University. Poll 16. Public Opinion Poll on Palestinian Living Conditions, the Peace Process, Rafah Operation and Sharon's Proposed Disengagement Plan. Question 31. Poll can be found at: http://home.birzeit.edu/cds/opinionpolls/poll16/results.html

12. United Nations Security Council Resolution 242, Paragraph 1 (ii).

13. Although it is certainly true that some parts of the now largely defunct 'Greater Israel' movement did seek to make from this a virtue out of necessity.

14. Malvina Halberstam, 'Belgium's Double Standard', *Legal Times*, 27 May 2003.

15. Ibid.

16. Ibid.

17. Alan Dershowitz, 'Amnesty International redefines "war crimes"', *Jerusalem Post*, 31 August 2006.

18. Ibid.

19. 'Rights group says U.S. response to Gaza "lopsided"', Reuters, 2 January 2009.

20. 'Bombing Gaza is not a solution', FT.com, 28 December 2008.

21. Dan Izenberg, 'Dershowitz: Int'l Court doesn't give just rulings', *Jerusalem Post*, 20 March 2008.

22. Charles Krauthammer, 'Israel's Day in Court', *Washington Post*, 16 July 2004.

23. It is worth noting that, by the logic of the disproportionate response argument, the United States and Britain were guilty of a massively disproportionate use of force against Hitler's Germany in World War II since fighting between the two most important Western Allies and the Nazis resulted in vastly more deaths, civilian and military, on the German side than on the American and British side. It is doubtful that Churchill and Roosevelt would have lost much sleep over accusations that their policies were not proportionate.

Chapter 4

1. It is true that there has been something of a resurgence of nationalist parties in some European countries in recent years and this trend needs to be watched closely. However, serious inroads have not yet been made in the mainstream in the sense that they have neither taken control of governments; nor do their ideological supporters have a strong presence in the media.

2. Cardinal Joseph Ratzinger, 'If Europe Hates Itself', published on the Communion and Liberation website at http://www.comunioneliberazione.org/articoli/eng/RatzAvv140504.htm

3. Preamble to the treaty establishing the European Coal and Steel Community. Available at http://www.ena.lu/

4. Fernando Savater, 'Europe, in need and needed', *El País*, 31 May 2003.

5. Mark Mazower, *Dark Continent: Europe's Twentieth Century*, Penguin, London, 1998, p. 404.

6. Ibid., p. 406.

7. Tamara Thiessen, 'Secular Europe avoids G-word: As EU members wrangled over their new constitution, a major sticking point was whether to keep god out of it', *Montreal Gazette*, 6 November 2004.

8. Vaclav Havel, *The Art of the Impossible: Politics as Morality in Practice*, First Fromm International paperback, 1998, p. 129.

9. Transatlantic Trends surveys available online at: www.transatlantictrends.org

10. The motion said: 'Schools should not be conduits for either the dissemination of MoD [Ministry of Defence] propaganda or the recruitment of military personnel.'

11. The words of Paul McGarr quoted in Alexandra Frean, 'MoD uses propaganda to recruit deprived pupils, teachers claim', *The Times*, 26 March 2008.

12. Robert Kagan, *Of Paradise and Power*, Alfred A. Knopf, New York, 2003, p. 3.

13. Ibid.

14. Ibid., pp. 73–4.

15. Robert Cooper, *The Breaking of Nations: Order and Chaos in the Twenty-First Century*, Atlantic Books, London, 2004, p. 160.

16. Ibid., p. 161.

17. Ibid., p. 162.

18. Michael Gove, *Celsius 7/7: How the West's Policy of Appeasement Has Provoked yet more Fundamentalist Terror – and What Has to Be Done Now*, Weidenfeld & Nicolson, London, 2006, pp. 11–12.

19. Sir Jeremy Greenstock interviewed on BBC Radio 4's *Today Programme* 12, January 2009. The interview, which is preceded by a conversation with Tony Blair, is available to be listened to at

http://news.bbc.co.uk/today/hi/today/newsid_
7823000/7823746.stm

20. 'EU legislators invite Hamas lawmakers to Brussels', Reuters, 3 November 2008.

21. During this period the author was working for Reuters and experienced this ruling first hand.

22. The press release is available at:
http://www.randomhouse.com/rhpg/medinaletter.html

23. Mick Hume, 'It's a festival of grovelling to terrorists', *The Times*, 12 August 2008.

24. Dorothy Byrne, head of news and current affairs at Channel 4, quoted in Patrick Foster, 'Channel 4 attacked for allowing Iranian "despot" to deliver a Christmas message; President accused of propaganda speech', *The Times*, 26 December 2008.

25. Ibid.

26. Patrick West, *The Poverty of Multiculturalism*, Civitas, London, 2005, p. 6.

27. Ratzinger, op. cit.

28. I was a schoolboy in the town of Ilkley in the Bradford Local Education Authority. I recall the shock of my teachers at what was happening a few miles away. A head teacher being fired for his political views was not supposed to happen in a democracy.

29. Ray Honeyford, 'If only they'd listened to me', *Daily Mail*, 5 October 2005.

30. Mariette le Roux, 'Dutch court orders prosecution of anti-Islam politician', Agence France-Presse, 21 January 2009.

31. Ibid.

32. Jack Lefley, 'Right-wing author is banned from Islam talk', *Evening Standard*, 23 January 2009.

33. For example, Trevor Phillips, as head of Britain's Commission for Racial Equality (which has since morphed into the Equality and Human Rights Commission) has argued that multi-culturalism has led to Britain 'sleepwalking to segregation'.

34. Douglas Murray, Director of the Centre for Social Cohesion, 'I am not afraid to say the West's values are better', *Spectator*, 6 October 2007.

35. Manfred Gerstenfeld, 'Behind the Humanitarian Mask: The Nordic Countries, Israel and the Jews', The Jerusalem Center for Public Affairs, Jerusalem, 2008, p. 22.

Chapter 5

1. Helen Nugent and Nadia Menhin, 'Muhammad now Britain's number 2 name', *The Times*, 6 June 2007.
2. Figures in this section are taken from Charles F. Westoff and Tomas Frejka, 'Religiousness and Fertility Among European Muslims', *Population and Development Review*, 33, no. 4, 2007.
3. Pew Research Center, *Pew Global Attitudes Project*: *Spring 2006 Survey*. http://pewglobal.org/reports/pdf/254topline.pdf. The Pew Global Attitudes Project bears no responsibility for the analyses or interpretations of the data presented here.
4. The figures only refer to those who had actually heard about the Hamas victory.
5. Yasmin Alibhai-Brown, 'Israel's friends cannot justify this slaughter', *Independent*, 19 January 2009.
6. 'Genocide in Gaza, Muslims Demand Action Not Words', MCB press release, 21 May 2004, http://www.mcb.org.uk/media/presstext.php?ann_id=90
7. 'MCB Demands Urgent Recall of Parliament to Discuss Lebanon', MCB press release, 4 August 2006, http://www.mcb.org.uk/media/presstext.php?ann_id=220
8. 'Another Israeli War Crime in Qana – UK Must Insist on Immediate Ceasefire', MCB press release, 30 July 2006.
9. Ibid.
10. 'Open Letter to the Prime Minister on Gaza', MCB press release, 30 December 2008.
11. 'Cartoons Row: Mandelson in blast at newspapers', Press Association (UK), 2 February 2006.
12. Kerstin Gehmlich, 'UPDATE 6 – Row over cartoons boils as Europe leaders urge calm', Reuters, 3 February 2006.
13. Katrin Bennhold, 'Trying to keep the lid on in France: Muslim

leaders warn of anger at cartoons', *International Herald Tribune*, 9 February 2006.

14. Ali Imam, 'WRAPUP 1 – EU backs Danes in cartoon row, Pakistanis enraged', Reuters, 15 February 2006.

15. 'Danish Muslims say apology in cartoon row not good enough', Agence France-Presse, 2 February 2006.

16. Ibid.

17. For other examples of what has been going on see Daniel Mandel, 'Preemptive Appeasement', *Weekly Standard*, 20 September 2007.

18. Daniel Schwammenthal, 'Europe's New Dissidents', *Wall Street Journal*, 4 February 2006.

19. 'Don't Be Provoked By Mischievous Elements Over Cartoon Row', MCB press release, 3 February 2006,

http://www.mcb.org.uk/media/presstext.php?ann_id=187

20. For evidence of the grudging nature in which the decision was taken see Vikram Dodd, 'Muslim Council ends Holocaust memorial boycott', *Guardian*, 3 December 2007. The move raised concerns that some affiliates of the MCB would leave the umbrella grouping in protest. Daud Abdullah, the MCB's deputy secretary-general, voted against it. Former Secretary-General Sacranie, who voted in favour of the change, explained the move in the article in the following terms: 'There are voices who have been attacking us from day one and trying to misconstrue our non-participation as antisemitism.' The key word in that quotation, of course, is 'misconstrue'. In other words, it was the way in which the policy played out in the public domain, how it looked, that most concerned him. This does not look like a recognition that the ethical basis on which the policy had previously been carried through was flawed.

21. Abul Taher, 'Ditch Holocaust day, advisers urge Blair', *Sunday Times*, 11 September 2005.

22. 'Holocaust Day: MCB regrets exclusion of Palestinian genocide', MCB press release, 27 January 2003,

http://www.mcb.org.uk/media/presstext.php?ann_id=24

23. There are signs that, in a long-after-the-horse-has-bolted

kind of way, the British government has begun to recognise that extremism in Britain's Muslim communities goes well beyond the fringes. Nonetheless, attempts to confront the problem have been met with fury by important sections of the opinion-forming classes. See, for example, Brian Whitaker, 'Alienating British Muslims', *Guardian*, 24 March 2009. Available online at: http://www.guardian.co.uk/commentisfree/2009/mar/24/islam-politics

24. L'Union des Organisations Islamiques de France – UOIF, press release, 21 January 2008, http://www.uoif-online.com/webspip/spip.php?article260

25. L'Union des Organisations Islamiques de France – UOIF, press release, 5 March 2008, http://www.uoif-online.com/webspip/spip.php?article284

26. See, for example, the press release by the UOIF on 20 January 2009, http://www.uoif-online.com/webspip/spip.php?article454

27. Ofri Ilani, 'German Turk takes on "anti-Semitic Islamic propaganda"', *Haaretz*, 12 October 2006, available at http://www.haaretz.com/hasen/spages/773459.html

28. See analysis of al-Rawi in Ian Johnson, 'Islam and Europe: A Volatile Mix', *Wall Street Journal Europe*, 29 December 2005.

29. Lorenzo Vidino, 'The Muslim Brotherhood's Conquest of Europe', *The Middle East Quarterly*, Winter 2005, vol. xii, no. 1, http://www.meforum.org/article/687

30. 'Sharia law in UK is "unavoidable"', BBC, 7 February 2008. See report, which also contains link to broadcast interview, at http://news.bbc.co.uk/1/hi/uk/7232661.stm

31. Patrick Wintour and Riazat Butt, 'Sharia law could have UK role, says lord chief justice', *Guardian*, 4 July 2008.

32. Vidino, op. cit.

33. Timothy Savage, 'Europe and Islam, Crescent waxing, cultures clashing', *Washington Quarterly*, Summer 2004, p. 27, available at http://www.twq.com/04summer/docs/04summer_savage.pdf

34. See 'Low Fertility and Population Ageing: Causes, con-

sequences and policy options, Rand Corporation', 2004 for a well-researched discussion on the subject. The report was compiled for the European Commission. It is available at http://www.rand.org/pubs/monographs/2004/RAND_ MG206.pdf

35. For a brief essay on this cautionary tale see J. R. Dunn, 'How Demography Fails', *American Thinker*, 18 January 2006, available at http://www.americanthinker.com/2006/01/how_ demography_fails.html

36. Westoff and Frejka, op. cit.

37. See Pew Global Attitudes Project, 'Muslims in Europe: Economic Worries Top Concerns About Religious and Cultural Identity', released 7 June 2006. Available at http://pewglobal.org/ reports/display.php?ReportID=254. The Pew Global Attitudes Project bears no responsibility for the analyses or interpretations of the data presented here.

38. Gaby Hinsliff, Ned Temko, Peter Beaumont, 'Cabinet in open revolt over Blair's Israel policy', *Observer*, 30 July 2006.

39. Aziz Al-Azmeh and Effie Fokas (eds), *Islam in Europe: Diversity, Identity and Influence*, Cambridge University Press, Cambridge, 2007.

40. Ibid., p. 4.

41. Ibid., p. 22.

42. Ibid., p. 44.

43. Ibid., p. 65.

44. Ibid., pp. 78–9.

45. Ibid., p. 208.

46. 'Europe's Muslims More Moderate: THE GREAT DIVIDE: HOW WESTERNERS AND MUSLIMS VIEW EACH OTHER', The Pew Global Attitudes Project, 22 June 2006. Available at http://pewglobal.org/ reports/pdf/253.pdf. The Pew Global Attitudes Project bears no responsibility for the analyses or interpretations of the data presented here.

47. See Melanie Phillips, *Londonistan*, Gibson Square, London, 2006.

48. From a press release by the Quilliam Foundation of which Hussein is the co-director, 28 December 2008.

49. Ed Hussein, 'Britain has a duty to Arabs', *Guardian*, 30 December 2008.

50. Tariq Ramadan, 'An Alliance of values', *Guardian*, 2 January 2009.

51. Manfred Gerstenfeld and Tamas Berzi, *The Gaza War and the New Outburst of Anti-Semitism*, Institute for Global Jewish Affairs, no. 79, 1 April 2009, published March 2009.

52. 'Islam and phobias – Canada', *The Economist*, 12 January 2008.

53. Mark Steyn, *America Alone: The End of the World as We Know It*, Regnery Publishing, Washington, DC, 2008 (paperback edn), p. xviii.

54. Bertrand Benoit and Silke Mertins, 'Brussels urged to publish anti-Semitism report', *Financial Times*, 24 November 2003, article available at http://search.ft.com/nonFtArticle?id= 031124006667&query=EUMC&vsc_appId=totalSearch&state= Form

Chapter 6

1. 'A letter to Blair – Your Middle East policy is doomed, say diplomats', *Independent*, 27 April 2004.

2. Vernon Bogdanor, 'Is the Foreign Office Arabist?', *Jewish Chronicle*, 22 February 2008. NB: There have been two Lord Janners of note in British political life. This quotation is attributed to the elder of the two, not his son Greville.

3. Hussein Agha and Robert Malley, 'Camp David: The Tragedy of Errors', *New York Review of Books*, vol. 48, no. 13, 9 August 2001.

4. Merkel's speech to the Knesset, 18 March 2008.

5. Gordon Brown's speech to the Knesset, 21 July 2008.

6. President Nicolas Sarkozy's speech to the Knesset, 23 June 2008.

7. Editorial: 'Brown's Courage', *Daily Mail*, 22 July 2008.

8. 'Merkel made weighty pledge to Israel: German critics', Agence France-Presse, 19 March 2008.

9. Ibid.

10. 'Merkel Addresses Israeli Parliament Amid Controversy', Deutsche Welle, 18 March 2008.

11. Denis MacShane, *Globalising Hatred: The New Anti-Semitism*, Weidenfeld & Nicolson, London, 2008, pp. 49–50.

12. Bat Ye'or, *Eurabia: The Euro-Arab Axis*, Farleigh Dickinson University Press, Madison, 2005.

13. Ibid., Chapter 4, pp. 52–9.

14. At the time the European Union was called the European Community and had nine members.

15. Bat Ye'or, op. cit., p. 84.

16. Venice Declaration, 13 June 1980. Article 4.

17. Rory Miller, *Ireland and the Palestine Question 1948–2004*, Irish Academic Press, Dublin, 2005, p. 89.

Chapter 7

1. It is not just ideology and interests that matter. Attitudes to Israel may also be influenced by religious considerations, by personal circumstances, or by anti-Semitic or philo-Semitic starting points. In some parts of Europe, the way in which politicians, activists and opinion formers relate to Israel is driven above all by their countries' response to the Holocaust. In Germany, the political culture is suffused with a historical guilt about the past. In Britain, by contrast, there is no sense of direct historical guilt about the Holocaust at all.

2. The Paris Manuscripts are more formally known as the Economic and Philosophical Manuscripts of 1844. They were published well after Marx's death, in 1932 in the Soviet Union.

3. I have made this argument before in shorter form in an article for Z Word, a website created by the American Jewish Committee: 'Europe and Israel: Worlds Apart?', June 2008. It is available at http://www.z-word.com/z-word-essays/europe-and-israel%253A-worlds-apart%253F.html

4. See Stephane Courtois, Nicolas Werth, Jean-Louis Panne, Andrzej Paczkowski, Karel Bartosek and Jean-Louis Margolin,

The Black Book of Communism: Crimes, Terror, Repression, translated by Jonathan Murphy and Mark Kramer, consulting editor Mark Kramer, foreword by Martin Malia, Harvard University Press, London, 1999.

5. There are several important works on this subject. An excellent example is Paul Hollander, *Political Pilgrims: Western Intellectuals in Search of the Good Society*, Transaction Publishers, 4th revised edition, 1997.

6. *The Criminal Alliance of Zionism and Nazism*, Novosti, Moscow, 1985.

7. Herbert Marcuse, *One-Dimensional Man: Studies in the Ideology of Advanced Industrial Society*, 1964. Available online at www.marcuse.org/herbert

8. Frantz Fanon, *The Wretched of the Earth*, Penguin Modern Classics, December 2001 edition.

9. Walter Laqueur and Barry Rubin (eds), 'Fatah: The Seven Points (January 1969)'. In *The Israel–Arab Reader*, Penguin, London, 2001, 6th edition, p. 131.

10. Ben Cohen, 'A Discourse of delegitimisation: The British Left and the Jews', originally written for the Institute for Jewish Policy Research, London, 2003, available at http://www.axt.org.uk/HateMusic/essay_cohen_delegitimisation.htm

11. Ibid.

12. The document was first published in *Neue Rheinische Zeitung*, no. 194, 13 January 1849.

13. Quoted in Manfred Gerstenfeld, *European-Israeli relations: Between confusion and change?*, Part II, The Jerusalem Center for Public Affairs, September 2007. www.jcpa.org

14. Emanuelle Ottolenghi, *Under a Mushroom Cloud: Europe, Iran and the Bomb*, Profile, London, 2009, pp. 85–6.

15. David Horowitz, *Unholy Alliance: Radical Islam and the American Left*, Regnery Publishing, Washington, DC, 2004.

16. This is also why defenders of Israel miss the point in putting the case for the Jewish state in terms of its liberal-democratic credentials, its commitment to equality for women, its unique

tolerance in the Middle East for the rights of gays and so on. To the radical Left, in the greater scheme of things, these values at best count for nothing; at worst they proceed from a capitalist framework which represents the antithesis of their world view.

17. For many, including the author, the war in Afghanistan was a just war of self-defence. The war in Iraq was not necessarily so. It is possible, though not certain, that Saddam Hussein could have been contained. That is debatable, as is the question of whether the war could have been justified on humanitarian grounds. The interventions in Kosovo and Bosnia were not exactly wars of self-defence but they were just wars because there was an overwhelming humanitarian case to support them. It is arguable that we should indeed have acted sooner.

18. The flip side of the demonisation of the opponent is the adoration of the leading supporters. The personality cult of radical Left leaders from Lenin to Fidel Castro, the badge wearing, the T-shirts emblazoned with the revolutionary heroes, is not in any way accidental. Just as one side is absolutely wrong, in every way and in every respect, the other side is absolutely right in every way and in every respect.

19. Paul Hockenos, *Joschka Fischer and the Making of the Berlin Republic*, Oxford University Press, New York, 2008, p. 114.

20. Ibid., p. 115.

21. Many have argued that this very fact may have led to a kind of resentment against the Jews. Capitalism, after all, was supposed to be irredeemably oppressive. Who on earth do these Jews think they are disproving radical Left thinking by having the temerity to be successful? Perhaps some among the radical Left do think this way. But the realities of the contemporary world refute everything about radical Left ideology, not just the social and economic prospects of once oppressed minorities.

22. Marcus Dysch, 'Shoah leaflet refers to gays but not Jews', *Jewish Chronicle*, 22 August 2008.

23. Paul Berman, *Power and the Idealists: Or, the Passion of Joschka Fischer and its Aftermath*, W. W. Norton, New York, London, 2007.

24. 'Has multiculturalism failed? And as a feminist, are you proud of Mrs Thatcher?', *Independent*, 25 February 2008.

25. Stephane Courtois et al., op. cit., p. xiii.

26. Judy Dempsey, 'Schroder's party pitches to left, Old rhetoric is revived amid a key race', *International Herald Tribune*, 20 April 2005.

27. George Orwell, *Selected Writings*, Heinemann Educational, London, 1976, pp. 32–3.

28. Naomi Klein, 'Enough. It's time for a boycott', *Guardian*, 10 January 2009.

29. Giles Fraser, 'Why is the Left so anti-Jewish', *Church Times*, 20 February 2009, http://www.churchtimes.co.uk/content.asp?id=70749. Retrieved 12 March 2009.

30. This applies even though some were themselves members of ruling communist parties. The social democratic scene in central and eastern Europe is littered with examples.

31. David Cronin, 'Israel's Czech mate', *Guardian*, 10 January 2009.

32. 'Unfavorable Views of Jews and Muslims on the Increase in Europe', Pew Global Attitudes Project, A Pew Research Project, 17 September 2008. The poll is available at: http://pewglobal.org/reports/display.php?ReportID=262. The Pew Global Attitudes Project bears no responsibility for the analyses or interpretations of the data presented here.

Chapter 8

1. The remarks that had been highlighted included: his letter to America's UN ambassador Zalmay Khalilzad in January 2008 calling for the Security Council to 'unequivocally condemn' rocket attacks on Israel from Gaza and affirming Israel's 'right to defend itself against such actions'; his remarks in Muscatine, Iowa, in March 2007 that 'nobody is suffering more than the Palestinian people' – remarks that were later subject to a clarification that that suffering was the self-inflicted consequence of

Palestinian terrorism; his speech to the American Israel Public Affairs Committee (AIPAC) in June 2008 in which he referred to Palestinian 'government funded text books filled with hatred towards Jews' and in which he famously argued in favour of the hard-line Israeli position that Jerusalem must 'remain undivided' as the capital of the Jewish state, a position from which he later appeared to back down in favour of the more nuanced stance that the status of Jerusalem was a matter for negotiation. His associations with the likes of pro-Palestinian academic Rashid Khalidi and several others were also scrutinised and fretted over.

2. Biden has said: 'If I were a Jew, I would be a Zionist. I am a Zionist. You don't have to be a Jew to be a Zionist.' His remarks are from an interview with Shalom TV in March 2007. The remarks were also quoted widely, for example in 'Obama's Zionist Wannabe Veep', *Palestinian Chronicle*, 2 September 2008.

3. During the Democratic primaries in April 2008, she told ABC television that the US could 'totally obliterate' Iran if it were foolish enough to attack Israel.

4. For example, at the end of 2008, amid the Gaza operation, Georgetown University Professor Michael Hudson was quoted by Al-Jazeera as saying: 'If you're identified with an Israel that is bombing indiscriminately and disproportionately, this is really good for Osama Bin laden, it's good for extremists all across the region and I fear that Americans as well as Israelis will now suffer.' Quoted Tom Ackerman, 'Gaza strikes challenge for Obama', Al-Jazeera, 29 December 2008. Retrieved 18 January 2009, http://english.aljazeera.net/news/americas/2008/12/200812291463395447.html

5. This works both ways. I do not exclude the possibility that there could be positive contagion from America to Europe.

6. Tim Montgomerie, 'British media could swing next US election', BritainandAmerica.com, retrieved 12 October 2008. Article available at http://britainandamerica.typepad.com/britain_and_america/2007/05/british_media_c.html. See also Eric Pfanner, 'U.K. press discovers Web bonanza in U.S.', *International Herald Tribune*, 2 July 2007.

7. See data from comScore and My Metrix.

8. Egypt and Jordan are exceptions, as I have stated elsewhere. However, they have done nothing to inculcate in their populations an acceptance of the full legitimacy of Israel as a Jewish state (quite the opposite), leaving the long-term durability of the peace agreements as an open question. What happens, for instance, if Egypt or Jordan become subject to *coups d'état*?

9. The use of Lebanon and Yugoslavia as models for what Israel should become was a common motif of far-Left discourse in the 1960s, 1970s and 1980s.

10. See Khaled Abu Toameh, 'On Campus: The Pro-Palestinians' Real Agenda', *Hudson New York*, 24 March 2009. http://www.hudsonny.org/2009/03/on-campus-the-pro-palestinians-real-agenda.php. As the author put it: 'During a recent visit to several university campuses in the U.S., I discovered that there is more sympathy for Hamas there than there is in Ramallah. Listening to some students and professors on these campuses, for a moment I thought I was sitting opposite a Hamas spokesman or a would-be-suicide bomber.'

11. Ricki Hollander, Eric Rozenman, Tamar Sternthal, 'Study: On Nation's Op-ed pages, Israel's voice is stifled', CAMERA, 5 February 2008. Article, with explanation of methodology, available at http://www.camera.org/index.asp?x_context=2&x_outlet=33&x_article=1439

12. Walter Russell Mead, 'Jerusalem syndrome: decoding The Israel Lobby' (The Israel Lobby and US Foreign Policy) (book review), *Foreign Affairs*, November–December 2007.

13. Abraham H. Foxman, *The Deadliest Lies: The Israel Lobby and the Myth of Jewish Control*, Palgrave Macmillan, New York, 2007.

14. 'An Interview with President Jimmy Carter', http://www.amazon.com/Palestine-Peace-Apartheid-Jimmy-Carter/dp/0743285026

15. John J. Mearsheimer and Stephen M. Walt, *The Israel Lobby and US Foreign Policy*. Penguin, London, 2008, p. 96.

16. Ibid., p. 386.

17. Unless they want to argue that 'Palestinian ambitions' refers

to their ambition over many decades of destroying Israel. One doubts that Mearsheimer and Walt actually meant that since it would fatally undermine significant pillars of their overall case. Predictably, they are in denial about the Clinton-brokered accords of 2000 and 2001. But even they cannot deny that offers were made and flatly rejected by Yasser Arafat.

18. Foxman, op. cit., quoted p. 58.

19. Quoted in full in 'Diplomat's [sic] letters to Blair and Bush', *Middle East Policy*, 1 July 2004.

Conclusion

1. Indeed, influential Arab writers can sometimes appear more moderate and considered in their criticisms of Israel than many in Europe. See, for example, Tariq Alhomayed, 'The Blood of Gaza ... A Business Venture', *Asharq Al-Awsat* (the pan-Arab daily newspaper which is printed in four continents), 28 December 2008. The article contains the ritual denunciations of Israel but also elaborates on the mendacity of Iran and Hamas in the Gaza 2008–9 conflict in a manner that was frequently absent in comment in the European press. Article available at http://www.asharqalawsat.com/english/news.asp?section=2& id=15189. Retrieved on 18 January 2009.

Another example during the same Gaza conflict came with a letter to *The Times* (Letters, 3 January 2009) from Dr Wafik Moustafa, Chairman of the Conservative Arab Network. Dr Moustafa said: 'Unreported in the mainstream British media, an increasing number of the Arab press and political commentators are openly condemning Hamas, and expressing an understanding of Israel's predicament.' There were not many British or European commentators showing such broadness of mind. The full letter is available at http://www.timesonline.co.uk/tol/life_and_style/court_and_social/article5435064.ece. Retrieved 18 January 2009.

2. Quoted in Manfred Gerstenfeld, 'Israel and Europe: An Expanding Abyss?', The Jerusalem Center for Public Affairs and the Adenauer Foundation, Jerusalem, 2006, p. 65.

SELECT BIBLIOGRAPHY

Al-Azmeh, Aziz, and Fokas, Effie (eds), *Islam in Europe: Diversity, Identity and Influence*, Cambridge: Cambridge University Press, 2007

Ardagh, John, *France in the New Century: Portrait of a Changing Society*, London: Penguin Books, 2000

Bauman, Zygmunt, *Modernity and the Holocaust*, Ithaca, NY: Cornell University Press, 2000

Bawer, Bruce, *While Europe Slept: How Radical Islam is Destroying the West from Within*, New York: Broadway Books, 2006

Berman, Paul, *Power and the Idealists: Or, the Passion of Joschka Fischer and its Aftermath*, New York and London: W. W. Norton, 2007

Brown, Anthony, *The Retreat of Reason: Political Correctness and the Corruption of Public Debate in Modern Britain*, London: The Institute for the Study of Civil Society, 2006

Burke, Jason, *Al Qaeda: The True Story of Radical Islam*, London: Penguin Books, 2004

Carter, Jimmy, *Palestine: Peace not Apartheid*, New York: Simon & Schuster, 2006

Cesarani, David (ed.), *The Making of Modern Anglo-Jewry*, Oxford: Basil Blackwell, 1990

Chesler, Phyllis, *The New Anti-Semitism*, San Francisco: Jossey-Bass, 2003

Clark, Victoria, *Allies for Armageddon: The Rise of Christian Zionism*, New Haven, Conn., and London: Yale University Press, 2007

Cohen, Nick, *What's Left? How Liberals Lost Their Way*, London: Fourth Estate, 2007

Conway, David, *A Farewell To Marx*, Harmondsworth: Penguin Books, 1987

Cooper, Robert, *The Breaking of Nations: Order and Chaos in the Twenty-First Century*: London, Atlantic Books, 2004

Courtois, Stephane, Werth, Nicolas, Panne, Jean-Louis, Paczkowski, Andrzej, Bartosek, Karel, and Margolin, Jean-Louis, *The Black Book of Communism: Crimes, Terror, Repression*, London: Harvard University Press, 1999

Cox, Caroline, and Marks, John, *The West, Islam and Islamism: Is Ideological Islam Compatible with Liberal Democracy?*, London: Civitas: Institute for the Study of Civil Society, 2003

Craig, Gordon A., *The Germans*, New York: Meridian, 1991

Davies, Norman, *Europe: A History*, London: Pimlico, 1997

Dershowitz, Alan, *Why Terrorism Works: Understanding the Threat, Responding to the Challenge*, New Haven, Conn., and London: Yale University Press, 2002

——, *The Case for Israel*, Hoboken, NJ: John Wiley & Sons, 2003

Evans, Richard J., *In Defence of History*, London: Granta Books, 1997

Fanon, Frantz, *The Wretched of the Earth*, London: Penguin Books, 2001

Ferguson, Niall, *The War of the World*, London: Allen Lane, 2006

Foxman, Abraham H., *The Deadliest Lies: The Israel Lobby and the Myth of Jewish Control*, New York: Palgrave Macmillan, 2007

Fukuyama, Francis, *State Building, Governance and World Order in the Twenty-First Century*, London: Profile Books, 2004

Garton Ash, Timothy, *History of the Present: Essays, Sketches and Despatches from Europe in the 1990s*, London: Penguin Books, 2000

Gerstenfeld, Manfred, *Europe's Crumbling Myths, The*

Post-Holocaust Origins of Today's Anti-Semitism, Jerusalem: Jerusalem Center for Public Affairs, Yad Vashem, World Jewish Congress, 2003

——, *Israel and Europe: An Expanding Abyss?*, Jerusalem: the Jerusalem Center for Public Affairs and the Adenauer Foundation, 2005

——, *European-Israeli Relations: Between Confusion and Change?*, Jerusalem: the Jerusalem Center for Public Affairs and the Adenauer Foundation, 2006

——, *Behind the Humanitarian Mask, The Nordic Countries, Israel and the Jews*, Jerusalem: the Jerusalem Center for Public Affairs, the Institute for Global Jewish Affairs, Friends of Simon Wiesenthal Center for Holocaust Studies, 2008

Gilbert, Martin, *The Routledge Atlas of the Arab–Israeli Conflict*, London and New York: Routledge, 2003

Glenny, Misha, *The Rebirth of History*, London: Penguin Books, 1993

Gold, Dore, *The Fight for Jerusalem*, Washington, DC: Regnery Publishing, 2007

Goldhagen, Daniel Jonah, *Hitler's Willing Executioners: Ordinary Germans and the Holocaust*, New York: Alfred A. Knopf, 1996

Gove, Michael, *Celsius 7/7*, London: Weidenfeld & Nicolson, 2006

Guttman, Robert J. (ed.), *Europe in the New Century: Visions of an Emerging Superpower*, London: Lynne Rienner Publishers, 2001

Harrison, Bernard, *The Resurgence of Anti-Semitism*, Plymouth: Rowman & Littlefield Publishers, 2006

Havel, Vaclav, *The Art of the Impossible: Politics as Morality in Practice*, First Fromm International paperback, 1998

Hazony, Yoram, *The Jewish State: The Struggle for Israel's Soul*, New York: Basic Books, 2000

Hockenos, Paul, *Joschka Fischer and the Making of the Berlin Republic*, New York: Oxford University Press, 2008

Hollander, Paul, *Political Pilgrims: Western Intellectuals in Search of the Good Society*, Transaction Publishers, 1997

Horowitz, David, *Unholy Alliance: Radical Islam and the American Left*, Washington, DC: Regnery Publishing, 2004

Howard, Michael, *War and the Liberal Conscience*, London: Hurst & Company, 2008

Huntington, Samuel P., *The Clash of Civilizations and the Remaking of World Order*, London: Touchstone Books, 2008

Hussein, Ed, *The Islamist*, London: Penguin Books, 2007

Iganski, Paul, and Kosmin, Barry A., *The New European Extremism: Hating America, Israel and the Jews*, London: Profile, 2005

Johnson, Eric A., *Nazi Terror: The Gestapo, Jews, and Ordinary Germans*, New York: Basic Books, 1999

Johnson, Lonnie R., *Central Europe, Enemies, Neighbors, Friends*, New York and Oxford: Oxford University Press, 2002

Judt, Tony, *Postwar: A History of Europe*, London: Heinemann, 2005

Kagan, Robert, *Of Paradise and Power*, New York: Alfred A. Knopf, 2003

Karsh, Efraim, *Islamic Imperialism: A History*, New Haven, Conn., and London: Yale University Press, 2007

Kupchan, Charles A., *The End of the American Era: U.S. Foreign Policy and the Geopolitics of the Twenty-First Century*, New York: Alfred A. Knopf, 2002

Laqueur, Walter (ed.), *Fascism: A Reader's Guide*, Harmondsworth: Penguin Books, 1982

——, *The Changing Face of Anti-Semitism*, Oxford: Oxford University Press, 2006

——, *The Last Days of Europe: Epitaph for an Old Continent*, New York: Thomas Dunne Books/St Martin's Press, 2007

——, and Rubin, Barry (eds), *The Israel–Arab Reader: A Documentary History of the Middle East Conflict*, London: Penguin Books, 2001

Lee, Stephen J., *Hitler and Nazi Germany*, London and New York: Routledge, 1998

Lewis, Bernard, *Semites and Anti-Semites: An Inquiry into Conflict and Prejudice*, London: Phoenix, 1997

——, *The Clash Between Islam and Modernity in the Middle East: What Went Wrong?*, London: Weidenfeld & Nicolson, 2002

——, *The Crisis of Islam: Holy War and Unholy Terror*, London: Weidenfeld & Nicolson, 2003

Lipset, Seymour Martin, *American Exceptionalism: A Double-Edged Sword*, New York: W. W. Norton, 1995

Lipstadt, Deborah, *Denying the Holocaust: The Growing Assault on Truth and Memory*, London: Penguin Books, 1994

Lochery, Neill, *Why Blame Israel?*, Cambridge: Icon Books, 2004

MacLean, Ian, Montefiore, Alan, and Winch, Peter (eds), *The Political Responsibility of Intellectuals*, Cambridge: Cambridge University Press, 1990

MacShane, Denis, *Globalising Hatred: The New Anti-Semitism*, London: Weidenfeld & Nicolson, 2008

Marcuse, Herbert, *One-Dimensional Man: Studies in the Ideology of Advanced Industrial Society*, Available online at www.marcuse.org/herbert, 1964

Markovits, Andrei S., *Uncouth Nation: Why Europe Dislikes America*, Princeton, NJ: Princeton University Press, 2007

Mazower, Mark, *Dark Continent: Europe's Twentieth Century*, London: Penguin Books, 1998

Mearsheimer John J., and Walt, Stephen M., *The Israel Lobby and U.S. Foreign Policy*, New York: Farrar, Straus & Giroux, 2007

Miller, Rory, *Ireland and the Palestine Question 1948–2004*, Dublin: Irish Academic Press, 2005

Morris, Benny, *The Birth of the Palestinian Refugee Problem Revisited*, Cambridge: Cambridge University Press, 2004

O'Brien, Conor Cruise, *The Siege*, London: Weidenfeld & Nicolson, 1986

Oren, Michael B., *Six Days of War: June 1967 and the Making of the Modern Middle East*, London: Penguin Books, 2003

——, *Power Faith and Fantasy: America in the Middle East 1776 to the Present*, New York and London: W. W. Norton, 2007

Pappé, Ilan, *The Ethnic Cleansing of Palestine*, Oxford: Oneworld Publications, 2007

Phillips, Melanie, *Londonistan*, London: Gibson Square, 2006

Prior, Michael, *Zionism and the State of Israel: A Moral Inquiry*, London: Routledge, 1999

Rubin, Barry, *Revolution until Victory: The Politics and History of the PLO*, Cambridge, Mass.: Harvard University Press, 1994

Ruthven, Malise, *A Satanic Affair: Salman Rushdie and the Wrath of Islam*, London: Hogarth Press, 1990

Said, Edward, *Orientalism: Western Conceptions of the Orient*, London: Penguin Books, 1995

——, *Culture and Imperialism*, London: Vintage, 2003

Sassoon, Donald, *The Culture of the Europeans – From 1800 to the Present*, London: HarperCollins, 2006

Schopflin, George, *Politics in Eastern Europe*, Oxford and Cambridge, Mass.: Blackwell Publishers, 1993

Scruton, Roger, *Thinkers of the New Left*, Harlow: Longman Group Limited, 1985

Sharansky, Natan, *Defending Identity, Its indispensable Role in Protecting Democracy*, New York: Public Affairs, 2008

Shepherd, Robin, *Czechoslovakia, The Velvet Revolution and Beyond*, Basingstoke and London: Macmillan Press Ltd, 2000

Shindler, Colin, *What do Zionists Believe?*, London: Granta Books, 2007

Shlaim, Avi, *The Iron Wall: Israel and the Arab World*, New York and London: W. W. Norton, 2000

Siedentop, Larry, *Democracy in Europe*, London: Penguin Books, 2000

Sternhell, Zeev, *The Founding Myths of Israel*, Princeton, NJ: Princeton University Press, 1998

Steyn, Mark, *America Alone: The End of the World as We Know It*, Washington, DC: Regnery Publishing, 2008

Wasserstein, Bernard, *Vanishing Diaspora: The Jews in Europe since 1945*, London: Hamish Hamilton, 1996

West, Patrick, *The Poverty of Multiculturalism*, London, Civitas, 2005

Wistrich, Robert S., *Anti-Semitism: The Longest Hatred*, London: Thames Methuen, 1991

Ye'or, Bat, *Eurabia: The Euro-Arab Axis*, Madison, Wis.: Farleigh Dickinson University Press, 2005

Zakaria, Fareed, *The Future of Freedom: Illiberal Democracy at Home and Abroad*, New York: W. W. Norton, 2003

INDEX